Robert McLean Calder, William Shillinglaw Crockett

A Berwickshire Bard

The Songs and Poems of Robert McLean Calder

Robert McLean Calder, William Shillinglaw Crockett

A Berwickshire Bard
The Songs and Poems of Robert McLean Calder

ISBN/EAN: 9783337006457

Printed in Europe, USA, Canada, Australia, Japan

Cover: Foto ©Thomas Meinert / pixelio.de

More available books at **www.hansebooks.com**

A BERWICKSHIRE BARD

The Songs and Poems

OF

ROBERT M^cLEAN CALDER.

EDITED, WITH INTRODUCTORY MEMOIR,

BY

W. S. CROCKETT.

Author of *Minstrelsy of the Merse*, etc.

J. AND R. PARLANE, PAISLEY.

JOHN MENZIES AND CO., EDINBURGH AND GLASGOW.

HOULSTON AND SONS, LONDON.

1897.

To the

Borders Association in London,

OF WHICH

ROBERT McLEAN CALDER

WAS

A PATRIOTIC MEMBER,

This Edition of his Songs and Poems

IS DEDICATED.

CONTENTS.

	Page
Prefatory Note ...	13
Memoir	17

I.—MEMORIES OF POLWARTH.

My Faither's Fireside	59
My Faither's Fiddle	61
Polart Burn	63
The Auld Schule Hoose on the Green	65
The Love o' my Schule-boy Days	66
The Auld Theekit Hoose	67
My Horn-spune an' Luggie	68
The Chimla Cheek	70
Langton Water	71
Langton Brig	74
Chousley Brae	76
The Auld Smiddy Door	77
The Packman's Loan	79
The Auld Barn-yaird	81
Penny's Brae	83
Jasper's Mill	84
The Quarry on the Hill ...	86
By Fogo Braes	88
The Kirk on the Brae ...	89
Up the Burn	90
Dancin' in the Barn	92
The Leadin' In at Polart ...	95
Aroun' the Village Thorn ...	98
Ane o' Oorsel's	100
In Days Gane Bye	101
Moorland Musings	104
When we were a' at Hame ...	106
I like my Ain Fireside ...	107
The Auld Folks o' the Village ...	109
Puir Wull's awa' ...	111
"Fasten's E'en" ...	113
Hallowe'en Memories ...	116
Hogmanay	117
The Blaeberry Plantin'	119
Davy's Ha'	121

	Page
Yiddum	123
Gaun to the Kirk at Polart	125
Lounsdale Haughs	129
Bygone Days	131

II. HAME SANGS.

St. Andrew's Day	137
The Thistle	139
It's Hard to Leave the Hame	142
I Love to Dream of Home	143
Hame-sick	144
My Boyhood's Hame	147
My Hame across the Sea	147
Far frae Hame	148
Sangs o' Hame	149
My Hame amang the Hills	150
My Heart is Hame in Scotland	151
Scotia's Sangs	152
Where the Heather is in bloom	153
Ance mair amang the Heather	154
I must come back	155
We hae been lang acquent	156
Home of Youth, I leave thee	157
We were a' brocht up together	158
We were Cronies at the Schule	159
When the Kettle's on the Swee	160
When the Bairnies say Guid-nicht	161
When auld frien's meet	162
The Wee Anes at Hame	163
Hame at E'en	165
An Auld Settler	166
The Gloamin' Hour	168
By the Burnie Side	169
On the road hame	171
Come Again	171

III. SONGS SET TO MUSIC.

Wait a-wee an' dinna weary	175
My Heart warms to the Tartan	176
When the Bairnies are frae Hame	177
Heaven is where our Father is	178
Kiss the Bairns for Me	179
Under the Orchard Trees	180
The Land of the Maple for Me	181
Constant Still	182
"Love will bide when Simmer's gane"	183
Little Bluebell	184
The little Patch of Sunshine	185
Hand in Hand	185

	Page
The Border Lads	186
Lassie Dear	187
When the Summer Buds unfold	188
"Shouther to Shouther"	189
The Muirland Glen	190
The little White Cot in the Clearing	191
My bonnie Border Lassie	192
Our Coortin' Days	193
When the Kye gang to the Muir	194
Where Duty Calls	195
Keep a Corner in your Heart for Me	196

IV.—POEMS FOUNDED ON FAMILIAR SCOTTISH PROVERBS AND SAYINGS.

Creep before ye gang	199
Come oot frae 'mang the Neeps	202
Doon at the Heel	204
Be as Guid as ye can	205
It micht hae been waur	206
Whustle on your Doug	207
When the Pat rins owre	208
Spit on your Hands	209
Dinna droon the Miller	211
Aye a Something	212
That's anither Sang	213
Keep the Chain on the Door	215
Mak' yoursel' at Hame	217
Ca' your Gird	218
Ca' Canny	219
A Kind Welcome Hame	221
Look in i' the By-gaun	222
Collie, will ye lick	223
Put out Hand an' help Yoursel'	224
What's the Guid	225
Haud your Wheesht	227
Up in Years	228
It's maybe just as weel	230
Auld Frien's	231
A Lift on the Road	233
Kiss an' Gree	235
Oor Side yet	236
Come awa' ben	237
Be Canny wi' the Cream	238
Haud the Kail het	240
Grip your Nettle tight	242
Fill an' Fetch mair	244
The Morn's anither Day	247
It's hardly worth your while	248
Look where you're gaun	250

	Page
Mair the Morn	252
A Man afore your Mither	254
At the Rich Man's Door	255
Simmer Frien's	257
It's a Sair Thing Trouble	259
At the Heel o' the Hunt	260
Never go Back on a Friend	261
It's a' the same to Me	262
The Morn we never saw	263
Kiss the Sair Place	265
Come in Ahint	266
Hunt the Gowk	268
Wait and Hope	270
Heaven is no' sae far awa'	271
When the days are creepin' in	272
I'll fecht till I dee	273

V.—MISCELLANEOUS POEMS.

The Royal Marriage	277
Robert Burns	279
A Royal Mouse	282
Welland Stream	284
The Sunset Hour	286
Dreaming of Mother	287
Draw in your Stool an' sit doon	288
Indian Summer	289
How shall we honour him	290
On the Death of David Kennedy, the Scottish Vocalist	290
Where shall our Loved Ones Rest	292
Mither's Bonnie Lass	293
Nae Mair	294
Faither's Ain Bairn	295
When Daddy Comes Hame	296
The Bairnie tak's after his Faither	297
To please the Bairns	298
The Waning Year	300
Birthday Musings	302
The Way-gaun o' the Year	304

ILLUSTRATIONS.

Robert M'Lean Calder	Frontispiece
North Side of Market Place, Duns	19
Polwarth Green and Thorn	25
Lantern carried by Lady Grisell Baillie	30
Polwarth Church (from a sketch)	35
Polwarth Church	127
Site of the Old Castle of Polwarth	167

PREFATORY NOTE.

SHORTLY after the death of Robert McLean Calder, the suggestion was made that a new and enlarged edition of his poetical writings would prove acceptable to many of his old friends and the public generally. Mr Calder, I believe, had intended to prepare such a collection, but circumstances at the time were unfavourable; and now since he has gone, that task has fallen to other hands. I gladly undertook, at the request of several who were interested in the proposal, the work of arranging the very large amount of material placed in my hands by Mr Peter Calder, London, brother of the deceased bard. The present edition contains but a tithe of what had been penned. It seems perfectly marvellous how, notwithstanding the demands of a busy professional life, Mr Calder found opportunity for indulging his poetic gift. It was his one hobby, and he appears to have been indefatigable in its cultivation. A preference has naturally been given to those productions based on scenes and incidents in his native Berwickshire. He was devotedly a man of the Merse; and one is glad to know that his name and work are lovingly cherished all over the county. At Polwarth, where his happy boyhood days were passed, a tangible reminder of his association with that historic hamlet is shortly to be erected. Polwarth is proud of her poet, and the little kirk on the brae, of which he so frequently wrote, will soon have added to it this fresh touch of interest and romance. We do well to so shrine the memory of our sons of song.

Though Robert McLean Calder cannot be ranked among the outstanding poets of his country, he at least deserves a worthy place on the roll of minor bards. He attempts no lofty flight. His productions are of the simplest character, and it is their very simplicity that wins our admiration and sympathy. He is essentially a poet of the home. The fireside, and the joys of domestic life—the ceaseless play of sunshine and shadow on the cottage and the hearth—the quiet, unaffected, untarnished round of rural labour—the vivid memories of past scenes and incidents—are the themes that have most stirred his soul and inspired his pen. He has not failed in the high mission he set before him—no aim more noble—to comfort and cheer his brethren of lowlier lot. There are many to-day in Berwickshire, and in other parts of the world, for whom life with all its toil and worry has become a sweeter existence because of the manful message of this humble singer.

The accompanying memoir, from lack of informative material, is necessarily confined to the main incidents of a somewhat uneventful career. But, indeed, for such a life there could not be expected the heavier manipulation of a complete biography. Such as it is, it reveals that the writer of the verses comprising this volume knew whereof he voiced so well and so truthfully the ups and downs which meet so many amid these changeful scenes. His message is earnest and faithful; and sent out now in new guise, it may serve to stimulate and strengthen other souls "speeding onward in the race of life."

It remains to acknowledge the courtesy of Miss Warrender, author of *Marchmont and the Humes of Polwarth ;* Messrs Wm. Blackwood & Sons, Edinburgh ; and the Editor of the *Border Magazine*, for the privilege of reproducing several of the illustrations.

W. S. CROCKETT.

TWEEDSMUIR,
    PEEBLESSHIRE,
        November, 1897.

A BERWICKSHIRE BARD.

MEMOIR.

ROBERT M'LEAN CALDER was born at Castle Street, Duns, Berwickshire, November 19th, 1841. He was the fourth child of a family of nine sons and one daughter born to George and Elizabeth Calder. The Calders had long been settled in the county. A common tradition of the family claims descent from the Thanes of Cawdor. The English Calders, it may be interesting to note, affirm the same ancestry. George Calder, who was born at Abbey St. Bathans, is described as a man of strong character and quick intellect, holding somewhat advanced views on religious and political questions, an extensive reader, and withal, "a man whose powers of mind were far above the ordinary run of a country villager." Bringing to his home in very early life a bride from the clan M°Lean, whose grand-parents had crossed from Mull and travelled south with Sir John MacDonald, who had inherited the estate of Whitehill, one can scarcely conceive of a happier alliance, or which contributed more to the general welfare of her family. The warm

Celtic character of the mother mirrored itself in more than one of her children; her keen intellectual faculties shone out, perhaps, most of all, in the subject of this memoir; whilst her deep religious convictions were a savour of sweetness and a source of strength to all who were privileged to know her. "My mother," writes one of her sons, "had a noble and refined mind, and high literary faculties; and had opportunity and time been granted her, she would, I am convinced, have left memorials of her talents; but my father married very young and family cares began early, and continued all through life. Her memory to me is very sacred, and I look upon her as one of the noblest spirits I ever knew—a gentle, unselfish, and heroic woman. I shall never forget my last interview with her by her deathbed, as I had unavoidably to leave for London. I fancy I see her, looking down at her thin, emaciated frame, and repeating clearly and distinctly, and with true eloquence —for she was a fine reader and reciter—

> 'Soon shall this earthly frame, dissolved.
>   In death and ruins lie;
> But better mansions wait the just.
>   Prepared above the sky.
>
> An house eternal, built by God,
>   Shall lodge the holy mind,
> When once those prison walls have fallen
>   By which 'tis now confined.'"

It is no exaggeration to say that such mothers are the saviours of the people. Their influence, unknown on the broader arenas of life, confined chiefly to the narrower boundaries of home, has nevertheless made itself signifi-

cantly felt through the character and life of those receptive souls whom a good Providence has blessed with a home atmosphere at once religious and patriotic. Young Calder had reason to be thankful for such a home, and for so faithful a mother. To her he owed his future, and the sterling, pure purpose that graced his life.

The town of Duns, though the largest, is not the county town of Berwickshire. But most of the business of the county is transacted there. And if not always a stirring place, it is a fair example of a Scottish market-town. Duns is associated with several important incidents in Scottish history, and not a few distinguished men, from Duns Scotus downwards, have been natives of the place. At Duns, George Calder followed the occupation of a baker and miller. It was a hard life, but he faced it manfully and kept up his spirit in wonderful degree in spite of many difficulties. In this uphill fight he was aided by the counsel and cheer of a wise and winning helpmeet. A woman of profound faith and gentle disposition, an excellent housewife, and just the kind of soul best fitted to lend inspiration to the humblest tasks was this Highland maiden whom he had wooed and won.

In 1846 the Calders quitted Duns. Henceforth their life was to be spent in a quieter sphere. Polwarth, to which hamlet they removed, is distant only a few miles from their former abode. The parish lies in almost the very centre of the county, and is, with one exception, the smallest in the shire. But it is one of the prettiest and fullest of romantic memories. Scottish song has shrined its sweet-sounding name. Scottish story has gathered around it a wealth of honourable association. Polwarth-on-the-Green is a name familiar to all lovers of the national minstrelsy. It would indeed be difficult to stifle the poetic feeling amid such surroundings. Nature has dowered the place with uncommon attractiveness, and there is the added charm of history in its most varying phases, whilst romance and old tradition have not wholly lost their *glamourie* amid the quick march of modern days. "The long brown slopes of Lammermuir seem to pause before making a rapid descent into the Merse, and the wooded crest of Kyles Hill looks boldly forth across the wide expanse of plain that sweeps to the foot of Cheviot; and there—where the heather ceases, and the rich grass fields run up among the sheltering plantations—nestles the little village, which for centuries has been known as Polwarth-on-the-Green. It is a singularly picturesque spot."[1] In form not unlike an English hamlet of the attractively romantic type, it gathers itself with a kind of easy, self-contented air around the one dominating feature of the place—the Green. "There are no formal rows of houses: ash trees of immense size and great age overhang the thatched cottages which are dotted about in groups of twos and threes. Each has its garden, bright with flowers; while interspersed among them are little hedged-in paddocks, where generally a pony is grazing. There are only about twenty inhabited cottages now, for the village is dwindling away: but within the memory of persons still alive, there were nearly double the number."[1]

[1] *Marchmont and the Humes of Polwarth*, p. 2—Miss Warrender. Wm. Blackwood & Sons, Edinburgh, 1894.

One is therefore not surprised to find the spirit of poetry at work in such a place, so primitive, so blessed of Nature, so rich in imperishable memories. Long before Allan Ramsay wrote his *Polwart-on-the-Green* an older song and melody had been current in the district. Both are now lost, all that survives being the first and last four lines of the *Tea-Table Miscellany* version:

> "*At Polwart on the Green.*
> *If you'll meet me the morn,*
> *Where lovers do convene*
> *To dance about the thorn.*
>
> A kindly welcome ye shall meet
>   Frae her wha likes to view
> A lover and a lad complete,
>   The lad and lover you.
>
> Let dorty¹ dames say na   ¹ saucy
>   As lang as e'er they please,
> Seem caulder than the sna'
>   While inwardly they bleeze:
> But I will frankly shaw my mind,
>   And yield my heart to thee;
> Be ever to the captive kind
>   That langs na to be free.
>
> At Polwart on the Green,
>   Amang the new-mawn hay,
> Wi' sangs and dancing keen,
>   We'll pass the heartsome day.
> *At nicht if beds be o'er thrang laid*
> *And thou be twin'd of thine,*
> *Thou shalt be welcome, my dear lad,*
> *To tak' a part of mine.*

A much more graceful composition, bearing the same title, was written early in the present century by John Grieve, an Edinburgh hat manufacturer, one of the

Ettrick Shepherd's most intimate friends, to whom he dedicated *Mador of the Moor*, and introduced as Bard the fourteenth in the *Queen's Wake* :—

> "'Twas summer-tide ; the cushat sang
>   His am'rous roundelay ;
> And dew, like clustered diamonds, hang
>   On flower and leafy spray.
> The coverlet of gloamin' grey
>   On everything was seen,
> When lads and lassies took their way
>   To Polwarth on the Green.
>
> The spirit-moving dance went on,
>   And harmless revelry
> Of young hearts all in unison
>   Wi' love's soft witcherie ;
> Their hall the open-daisied lea,
>   While frae the welkin sheen
> The moon shone brightly on the glee
>   At Polwarth on the Green.
>
> Dark een and raven curls were there,
>   And cheeks of rosy hue,
> And finer form, without compare,
>   Than pencil ever drew ;
> But ane, wi' een o' bonnie blue,
>   A' hearts confessed the queen,
> And pride of grace, and beauty too,
>   At Polwarth on the Green.
>
> The miser hoards his golden store,
>   And kings dominion gain ;
> While others in the battle's roar
>   For honour's trifles strain.
> Away such pleasures, false and vain
>   For dearer mine have been
> Among the lowly, rural train
>   At Polwarth on the Green."

POLMAETH GREEN AND THORN.

Both of these lyrics refer to a very ancient and pleasing custom which long prevailed at Polwarth, and is founded on the following tradition. " In the time of Robert II. (1371-1390) Sir Patrick de Polwarth died, leaving an only child, Elizabeth, the last of her race. She carried the broad lands of Polwarth and Kimmerghame into the Sinclair family by her marriage with Sir John Sinclair of Herdmanston. Their great-grandson, John Sinclair, died in the fifteenth century without male issue. The estate of Herdmanston devolved on his brother, Sir William Sinclair (from whom the present Lord Sinclair is descended), but his lands of Polwarth and Kimmerghame went to his daughters, Marion and Margaret. The heiresses were young and beautiful; and among the many suitors that flocked round them, those that met with the greatest favour in their eyes were two brothers, George and Patrick. the young Humes of Wedderburn. The ladies' uncle, Sir William, fearing that their lands should go out of the family, not only refused his consent, but removed his nieces from their castle of Polwarth to lonely Herdmanston, his stronghold on the northern slopes of Lammermuir. Though closely immured, they contrived, by the help of an old beggar woman, to send a message to Wedderburn. A day or two later, a gallant train, headed by the two young lovers, rode over the hills and drew rein beneath the castle walls. An angry parley followed the demand for the restoration of their lady-loves; but the " Men o' the Merse " were too strong to be resisted, and Sir William had the mortification of seeing the heiresses borne away in triumph. The double marriage was celebrated at Polwarth, and the wedding-dance took place around the thorn tree."[1] In commemoration of this incident all future marriage-parties danced round the thorn, and the custom continued in force for several centuries, but gradually ceased in consequence of the privacy with which marriages are now conducted, and the fall of the original tree.

Another rhyme of unknown origin celebrates this curious old-world custom.

> " At Polwart-on-the-Green
> We oft hae merry been,
> And merry we'll be still
> While stands the Kylie's hill :
> And round the corn-bing
> We'll hae a canty fling ;
> And round about the Thorn
> We'll dance till grey-e'ed morn
> Shall lift her drowsy bree
> On mountain, vale, and lea.
> At Polwart-on-the-Green
> Our forebears oft were seen
> To dance about the Thorn,
> When they gat in their corn :
> Sae we their sons wha be,
> Shall keep the ancient glee,
> Nor let the gree gang doun
> While Polwart is a toun."

But the poetical associations of Polwarth are of an earlier date than Ramsay's or Grieve's day. It is a remarkable feature that these are chiefly connected with one family—the Humes, the great house of the district, the overlords and owners of the entire parish.

[1] *Marchmont and the Humes of Polwarth.* p. 15.

The ancient Border house of Hume, of which the Polwarth Humes were a not unimportant branch—represented still by an Earldom—has long played a prominent part in Scottish history. Not a few of its members have filled conspicuous positions in both Church and State. Some have signally distinguished themselves in military affairs, while peace has bequeathed its honours no less renowned. In the republic of letters the Polwarth family is worthily remembered, and Scottish poetry is indebted to several for their cultivation of its art.

Sir Patrick Hume of Polwarth, the sixth laird, a noted favourite at the court of James VI., is remembered for his share in the famous "Flyting betwixt Montgomerie and Polwart," a somewhat scurrilous composition in which the contending parties do not hesitate to hurl at each other the most opprobrious epithets, yet with all good feeling, and not, as one would imagine, the bitter outcome of a real quarrel. Sir Patrick is the author of a more sensible poem, *The Promine*, addressed to the king, and favourably received by his majesty. Alexander Hume, Sir Patrick's brother, minister of Logie in Stirlingshire from 1597 to 1609, a gifted poet-preacher of the Scottish Kirk, preserves his memory in those *Hymnes and Sacred Songs* which long delighted the hearts of the pious Lady Culross and her Presbyterian followers. The principal poem in the collection—The Day Estivall—is Hume's masterpiece. It is one of the finest descriptive poems in the language, and no doubt received much of its inspiration from the witching scenery around the Ochils. Alexander Hume is also the author of some six tractates on religious subjects; one of these being a telling defence of church government by Presbytery, which gained for him the commendation of Row the historian as one of the "faithful witnesses against the hierarchy of prelacy in this kirk." In the seventeenth century flourished another Patrick of the same noble house, a learned commentator on Milton, and a writer of Latin odes. But the best known versifier of the family was Grisell. No name is held in devouter memory by the men and women of the Merse than that of their sweet-faced girl-heroine. The story of how, amid the perilous times of

LANTERN CARRIED BY LADY GRISELL BAILLIE.

the Reformation, she displayed such undaunted courage and touching filial devotion, is known to all readers of Scottish history. Every boy and girl in the county treasures the tale, although they may not understand its historical setting. How many from far and near have peered into that vault beneath Polwarth Kirk and conjured up the incidents that seem still to survive in its gloom! It is one of the sacred shrines, not only of the shire, but of the whole country, weirdly testifying to a dark and trying period in the religious life of the nation. Amid the bitterness of exile-life in Holland, Grisell Hume found time to fill a manuscript book with poems of her own composition, and it is possible that the gem, *Were na my heart licht, I wad die*, without which no collection of Scottish song is complete, was penned during those toilsome days. After she happily wedded, when the darkness of persecution had passed, George Baillie of Jerviswood and Mellerstain, son of Robert the martyr, and frequently styled the "Scottish Sidney," Polwarth church and parish were more closely knit to her heart than ever, and memories of her sunny life consecrated the district for many generations.

Here then, amid such scenes and associations, Robert Calder passed his happy boyhood. The place accorded well with his nature. An intelligent, keen-eyed, knowledge-loving lad, he did not fail to store his mind with the rich lore of the district. He became familiar with the many traditions which clung to cot and hall. The fortunes of the Marchmont family; the story of the heiresses; of the slaughtered Laird of Murlierig; of the Black Well; of the Witches' Knowe; of the Packman's Brae; of the Haugit-man-Hill; of the Covenanters' march through the parish; of Cromwell's troopers at Choicelea; all these and many others were discovered and held in high veneration.

At Polwarth he was sent to the Infant School, instituted and kept up by the late Lady Hume-Campbell. In musical matters he must have been a precocious child, for we are told that although not yet five years old, he was frequently made to stand on the master's chair to lead the other children in their simple songs. Afterwards he attended the parish school, taught by the late Mr Smith; but his time there was brief enough. "The three R's were as far as I got," he wrote, "for at the early age of nine I hired out at the farm of Raecleughhead in the humble occupation of 'herding craws,' and varying this with cutting thistles or gathering 'rack.' During this time, and also later on when herding sheep on the moors by Kyles Hill, I supplemented the meagre education I had received by taking my books with me to the field and the hill-side, and improving my leisure hours in studying educational text-books and generally reading everything I could borrow in the village. My father and mother—the former being a man of more than ordinary intelligence, and the latter having decided poetical ability—encouraged me in every way in these efforts to improve my mind." Such an experience is by no means uncommon. Many of the most gifted and distinguished men of modern times have passed to eminence along this way.

From the hill-sides and the quiet retreats of romance-haunted Polwarth, he returned to Duns. His uncle, Mr Robert McLean, a leading draper in the town, wished him to turn his thoughts towards a commercial career, and to this particular calling he apprenticed himself for what were destined to be five pleasant and profitable years. During this period he sought to further improve his education by attending evening classes, and also by studying music under the late Rev. Daniel Kerr, United Presbyterian minister, who was one of the pioneers in the introduction of the sol-fa system into Scotland. After three sessions at the music classes he took a certificate of proficiency in both notations when in his sixteenth year. It was during this time, too, that he began weaving his thoughts and observations into verse and venturing to contribute to the local newspapers. In his manuscript book the first insertion, of date 1858, bears the title, "The Hawthorn Tree," and as a specimen of our bard's early musings, it is herewith printed:

'Twas on a summer's sunny eve when nature sought to rest.
The setting sun still lingered in the gaily purpled west;
'Twas then I heard a maiden sing, " 'Tis pleasure dear to me
To meet my Shepherd Laddie by the hawthorn tree."
　　By the hawthorn tree, by the hawthorn tree,
　　To meet my shepherd laddie by the hawthorn tree.

O! sweetly sang that merry maid as she skipped o'er the green:
A happier, smiling face, I trow, in Polwart ne'er was seen.
Sae rosy was her cheek, and sae brightly shone her e'e.
When she met her Shepherd Laddie by the hawthorn tree.
　　By the hawthorn tree, etc.

When met and clasped in fond embrace, O! who their joys can tell?
Sae fondly lo'ed that shepherd lad his ain dear Isabel.
Nae lad she lo'ed like him, aye sae blithe and gay was he,
When she met her Shepherd Laddie by the hawthorn tree.
　　By the hawthorn tree, etc.

The journal which looked thus kindly on the young lyrist was the *Berwick Advertiser*, and during the remainder of his stay in Duns he continued to be a regular contributor to its columns.

Among his acquaintances during those years at Duns was a youth, a pupil-teacher in the parish school, Robert Pringle, afterwards a noted educationist and poet. "Many happy rambles we had together amid the rural scenery of the neighbourhood, drinking in inspiration for the early efforts of our poetical effusions."

Pringle was also a native of Duns, born in the same year as his friend. After passing with distinction through the Training College at Edinburgh, he was appointed Latin Master in Forfar Academy, and is now settled near Manchester as the head of a large institution. He has published several scholastic works of high merit, and is well known as a writer of thoughtful and graceful verse. Both young men kept up for many years a regular poetical correspondence. Apprenticeship over, like so many others in the same line of business, Calder was bent on seeing for himself the more fashionable life and keener enterprise of London. Accordingly, having obtained a situation in the extensive establishment of Messrs Marshall and Snellgrove in Oxford Street, he bade good-bye to the simple rustic life of the Merse, for the more stirring scenes of the million-peopled city. While here, he was one of a band who started an illustrated paper called the *Tomahawk*, to which he contributed a series of poetical sketches, entitled, "Job Lots from behind the counter," and many others. From this situation he passed into the employment of several other firms, and for a short time also was engaged in business in the Isle of Wight and in the Lincolnshire town of Stamford. Then he was led to consider seriously the question of emigration. Several of his acquaintances had crossed to America, and were fallen on prosperous times. London offered many facilities, and had many attractions for young men in business; but even London did not possess the enterprise and go-aheadness so characteristic of its Western rivals. Thus were many well-meaning and industrious young mercantile assistants constrained to try what fortune might bring them in the Greater Britain beyond the seas. Along with this we must place Calder's inherent passion for travel, for sight-seeing, for romance, for a life of novelty and change.

POLWARTH CHURCH.   *From a Sketch.*

Accordingly, in 1866, he took his departure from London and sailed for New York. The American Civil War had happily ended, but the joy of the victors had been marred by regret at the assassination of Lincoln, the Good President. Better times, however, had dawned for the Republic. Commerce was revived, and a more

peaceful spirit shed its hopeful influence on all classes.
Breathing freely, there was now room and due occasion
for men to seek anew the common pleasures and relax-
ations of life. And, among others, the concert-room
and the theatre, where the soul might be soothed and
inspired by a good song well sung or a noble drama
skilfully represented. Mr Lloyd, of the famous Lloyd
and Bidaux's Minstrels, was at New York arranging for
an extended tour in the States. To him the young
emigrant was introduced, well armed with commenda-
tions as to his character and musical gifts. Mr Lloyd
at once enlisted his services, and Calder very soon became a most popular member of the troupe. Within
the next three or four months they had visited many of
the chief cities and towns, being everywhere enthusiastically received. This was just the kind of life Calder
enjoyed. He saw the country, he learned much in the
school of human nature, and was able in after years to
turn to good account those first experiences of the
American Continent. This engagement being ended,
he turned his thoughts in the direction of Canada. It
was really with the intention of settling in Canada that
he had gone out. But he was all the better able to
do this from the extra dollars he had earned in the *role*
of minstrel. In 1867 he crossed into the newly formed
Dominion. The British North America Act had just
been passed. The Provinces of Ontario and Quebec,
Nova Scotia and New Brunswick, were united under the
name of the Dominion of Canada. At Chatham, in
Ontario, he succeeded in finding a situation in the dry
goods establishment of Mr John Hyslop, a native of
Galashiels. Here were spent some of his happiest years.

The town of Chatham has a population of nearly six thousand, the Scottish element largely predominating. Mr Calder had ample scope for his eminently social qualities amongst this community. Few men were more widely known. With heart and soul he entered into the life of the town, unselfishly giving up his time and talents for its pleasure and welfare. He was a constant contributor to the local newspapers and wrote regularly for the other journals of the country. Not a week passed without something from his pen in the *Chatham Banner* and the *Scottish American Journal*, a paper which has done much to foster the literary tastes of Scottish Americans. He wrote generally under a *nom de guerre*, but the author's real name was well enough known. Naturally he came to be recognised as a leading spirit in the social life of the town. The clubs sought after him. The various societies found in him a vigorous upholder. He was a host in himself. He possessed an attractive personality. Old and young alike were his friends. Citizenship bound them together; but in the case of very many there was something stronger than citizenship—the ties that knit them to the sundered homeland of their fathers. The Scot is said to yield to no nationality in patriotic feeling. He carries with him wherever he wanders a big bit of his country, in the traditions with which his memory is stored and the songs which frame themselves upon his lips. All the world over the distinctively Scottish Associations are doing admirable work in the fostering of that *perfervidum ingenium Scotorum* amongst all who in any way are allied to this little northern land. In Canada almost every town has its Caledonian

Society or other Scottish Institution. Certain it is that among the most loyal sons of Scotia, whose lot is now cast far from her shores, are those who have thus banded themselves together for the maintenance of the old home life amid a foreign environment. The stranger in a strange land does not readily forget the land he has left behind, and as the years speed their flight, each one but makes firmer the bond that unites him to the dear memories of the past. The Scottish community at Chatham had established a St. Andrew's Society. On the very first celebration after his arrival in the colony Mr Calder took a prominent part in its proceedings. He was then in his twenty-sixth year, and had won an assured place in the hearts of very many Scoto-Chathamites. Year after year he was present at the gatherings of this flourishing society, and on one occasion, at a Burns's Anniversary, proposed the toast of the evening in a speech full of poetic fire and characterised by fine discrimination and high literary merit. He composed verses for these celebrations and sang them himself. Endowed with a rich tenor voice—he was, according to one critic, one of the finest tenor singers in Canada—and possessing a masterly knowledge of music, his songs were rendered in the most pleasant manner, with correct expression and true feeling. Possibly his greatest achievement was the gaining of the gold medals awarded by the St. Andrew's Society of Ottawa for the best poems on Saint Andrew's Day and the Marriage of the Princess Louise. The Committee had great difficulty in awarding the prizes, from the fact that the several poems sent in were nearly equal. Among the competitors were some of the best writers of Scottish poetry in Ontario and Quebec. Both medals came to Chatham, worthily inscribed with the name of Robert McLean Calder. "Saint Andrew's Day" will be found among *Home Songs* of the present volume, and "The Royal Marriage" under *Miscellaneous Poems*.

He had not yet reached his thirtieth year, but all over the Dominion, and in many of the States, his name was now becoming well known, and by the banks of the Canadian Thames he was more sought after than ever. Chatham was his adopted home, and to Chatham he gave his best. His Manuscript Book records only a tithe of his labours for the town. He was in evidence in all departments of its history. Not that he was obtrusive or pushed himself into its various undertakings. These were brought under his notice, and if help were needed, he was not the man to refuse. Had he gifts in the way of organisation, of singing, of reciting, of penning a simple song for any special occasion, then it would be done and no more said about it. He was passionately fond of music, and was an accomplished teacher of the art. Curwen's Sol-fa method, which has done so much to popularise and simplify musical instruction, was unknown in Canada. Mr Calder was the first to introduce it, and he did so with conspicuous success. For eleven years he held the post of precentor in Saint Andrew's Presbyterian Church at Chatham, and during a brief residence in Toronto he was also precentor in Bay Street Presbyterian Church, the pastor of which was the Rev. Dr. Jennings, a fellow-student of the late Rev. Dr. Ritchie of Duns. As a leader of church praise he was very popular in Canada, and held strong but sensible views on the subject. He did not believe in mere choir singing, and had a system of his own whereby the congregation as well might become acquainted with any new or difficult tune. " It was the testimony of many Canadians whom I met on their visits to England, that after he left they never got a leader to properly fill his place."

" He had fine musical abilities, and could sing a song in splendid style. He was the life and soul of a social party. When in Canada he was a great friend of David Kennedy, the Scottish vocalist. I remember him telling me that one night when talking with Kennedy about Scottish song, he asked him if he had ever introduced 'The Laird o' Cockpen.' Kennedy said he had never seen anything in it. My brother differed from him, and offered to sing it. He did so, and acted the song as it should be done. Kennedy was struck with his performance. He practised it, and introduced it at a concert on my brother's model, and it became at once one of his most popular representations."

The town of Chatham could also boast of a Dramatic Club. " Rob Roy " was the piece produced during the season of 1868, and Mr Calder in the part of the hero— *Frank Osbaldistone*—" represented the character to perfection." " His songs added materially to the success of the play, and were repeatedly encored." Few clubs in the Province could have taken hold of a drama of the character of " Rob Roy " and carried it through so triumphantly. Other representations followed. Mr Calder took a prominent part in most of them, and was on more than one occasion " decidedly the star of the evening." Through his exertions a local minstrel troupe of ten artistes was got together, and all were effectively drilled by him for their respective parts. Chatham concert-goers were fully benefited by Mr Calder's residence in their midst. Men with his powers of organisation and gifts of song are always in demand.

In all these undertakings he acted without the slightest thought of reward. He was one of the most unselfish of men. Hard at work all day behind the counter, his spare hours were devoted to his own mental improvement and to furthering the happiness of very many in Chatham. But his stay there was about to be broken. He accepted of a new situation in Toronto as clerk and book-keeper in the American Hotel, and arrived in that city early in 1869. In Toronto, which has probably the largest Scottish population of any city in Canada, he was at once quite at home, being as much a favourite in its musical circles as during his residence in Chatham. The Caledonian Society of Toronto enlisted his services for its annual Hallowe'en Concert, "where his clear tenor voice of ample power was very advantageously displayed." Toronto, however, with all its attractions, its strong Scottish life, and the presence of several old acquaintances, was only second in his eyes. " He has come to the conclusion that Chatham was the best place after all, and he has returned to his former situation. He will be welcomed back by our citizens, by whom he was universally esteemed during his stay amongst us. He is likely to remain here permanently this time." Such is the announcement of one of the local newspapers in Chatham. In December, 1869, he took part in the annual celebration of the St. Andrew's Society of Chatham, when his new lyric, "The Land of the Maple for me," was sung in public for the first time. Towards the beginning of 1870 he paid a visit to the States, and wrote from Philadelphia a series of racy letters for the *Banner*. In July, 1871, he was back to the old country and revelling among the scenes of his youth. To his favourite *Banner* the promise had been made that he would contribute a number of "Notes by the Way." The first of these, dated July 31, 1871, is characteristically penned "From Polwarth-on-the-Green." The hamlet of his boyhood was a blessed vision for the wanderer's eyes. His parents were still there, but there were blanks in the family circle, and not a few old familiar faces were wanting from well-remembered haunts. There is ever a touch of sadness ready to break in on the gladness one naturally feels on being back at the old home after a few years' absence. The memories of the past are strikingly vivid. We seem not alone in imagination to re-live the dead days, but as if again we were actually experiencing all they brought to us of joy or sorrow. Nowhere can this feeling be better understood than through the life of a Scottish village. Here, for the most part, each one understands the other. History lies like an open page; the little details of life are known all around, yet the sense of neighbourliness, in a true community, cannot but assert itself. Young and old have much in common. It is true that rivalries and jealousies come sometimes too frequently to the front; but to the wanderer returning for awhile to the scenes of his childhood, these are all forgotten, and friendship hallows the hours.

August, 1871, was a memorable month in Scottish annals. The centenary of the birth of Sir Walter Scott was being celebrated. All over the country, from crowded metropolis to remotest hill-country hamlet, the patriotic sense of old Scotia was not slow to pay honour to the memory of one of her most illustrious and heroic sons. The man of letters, as poet and romancist, who wrought as Scott did for his country's best weal, is worthily styled a hero, and worship of the heroic in Scott can never be misplaced. Mr Calder attended two of the commemorative gatherings—at Edinburgh, where Scott was born, and at Galashiels, so near Abbotsford where he died. He was disappointed with the open-air demonstration at Edinburgh. "It did not come up to a State fair," he heard one Yankee remark at the hotel dinner-table. But of course the real literary celebration was a much different thing. That at Galashiels appears to have satisfied him. "Taken as a whole, it was a grand success, and as far as outward display goes, was far ahead of either Edinburgh or Glasgow."

At length, after three months' touring about Scotland and England, he returned to Canada, and commenced business on his own account in Chatham. He was almost immediately thereafter appointed precentor in St. Andrew's Church, and elected secretary of the St. Andrew's Society. This same year he won the prize medal for his poem on the Royal Marriage. But although he still took a keen interest and a large share in the literary and musical life of the town, he found that managing a business of his own demanded a curtailment of his former actively public work. A commercial career he was beginning to see required concentration, and so he set himself to keep pace with the pushing business methods of the West. His duties as choir-master were a sufficient relaxation from the hard, sometimes dull, routine of shop life. These he maintained with an energy born of real love for the subject, and with appreciation by all who were privileged to have him as interpreter of sacred praise.

And so the years sped on. His common-place book does not reveal much regarding this time. It is almost certain that during the next years his mind was fully occupied with his daily employment to the exclusion of many of those large-hearted and generous services which were the delight and passion of his life during the earlier years at Chatham. Sorrowfully has it to be recorded that he was troubled by business anxieties. He succeeded well until the introduction of Sir John Macdonald's Protective Policy, which went far to crush trade in the Canadian border towns. His health, also, had grown somewhat indifferent. Though never of a vigorous constitution, he was strong and wiry enough. But the worries through which he was called to pass told heavily on his general health. Nothing so impairs the physical framework like mental anxiety.

Very reluctantly did he resolve to give up. Had he remained, it might have meant more than complete ruin both financially and physically. To the regret of many kindly and good citizens in Chatham, he announced his intention of returning to England. He was the recipient of many messages of sympathy and fervent God-speeds for the future. Parting gifts were devised and cheering words arranged to be spoken. A number of friends determined to tender him some slight evidence of their esteem and acknowledgment of his valuable services in so many musical entertainments for benevolent objects. The following address was presented, accompanied by something more tangible :

"We, the undersigned, have learned with regret that you are about to quit Chatham, where you have lived so long and gained so many friends. Your gentle courtesy, and musical and poetical talents often delighted us in many a merry meeting ; while your strict integrity and unswerving loyalty to good principles have won our unfeigned respect. It is therefore only right and becoming that we should, on this occasion, testify in some tangible way our genuine appreciation of your character. This testimonial we have put in the form of a purse containing one hundred dollars, which were contributed in the shares expressed after our respective names. Accept then, we beg of you, this small sum as an earnest of our hearty goodwill towards you, as an expression of our esteem for your many talents and virtues, and be assured that we will watch with interest your future career wherever you may be."

His choir likewise presented him with an address, a gold watch, and other valuable tokens of respect.

"We, the members of St. Andrew's Church Choir, who have spent so many pleasant and profitable hours under your efficient leadership, regret very much that your new sphere of action compels you to sever your connection with us, and cannot allow you to leave without showing in some way our high appreciation of your abilities as a leader, of your gentlemanly conduct towards us, and your willingness at all times to aid in our entertainments with your musical talents. We therefore beg of you to accept the accompanying gift, not as compensation for the benefits which we have derived from your instruction, but as a small token of the respect and esteem in which you are held by us as a friend. In so doing, we feel confident we are expressing the sentiments of the entire congregation of St. Andrew's Church. We wish you a pleasant voyage, many happy meetings of long-divided friends, and a speedy return to our beloved country, where you will always be a welcome visitor in our Canadian homes."

Many other friends were glad to testify to their admiration and love for one who had endeared himself to them by his sterling qualities and supremely amiable disposition. He had spent in all fifteen years in Canada; perhaps, in spite of much pain, the happiest and best part of his life. He pursued there the life of a true Scotsman. Amid success he was not puffed up. Amid adversity he learned how to suffer patiently, knowing that he who endureth to the end shall behold the passing of all shadows. The last entry in his diary is from a newspaper extract:—" Mr Calder bade goodbye to his Chatham friends on Monday evening, and departed on the night express for New York *en route* for England. A large number of friends were at the station to see him off and wish him a safe voyage." He arrived in London about the middle of October, 1882. From that time until his death, he was associated with his brother, Mr Peter Calder, in the shoe-trimming and embroidery trade, a long-established and flourishing business.

From his settlement in London in 1882, he began to take a close interest in all Scottish affairs. Specially was he drawn to the study of Border life and poetry. His native Berwickshire had many attractions for him, and scarcely a week passed without some poetical contribution to the newspapers of that county. His name became better known than ever. His early essays in rhyme in the same journals pleased, for the most part, his own acquaintances; his productions now attracted the attention and secured for him the friendship of an ever-widening circle of readers. He made yearly pilgrimages to Scotland, and renewed many happy days at Polwarth. But the old home had been broken up. His mother had passed away in 1875, and the father a few weeks previous to his son's return. Comparatively few remained in the place of their birth of those who had been his schoolmates and early associates. Nearly all the old "worthies" and "characters" had disappeared. New faces met his as he wandered through each well-known haunt. No wonder that he bewails in touching rhapsody the sad changes which had come over this sweet and blessed spot!

In 1887 an event of considerable importance occurred in the life of our bard. This was the publication of *Hame Sangs*, a small volume of 140 pages, containing a selection of his best work (London: King & Co., 50 Booksellers Row, Strand); a brief prefatory note tells that "the themes being homely, are treated in a homely way: still, they may serve to echo the sentiments of Scotchmen who have wandered far 'owre the sea,' and who yet retain a strong affection for everything pertaining to their native country." The little book was most favourably received by both the press and public of Britain and America, and the author was honoured with kind and encouraging letters from many eminent Scotsmen at home and abroad. The Marquis of Lorne thanked him for his "pleasant verses." Mr Gladstone "heartily entered into the spirit of his verses." Professor Blackie characteristically wrote that "they are full of nature, and love, and truth, and fine wisdom. As genuine Scottish feeling *The Thistle* is an excellent glorification of our kingly weed, and *The Royal Mouse* is a poem that would have done credit to Burns. *Under the Snow* is a beautiful elegy." Madame

Antoinette Sterling—that most consecrated songstress of our time—"read the book with great pleasure." From across the Atlantic many appreciative tokens came to the grateful author. The Canadian journals were unanimous in its praise. The *Chatham Planet* avowed that "to read some of his more pronounced stanzas you can easily fancy yourself perusing a page of Burns. He has the true ring of Scottish poetry, the style of versification, the rugged metre, all very perfect, and he may fairly be classed among the best of the Scottish poets." This was high praise indeed, but not undeserved. A large number of criticisms were couched in similar strains. *Hume Sangs* proved a popular addition to Scottish minstrelsy; almost the whole of the first edition being bought up immediately on publication. It was the author's intention to have issued a second volume of verse, but the time for that never came. Into other hands that task has fallen, and the fulfilling of it has been a labour of love. For the next eight or nine years little has to be recorded in what was now a comparatively quiet and uneventful life. Business claimed its due attention. But verse-making was not discarded, nor did interest flag in British and Colonial politics. Mr Calder's political leanings were on the side of Advanced Liberalism; and on not a few occasions he rendered yeoman service to the cause. He was a member of the Pimlico Radical Club, and wrought hard by voice and pen on its behalf. Many of his musings breathe a strongly democratic spirit; but always well tempered with the divine principles of Christian brotherhood. "His sympathies were very broad, and his intense hatred of oppression and wrong often led him to take extreme views on the question of Socialism; but in the main he adhered to the Socialism of Christ." But his tastes were not in the direction of politics and noisy public meetings. His delight was to get home after business to the cosy fireside with his books—the best companions of his life—and there, surrounded with all that recalled incidents and reminiscences of the past, he would sit and muse, and shape his thoughts into some sweet song.

With one Association in the metropolis he closely and enthusiastically identified himself. This was "The Borders Association in London." All over the world, wherever Border men have settled, they have clubbed together in this way for the promotion of good fellowship and the preservation of the patriotic feeling. It is computed that there are somewhere about one hundred thousand Border men and women in London. From amongst these, several of the keener spirits formed themselves into the above Society, which has been of incalculable benefit to many new-comers from the Borderland. Mr Calder threw himself with characteristic ardour into the undertaking, and all along was an especial favourite; in fact it was largely owing to his exertions that the Association was begun. He was poet-laureate, and voiced in appropriate song the feelings of every member.

The following is part of a letter from the secretary of the Association:—"Mr Calder was a most valuable member, and his earnest work therein formed the groundwork of the Association. His assistance at our meetings was very much appreciated by all, and during the later part of his life, when disease had laid hold of him, and he no longer could attend the meetings, his thoughts were with his fellow-Borderers; and in a letter I had from him just about the time before he took to his bed, he says, 'I am sorry I cannot attend the meeting of the Border Raiders, being too ill; I am only a shadow of my former self, and am as weak as a kitten and as thin as a net-stabb. Another thing my illness has done, it has knocked all the poetry out of me. The machine won't work.' I visited him a day or two before he died. His thin wasted face lit up when I entered the room; he thanked me for the good wishes I conveyed to him from the members, and he said, 'I'll just need to try and warsle through,' which unfortunately for all he did not. The Association lost a well-beloved member, and I a good friend and wise counsellor."

A visit to Scotland for a few weeks during 1895, when he witnessed the celebrations at Earlston in connection with the taking over of the Tower of Thomas the Rhymer by the Edinburgh Border Counties Association, was the last visit he made to his native country and county. He was never happier than when down in Scotland on his annual holiday; and he always looked forward with keen anticipation to that pleasure. But he was then not at all in good health. The illness which ultimately cut him off was manifesting itself. The clear bracing airs of Tweedside, the romantic spell of the Border country, and the genial companionship of many whom he had come to recognise as attached friends, did much to inspire him with the hope that he might yet recover. But that was not to be. He got back to London and resumed work at

Warwick Street. The spirit was willing as ever, but the body was becoming gradually feebler. At length he had to take to his room, then to his bed, until finally it was only too apparent that his work was over.

"His last days were passed in singular patience and resignation. He did not like to converse long, he was so weak. He told me he liked best to lie and think, and that he felt quite happy in his contemplations. I had many opportunities of reading to him, and many a hallowed conversation we had when he felt more able for it. I told him one morning that I did not know a line he need regret having written. He said he never wrote anything with the intention of hurting any one; but he added, 'I must now begin to act up to my own philosophy.' I would add that a gentler or more unselfish soul never lived. He was a true child of nature, without any ambition to be rich, contented when he had enough, and ever ready to help the needy to the utmost of his means. His loss to me can never be repaired." So writes the brother who came closest into his life.

On Monday, April 13, 1895, Robert McLean Calder entered on the last of all journeys, and in that journey he was not alone. In life he had learned to know whereon to lean whenever the shadows of the valley might gather. He was in his fifty-fifth year. At the close of the week all that was mortal of one who had sung so sweetly was laid to rest in Norwood Cemetery, in presence of a large number of friends and admirers, and his brother pronounced over the grave, when dust had mingled with kindred dust, those final words,

" Here lies one who possessed one of the most unselfish spirits that ever inhabited a human frame."

For one who had sung so much of love it is surprising that he never married, but in contentment with his lot, strove to make better and brighter the larger life of those who came into contact with his own. Yet many mourn him among his own kin, and for them there is to-day the supreme satisfaction that their departed dead did not live in vain.

The announcement that Robert McLean Calder, "the Berwickshire Bard," had for ever ceased his singing, was received with feelings of deep regret by all classes in Berwickshire, and through all the wide Border. Since 1882 his name had been prominently before the readers of the county newspapers in the weekly contributions to which so many looked forward with pleasure. He was distinctively a Merse poet. His effusions were largely inspired by Merse manners, traditions, and scenery. The *patois* of Berwickshire is uppermost in his song. He did not attempt much beyond his native doric. To write in praise of the places endeared to him from long association was the delight of his life. And what was a joy to him begot joy in others. Like Burns, there was ever present to him

> "A wish that to my latest hour
>   Shall strongly heave my breast,
> That I, for puir auld Scotland's sake,
> Some usefu' plan or book could make,
>   Or sing a sang at least!"

The poet's mission is to cheer and elevate, to brighten the common round of life, to instruct, and to amuse. A perusal of the pages that follow will show how well our poet satisfied this high ideal. If it cannot be said that his verse always exhibits a polished gracefulness, it is none the less true that in it there is manifested the soul of a genuine singer who understood the mysteries of human nature, whose heart beat in close sympathy with the material universe, and whose song has lighted up with true beauty the simple annals of the poor, the holy charms of home, the pure joys of love, and the honest humility of country life. He was at his best when he took homely themes, early recollections and phases of nature for his verse, and in these he seemed to revel with ceaseless delight. Possibly rhyme came too easy to him, and he might have been more effective if he had revised and pruned a little more carefully. Yet he won for himself a recognised and honoured place among the bards of Berwickshire, and when death made void the sphere he filled, many hearts were made sorry at his too early departure.

To Mr Peter Calder, London, I am indebted for the following interesting reminiscences:

"My brother could never write poetry to order. I have often suggested a subject to him, and asked him to write something upon it, but very seldom could I get him to do anything in this way. Many of the best things he did came to him as an inspiration. He told a friend that he wrote the poem on *Saint Andrew's Day* on a sudden impulse. He went to bed, and woke up in the middle of the night, dressed himself, and wrote the poem straight off, and again retired. In the morning he posted the verses without any revision. It gained the prize medal. One of his most popular songs—*My heart warms to the Tartan*—was written under the following circumstances. He had to go up Oxford Street one night on business, and passing along the street, he stopped to look into the shop of Peter Robinson, when, admiring the new fashions, he heard in the distance the sound of the bagpipes. The Highlanders were marching along the street. Instantly the words came to his lips, 'My heart warms to the tartan.' He took out his pocket-book and at once wrote off the song in a few minutes. When he came home he told me the circumstances and read the words. The next week they appeared in the Berwickshire papers, and shortly afterwards were set to music by John Wilson of Glasgow, and published. *A Woman's Song*—a very pretty piece—was thus suggested: One morning, on a dull November day, when having his breakfast, his landlady called his attention to a sunbeam dancing on the opposite wall, and made some remark about a glint of sunshine bringing hope amid the gloom. Next morning he read her the poem I allude to. He told me that one very stormy morning, as he was going to business, he buttoned up his coat and said to himself, 'We maun just warsle through'; and before he got to the house he had composed the poem of that title. The poem, *Heaven is no' sae far awa'*, eminently expressed his own feelings. He could always extract the intensest pleasure from the quiet contemplation of nature. He told me one day that he would rather go out into the park or the fields in the company of a little child than with men to converse with. He was always at home amongst children or flowers, or roaming amidst nature's wildest scenes 'far from the madding crowd.' My brother possessed the soul of a true poet; in fact, I often thought that on many points he strongly resembled Burns. His politics, for example, would have cheered the heart of Robin; and in religious leanings he was much the same. He had a profound belief in the loving Fatherhood of God. He could not understand the man who professed the religion of Christ, and rode rough-shod over his fellow-men to further his own ambitions and ends. He had a firm faith in practice, and very little in profession. He carried a very small lamp, but a good supply of oil; and, perhaps unfortunately for him, his keen powers of detecting inconsistency in others prevented him from permanently allying himself to any particular church. He was more the scribe sitting at the foot of the Mount of Transfiguration, rather than the disciple entering into the inner circle to the presence of Christ, but adoring at a distance, his natural timidity keeping him back from ostentatious display. The Sermon on the Mount was to him real and literal. He had much in common with Count Tolstoi in his teaching, and believed the Church of to-day had wandered far away from the real teachings of the Master."

I.

Memories of Polwarth.

"There's nae place like ane's native place,
   Nae hame like ane's first hame;
It matters na hoo puir an' cauld,
   Oor love is a' the same.

We're drawn by some mysterious tie
   That nae man e'er defined,
To the sacred spot, hooe'er remote,
   Where licht first on us shined."

— *William Brockie.*

I.

MEMORIES OF POLWARTH.

MY FAITHER'S FIRESIDE.

Oh! the hame of my childhood, hoo can I forget
The bright scenes that cling to my memory yet,
Thro' lang years o' absence frae that cherished scene,
Wi' ocean's wide billows careering between!
My heart never yet has forgot the bright days
When as younkers we speeled up the heather-clad braes—
Or the sweet hallowed spot where true love did preside,
In the auld cosy neuk at my faither's fireside.

Nae distance or time can ever erase
Frae my heart the gay scenes o' my dear native place,—
The auld theekit cot, wi' the stile in the yaird,
The byre an' the barn where the poultry were reared ;
The bonnie thorn trees that grew on the green,
An' the burnie meandering sae crystal an' sheen ;
But the scene aboon a' that has stood time an' tide,
Is the auld cosy neuk o' my faither's fireside.

Hoo aften in dreams o' the nicht I am there,
An' mingle wi' lang-parted cronies ance mair,
As there, in his auld elbow chair in the neuk,
My faither sits readin' some paper or buik ;
My mither is mendin' my corduroy breeks
I had torn in some o' my mad speelin' freaks,
While my ae sister, Aggie, oor suppers provide,
Ere sleep reigns owre a' at my faither's fireside.

Or again, amid innocent laughter an' din,
We callants wad gather oor peeries to spin
On the muckle hearth-stane, where the dancin' glint
O' the big peat fire shone on faces content ;
Faces frae cares an' griefs mair free
I never hae seen 'mang the prood an' hie,
Nor hearts as free frae a' envy an' pride,
As gathered langsyne roun' my faither's fireside.

On cauld winter nichts, when the wind an' rain
Patterin' fell on the window pane,
We hae danced for hours to the fiddle's strains,
Or got in a corner a' oor lanes.
To tell owre stories, aft tauld before,
O' ghaist an' bogles, an' warlock lore,
Or sung the sangs that are Scotia's pride,
That sounded sae sweet at my faither's fireside.

My faither's auld neebours wad aften pop in,
Just to hae a bit crack owre what was gaun on,
The news or the gossip frae steadin' or toun,
Gin the craps were thrivin' or markets were doun ;
And listenin' to a' as they cracked sae crouse,
I sat in my corner as quiet 's a mouse,
Till my een nae langer open wad bide,
An' I dosed sae snug by my faither's fireside.

There 's no' a scene o' those days o' yore
I 'll e'er forget while I 'm to the fore :
The dance an' fun at the harvest kirns,
The fishin' splores in the muirland burns,
Climbin' for scroggs in the auld kirk park,
Or playin' at bogley whan nicht grew dark,
Or spaein' fortunes as we sat side by side,
On oor cutty stools by my faither's fireside.

Nor hae I ever the lessons forgot
The Bible lessons my faither taught,
Or the solemn stillness reigning there
When we read the buik, or we knelt in prayer ;

E'en noo I remember his solemn words,
An' my mither's counsels my heart still hoards,
As she sought in prayers my young heart to guide
An' I knelt at her knee by my faither's fireside.

But those days are gane, an' will ne'er return,
Yet oft wi' sic thochts my heart does burn,
As my youthfu' days I live owre again,
Forgettin' my manhood's sorrows an' pain;
An' oh! gin I could my wish but hae
To visit that spot noo far away,
I'd joyfully cross owre the foaming tide
To spend my last days by my faither's fireside.

MY FAITHER'S FIDDLE.

Hoo aft in happy times gane by,
When but a wean some three feet high,
My heart has been elate wi' joy
   As, chair astriddle,
I'd aft alane delight to try
   My faither's fiddle.

Or when the weary day was dune,
An' by the ingle gather'd roun',
I've watched whene'er my dad took doon
   The auld green bag,
I wearied sae to hear the tune,
   "An' rax my leg."

An' when we heard the tuning notes,
We sune were aff oor cosy seats
Beside the fire o' blazin' peats;
   Up to the floor,
When flingin' aff oor heavy boots
   We raised a stoure.

Nor did we cease the mirth an' glee,
Till tired an' wearied sair were we:
Wi' hearts as licht as licht could be
   We sought oor rest,
An' in sweet slumber closed oor e'e,
   An' pillow press'd.

When stack-yairds were wi' plenty clad,
An' farmer-boddies' hearts were glad,
I've seen the hinds gang dancin' mad
    When work was dune,
An' ilk blithe lass wad pick her lad
    An' dance like fun.

But when the harvest kirn took place,
Then joy was seen in ilka face,
An' lasses wi' a witchin' grace
    Sae neat an' braw,
Made Jock an' Tam alike confess
    "That it beat a'."

An' when thy canty strains began,
Thou kept them a' in mirth an' fun,
An' auld an' young wi' noise and din
    Made rafters ring,
Till daylicht tauld the nicht was dune—
    New cares to bring.

I've seen thee, too, on auld year's nicht,
Mak' lads' and lassies' hearts beat licht,
An' youngsters' faces beam sae bricht,
    An' hearts beat high
Wi' expectation and delicht,
    An' purest joy.

Then, when the partners danced and reeled,
Then loud and lang the music pealed,
While cat-gut held thou wadna yield,
    Tho' sair the tussle,
Exceptin' when the fiddler chield
    Wad weet his whustle.

Wi' gallant lads an' maidens coy,
An' youngsters daft wi' mirth an' joy,
I've seen the merry nicht slip bye,
    Till new year's morn
We welcomed in wi' blithe strathspey
    Around the thorn.

Oh! aften hae I blessed thy power
To yield us thus a happy hour,—
To sweeten a' that sad and sour
    Oppressed my heart,
An' gie auld care a canty clour,—
    His richt desert.

Still, when I hear thy canty sound,
I'm to my feet wi' lichtsome bound,
Or when the merry sang gangs round
    Wi' heartsome glee,
Nae mair wi' grief my heart does stound;
    Frae care I'm free.

Or when wi' plaintive accents played,
When sang o' lover lowly laid
Throws o'er my soul a holy shade
    Wi' heart richt sair,
I've sorrowed for the hapless maid,
    To fancy fair.

Lang may thou cheer my droopin' heart
Ere I frae this world's sorrows part,
An' when I feel the keen, keen dart
    O' grief an' pain,
I'll seek to soothe the bitter smart,
    Thy canty strain.

POLART BURN.

The frost has nipt the heather bloom,
    The brackens hing their dowdie leaves—
The hips are red upon the brier,
    An' paitricks whirr amang the sheaves:
Nae mair the bees roam owre the muir,
    Or, laden wi' their sweets, return,
As I, to sniff the cauler air,
    Stray up the glen by Polart burn.

Here mony a happy day we spent
    When we were laddies at the schule:
We sought the heather-linties' nests,
    Or gump'd for mennents in the pool:

We wist nae hoo the time sped on,
   Until we heard the cowboy's horn :
Yet, laith to lea', we linger'd on
   'Till gloamin' fell o'er Polart burn.

We've wander'd 'mang the heather knowes,
   When frae oor feet the muir-cock whirr'd,
Or wander'd by the lower haugh
   Where first the cuckoo's note was heard :
Syne hameward we would tread its banks
   To watch the moss-grown mill-wheel turn,
Or note the foamin' mill-race rush
   To blend its flood wi' Polart burn.

There, wi' the love oor boyhood knew,
   We wander'd—prodigal o' time—
When eyes were brighter, lips mair sweet,
   Than ever met wi' in oor prime ;
Noo sad the memory that comes back,—
   Its brightness never can return,—
An' phantom hopes float 'mid the haze
   That e'ening brings o'er Polart burn.

The schuleboy friendships then begun
   Hae still grown closer year by year,
Tho' a' oor mates are scatter'd wide,
   In cauld nor'-land, or southern sphere :
And scarce a simmer time comes roun'
   But ane or ither maun return
To see ance mair their native hame
   An' boyhood's haunts by Polart burn.

An' noo, amid the city's stir,
   The busy mart, an' crowded street,
Aft will my fancy wander free,
   Ilk shady nook and calm retreat ;
Or as beside my fire I sit,
   Inclined o'er bygane joys to mourn,
The sunny glints come back again,
   Whene'er I think o' Polart burn.

THE AULD SCHULE HOOSE ON THE GREEN.

Oh! weel I remember the schule hoose
    That stood fu' snug 'neath the trees,
Where the blaeberries grew in the plantin',
    And the heather invited the bees;
Where the bairnies' voices rang merry,
    As, wi' faces an' daidlies sae clean,
They scampered awa' thro' the bushes
    To the auld schule hoose on the Green.

Oh! I mind when mysel' a bit laddie,—
    When life wore its sunniest smile,—
How blithely wi' licht heart I lilted,
    As I scampered through hedge-slap an' stile:
Or climbed the scrogg tree in the meadow,—
    Or waded the burn clear an' sheen,
Tho' aften I loitered owre late for
    The auld schule hoose on the Green.

Still mem'ry delights to dwell upon
    The scenes o' those happiest days,
The burn where we gumpit for mennents;
    Or the bluebell an' gowan-clad braes
Where we twined flower wreaths for the lassies—
    For Mary, an' Lizzy, an' Jean,
Wha ilka morn toddled there wi' us
    To the auld schule hoose on the Green.

Oh! I mind o' that wee theekit schule hoose
    Wi' the rose bushes grown at the door,
An' the apple trees in the wee garden,
    Wi' bonnie white blossoms hung o'er;
The desks where we scribbled our copies,
    Or aftener, ate sweeties unseen,
While the lassies were clippin' and shoowin'
    In the auld schule hoose on the Green.

An' still aft I think o' the plantin
    Where the geans an' the blaeberries grew,
For aften we've sat there an' feasted
    Till our faces an' daidlies were blue;

An' oor legs wi' the whuns were a' scartit,
　　But whilk we ne'er cared for a preen;
We were blithe as the lambkins that sportit
　　Near the auld schule hoose on the Green.

An' weel can I mind how we huntit
　　The squirrel high up the fir tree,
Or the young cusha doo that had ventured
　　Oot the nest afore it could flee.
Where we shunned the deep well where the hunter
　　Had fa'n in, an' ne'er was mair seen,
When the bell ca'd us back frae oor sportin'
　　To the auld schule hoose on the Green.

Oh, aften I think o' those playmates
　　Noo scattered far, far frae their hames,—
Where the laddies still search in the plantin'
　　For the trees where we cut oot oor names,
While they tell ane anither the story, —
　　That in many a strange foreign scene
Are the laddies wha years were before them
　　At the auld schule hoose on the Green.

I ken na if e'er I may wander
　　Again by that auld cherished spot,
But those bright cloudless hours o' my childhood
　　An' those playmates shall ne'er be forgot:
While deeply engraved on my mem'ry
　　Shall aye be each fair hallowed scene,
As in fancy I aften shall linger
　　By the auld schule hoose on the Green.

THE LOVE O' MY SCHULE-BOY DAYS.

There's a langsyne fancy comes back to me
　　When I think o' my Scottish hame;
There's a lowe o' love that rekindles again,
　　That brings back a dear ane's name;
An' ance mair I wander the bonnie glen
　　Where the clear wimplin' burnie plays,
An' the primrose blooms on the banks I roamed
　　Wi' the love o' my schule-boy days.

The flowers were gay in their brichtest hues,
　　And the woods in their freshest green ;
An' there wasna a cloud to darken the sky,
　　Or a sorrow to mar the scene ;
Oor voices rang wi' as merry a lilt
　　As the birds that sang on the sprays,
As I daidled aboot in the simmer hours
　　Wi' the love o' my schule-boy days.

The burnie murmurs the same auld sang
　　By the banks where the hazels grow,
But it has nae langer the cheerie soun'
　　That it had in the lang ago :
For it tells o' my schule-mates scattered wide,
　　Far awa' frae its banks an' braes,—
An' it tells o' a mound near by, where sleeps
　　The love o' my schule-boy days.

It canna be sinfu' to cherish the thocht,
　　That when dune wi' this warl' o' toil,
We'll meet in that bonnie land aboon,
　　As if parted a little while ;
That the years gane by will seem as a day
　　When freed frae earth's dreary haze :
An' in happier scenes ance mair I'll renew
　　The love o' my schule-boy days.

THE AULD THEEKIT HOOSE.

Just owre the wee briggie that crosses the burn
　　That rins by the fit o' the Green,
There's a humble bit cottage wi' ivy-clad wa's,
　　Where mony blithe days I hae seen :
The inside is hamely, yet tidy an' neat,
　　Its inmates are kindly an' douce,
An' there's aye a warm welcome whenever I ca'
　　On the folks at the auld theekit hoose.

Hoo cantie we've been by the auld ingle-side,
　　When the lang winter nichts had set in ;
We sat in the glow of the cheery peat fire,
　　When the story an' sang wid begin ;

We sang the sweet lilts o' oor ain native land,
  When our heroes were Wallace and Bruce,
Or listened to auld-farrant tales that were tauld
  In the neuk o' the auld theekit hoose.

'Twas a picture o' hamely contentment an' cheer,
  That riches or state couldna bring ;
Auld Jock by the ingle, his pipe in his cheek,
  Was as happy as kaiser or king.
Auld Babbie sat there wi' her wark on her knee ;
  On the hearth stane lay Rover an' puss ;
For even the cats an' the dongs would agree
  'Neath the roof o' the auld theekit hoose.

Whene'er I return to the auld village Green,
  To the scene o' my boyhood's bright days,
The joys o' the past come again to my heart
  As I roam by the burnies an' braes ;
An' here wi' auld cronies, still faithfu' an' true,
  We meet a' sae frien'ly an' crouse,
To crack owre the scenes o' the happy langsyne,
  In the neuk o' the auld theekit hoose.

MY HORN-SPUNE AN' LUGGIE.

Oh ! weel I mind my boyhood's hame,
  An' a' its scenes sae cheerie,
An' thochts come back that pleasures gie
  When life is wairsh and drearie :—
The humble cot, wi' but an' ben,
  The ingle-neuk sae snug aye ;
The weel-scoored bink where stood my ain
  Wee horn-spune an' luggie.

My life has hain its ups an' doons,
  Wi' joys an' sorrows blended,
An' yet these scenes come back, as gin
  My childhood ne'er had ended :
The village Green 's the same as when
  We played at ba' or muggie,
Whilk gied a zest to mony a feast
  Oot horn-spune an' luggie.

That horn-spune wi' whistle in 't,—
    That luggie brichtly polished,
Are just as real to me, tho' a'
    Youth's dreams hae been demolished :
But tho' the glamour's gane for aye.
    An' life's noo geyan ruggie,
A glint o' joy comes back at sicht
    O' horn-spune an' luggie.

I like to see the dear auld spot,
    The cot where I was born in,
Nor feel a shame in speakin' o'
    The struggles o' life's mornin' ;
I raither pride me in the fac'
    That puirtith was mae bogie,
An' frugal lessons were imbibed
    Frae horn-spune an' luggie.

Sin' then, I've mixed amang the great,
    Wi' titles an' distinctions,
An' sat at mony a festive board
    In gay an' gilded mansions ;
But gie to me, 'boon a' their stews,
    Or wines that just befog ye,
A feast o' halesome parritch oot
    O' horn-spune an' luggie.

Auld Scotia's sons the warld owre
    Hae shown a sturdy valour :
They mak' a name where'er they gang,
    An' lauch at thoucht o' failure.
Tho' hard the struggles o' their youth,
    Wi' whiles a scrimpit coggie,
They've speeled the brae to walth an' poo'er
    Frae horn-spune an' luggie.

The sturdy chiel's frae Scotland's hills
    Hae shared war's strife an' glory,
An' left a record o' their deeds
    Embalmed in sang an' story :

An' where owre distant lands they range
    To share life's stern tug aye,
May they look back wi' honest pride
    On horn-spune and luggie.

THE CHIMLA CHEEK.

The snaw lies deep on the muirlands,
    An' drifts are in valley an' cleugh,
The win' blaws keen through the plantins
    An' sighs wi' an eerie sough,
As hame frae my wark I hurry
    The humble comforts to seek,
Where the wife an' weans are enjoyin'
    The warmth o' the chimla cheek.

Nae grandeur is there to entice me,
    But oor table's ne'er scant o' fare,
We've aye had eneuch for oor needs yet,
    An' we dinna hanker for mair;
There's a farl o' scones on the girdle—
    The kettle is hung on the cleek,
An' a halesome supper awaits me
    When I win to my chimla cheek.

Then the bairnies, red-lippit and rosy,
    Bright-e'ed, broon-leggit, and clean
Their mither looks after the rognies,
    An' keeps them as neat as a preen;
An' when they hae put on their gownies
    The dreamland o' slumber to seek,
They maun cuddle awhile wi' their daddy
    In the bleeze o' the chimla cheek.

An' when I'm alane wi' my Mysie,
    An' we con owre the days that are gane,
I mony times speak o' oor courtin',
    An' my speirin' gin she'd been my ain:
For it wasna when roamin' the woodlan's,
    Or in nature's sweet neuk—sae to speak,—
I wooed her an' won i' the glimmer
    O' the auld folks' ain chimla cheek.

Sin' then we hae had oor misfortunes,
   But oor pleasures hae no' be sae sma':
'Twas for better or waur when we marriet,
   An' we 've stuck to ilk ither thro' a':
We ne'er were ambitious or worldly,
   Nor afar for oor joys did we seek,—
Frae the rough storms o' life there's nae haven
   Sae safe as oor ain chimla cheek.

We envy nae ithers their pleasures,
   Be they great folks i' mansion or ha',
We ken that the richest hae troubles
   'Mid their housin' an' buskin' sae braw:
Sae contented we 'll toddle togither,
   While the blessin' o' Heaven we 'll seek
On the simple and innocent pleasures
   That brichten oor chimla cheek.

LANGTON WATER.

GREEN are thy banks, thou bonnie stream,
   That windest sweet by wood and field,
Where summer's flow'rets, blooming sweet,
   Their fragrance to the zephyrs yield.
Thy scenes are ever fair and bright,
   'Neath springtide's smile or summer's glow,
When with rich autumn's bounty crowned,
      Or winter's snow.

Far up amid the heathery hills,
   There, murmur first thy tiny rills;
Then, flowing on through mead and dell,
      The burnies meet,
With many a gurgling rippling swell,
      In calm and fair retreat.

Now thro' the deep and craggy glen;
      Now sleeping 'neath the hazel's shade,—
Now rushing on thy course again,
   Making the valley's echoes roar
   As o'er the linn thy waters pour;
   Now calm and peaceful as before
      On thro' the silent glade.

Thy course is marked by many a scene,
    Rugged, yet fair and bright,
Where fitful thro' thy leafy screen
The sun's refreshing rays are seen,
    Or Luna's silvery light;

Where, hanging in thy rugged steeps,
    The honeysuckle blooms,
And the trailing ivy creeps
    Where the sunshine never comes;

Where the cowslip and the fair primrose
    Lift up their modest heads,
And fling their fragance all around,
When hushed is every sound,
    As they catch the dewdrops' pearly beads
When day draws to its close.

When first Aurora's golden beams
O'er the eastern hilltops stream,
    Then sweet the forest warblers sing
Their happy songs of love,
Which echo thro' the grove
    Till woods and valleys ring.

Oh! how I love to roam along
    By many a sylvan scene,
And listen to thy song,—
        As oft in days of yore
        I wandered on thy pebbled shore,
    And happy was, I ween;
But now sad are the thoughts that rise,
And oft the tear-drops fill my eyes,
As thou recal'st the days gone by
When gayest of the gay was I.

Oft with the loved of childhood's days
I've sported on thy gowany braes;
Thy richest spots full well we knew—
The copse where the wild apples grew
    And where the hazels hung,

Down o'er the deep and craggy rock,
Where oft the echoes were awoke
By ringing laugh of mirth and joy
From many a fair and happy boy,
    The clustering boughs among.

Oft, too, we've gone a-nesting there,
    For we knew each shady nook
    And slaethorn bower,
Where the linnets loved their young to rear,—
    Where they loved to lave in the limpid brook
    At the sultry noontide hour:
We've watched the bee on the opening flower,
    And oft, in merry chase,
We've run o'er the glade for many an hour
    Chasing the gaudy butterflies—
    To us a rich and wondrous prize—
        'Till o'er each happy face
The rosy glow of health was spread,
And home again we sped.

There, too, I've often happy been,
    When, with the maid I loved,
    By thy sweet banks we roved
In some sequestered scene,
    Away from all the vexing cares
    Which marked my growing years.

But, ah! where is that maiden now?
    By thee, sweet stream,
She lieth low!
    No more her smiles, like sunshine's glow,
    Shall play around her brow;
    No more her dazzling eyes shall beam,
Or evening's balmy air
Dance 'mid her golden hair.

She sleeps, and on thou murmurest still:
    And thus I love to wander here
To listen to thy purling rill,
    As if her voice still met my ear,
    And bade my drooping spirits cheer
        With visions of a coming joy:

When, all my wanderings o'er,
I'll fly to you bright peaceful shore,
Where, to the loved ones gone before.
Sorrow and sighing come no more,
    And tears no more shall dim the eye,
      For there at last
      All griefs of earth are past.

But, lovely stream, still here I'll rove,
And list the songsters of the grove ;
Here at the opening dawn I'll come,
Here at the eventide I roam,
    While sweetly thou shall gurgle on ;
And tho' thou dost remind me still
    Of joys for ever gone,
        Yet will
I love thee, peaceful, murmuring rill.

LANGTON BRIG.

I WANDER at the gloaming tide,
    That lovely, heart-entrancing scene,
Where Langton waters sweetly glide
    The mossy-covered banks between :
With soul attuned to evening's charms,
    I view the scene so calm and fair,
Where giant trees stretch forth their arms,
    As toying with the evening air.

The birds sing sweet in every grove,
    Their notes re-echoing through the dell
With tenderness—no lay of love
    From art-taught song could charm so well :
I watch the swallows skim the mead,
    The troutlets leaping in the burn,
The midges to its rippling dance,
    The rabbits sport 'mid rush and fern.

How oft ! in careless mood, I've strayed
    The verdant haughs, where cowslips bloomed,
At dewy morn, when scented briers
    The gentle toying breeze perfumed ;

And oft at eve, as now I rove
   In sombre mood to muse and dream,
Or from the brig surveyed the pool,
   Where minnows through the water gleam.

My thoughts go not to castle walls,
   Nor richly wooded wide demesnes,—
The simple scenes of vale and hill
   Are hallowed by the poet's strains ;
And these come back in whispered notes.
   The evening breezes waft along
"'Mong Langton's blooming woods," where oft
   Has Sutherland attuned his song.[1]

Here by this spot for ages past
   Have love-sick wooers careless strayed.
That hour so dear to wooing hearts,—
   The magic hour 'tween light and shade :
With whispered joys, they conjured up
   The coming days, bright as a dream,
Or bending o'er the brig's low wall
   They watched the shadows in the stream.

I picture them in after years,
   Hard toilers in life's chequered race :—
Their hopes and joys crushed 'neath life's load,
   Like dreams the morning rays efface :
Yet others come -the same old tale
   To muse and sigh, or fondly dream,
To find life's pleasures at the best
   Are but a shadow in the stream.

Yet find I pleasure here, to muse
   When evening's shades creep softly down,
Like one escaped from strife and toil
   And warping cares of life in town :
My heart feels lighter for the time,
   As, brushing present clouds away,
I revel in the past once more,
   And feel the joys of youth's bright day.

---

[1] William Sutherland, the "Langton Bard"; see *Minstrelsy of the Merse*, page 137.

CHOUSLEY BRAE.

Oh! lang's the stretch frae Langton Kirk
    Until ye turn by Chousley farm,
Wi' ne'er a shelter frae the sun
    When simmer days are glintin' warm :
But when the gloamin' shadows fa'
    An' zephyrs sigh at close of day,
A quiet meditative walk
    You may enjoy up Chousley brae.

'Tis then that lovers may be seen,
    When ilka bird has sought its rest,
When dew-beads hing on flower an' spray,
    An' love-licht blushes in the west;
The saft-drawn sighs, the whispered vows,
    Beguile the erstwhile tedious way;
An' tho' the road were twice as lang,
    They'd loiter still up Chousley brae.

Frae mony a vantage point is seen
    The oot-spread garden o' the Merse,
An' auld historic Border scene,
    The theme o' mony a poet's verse;
Nae foreign shores, tho' e'er sae grand,
    Where Flora smiles in garments gay,
Can boast a scene sae sweetly bricht,
    Or match the view frae Chousley brae.

Yet when the winter storms are rife,
    An' snaw lies deep in wreath an' drift,
When snell win's frae the Snuffy-holes
    Send clouds careerin' owre the lift,
Oh! lang an' dreary seems the road
    That in the simmer bloomed sae gay,
An' shelterin' beild ye vainly seek,
    Till owre the tap o' Chousley brae.

Wi' boyish een I've viewed the scene,
    An' longed to roam that fairy land,
An' like the lave, I failed to see
    The humble pleasures near at hand;

But noo, when I hae roamed the warl'
   An' found its boasted joys decay,
I, weary, turn wi' jaded heart
   To simple scenes like Chousley brae.

An' like a boy, I feel again
   As when we sought the lintie's nest,
Or gleaned the roadside flowers that grew
   To please the lassies we lo'ed best;
An' memory will bring back again
   Oor boyhood's frien's, noo far away,
To fill the void that years hae brought
   Since youth's bricht hours by Chousley brae.

Noo whae'er walks this langsome steep,
   When winter snaws clead hill an' dale,
Or when the glaur clogs ilka fit,
   An' strength an' spirit seem to fail,
Briest up the hill—owre Crummie staps,
   A Polart welcome will repay
The weary walk by day or nicht
   Owre toilsome, cheerless Chousley brae.

Sae like life's journey; unco steep
   'Mid simmer's glare or winter's snaw,
We bravely maun pursue oor way,
   Nor heed the storms that roun' us blaw:
An' when we've reached the shelterin' turn,
   May we in life's declinin' day
As kind a welcome meet at last
   As when we've briested Chousley brae.

THE AULD SMIDDY DOOR.

When a' aroun' the clachan,
   Frae the plantin' to the schule,
There's no' a body stirrin',
   An' the gloamin' hour is still,
There's aye ae grand exception,
   For at almaist ony hour
There's sure to be a gatherin'
   At the auld smiddy door.

There 's the smith himsel' fu' jolly,
　　Just cam' oot to get the air ;
An' the wright frae cross the corner
　　Comes the latest news to speir :
There 's Will, an' Jock, an' Davy—
　　Weel, maybe half a score,
For a quiet crack foregathered
　　At the auld smiddy door.

They talk aboot their "acres"—
　　Hoo the hay an' tatties grow ;
An' hoo the calves are thrivin'
　　At the near-by whinny knowe ;
What price the pigs are fetchin'
　　What feed is in the muir ;
It 's a sort o' village council
　　At the auld smiddy door.

An' there 's the fun an' daffin',
　　Tho' it 's hardly fair to tell,
As the buxom village lasses
　　Are comin' frae the well ;
For tho' there 's wells fu' plenty
　　Wi' the clear springs runnin' owre,
They raither like the chaffin'
　　At the auld smiddy door.

The tailor draps his needle,
　　An' gangs oot to tak' a turn,
The mason's mell and trowel
　　Are laid aside till morn :
E'en the dominie rejoices
　　That the schulin' time is owre,
An' they 're a' at leave to danner
　　To the auld smiddy door.

Ye talk aboot yer councils,
　　Or e'en yer County Boards,
Yer Parliamentary Hooses
　　O' Commons and o' Lords ;

It is only waste o' pouther
  To pit thae cliques in power—
They could rule the hale clamjamfry
  At the auld smiddy door.

They would oust the County Council
  For the taxes they impose;
An' baith Salisbury an' Gladstone
  They are ready to depose;
They will hae nae troke wi' Harcourt,
  An' wad boycott e'en Balfour;
For they'd settle a' the business
  At the auld smiddy door.

But they no' forget the wanderers
  Wha are passin' day by day:
An' them that are deservin'
  Are helped upon their way;
For, no' like ither gatherin's,
  Where they wrangle by the hour,
It disna end in talkin'
  At the auld smiddy door.

May they lang be spared to gather
  On the auld familiar spot,
To discuss their wrangs, an' settle
  Hoo they may improve their lot;
An' ne'er may spite or rancour
  Come except to get a clour
Frae the worthies wha foregather
  At the auld smiddy door.

THE PACKMAN'S LOAN.

A QUIET road by the plantin's side,
  Close by the village Green,
That gangs by the name o' the Packman's Loan,
  Sae ca'd frae a tragic scene:
For gossips tell o' a fair held near,
  Where a murdered packman fell,
An' near the hedge is a moss-grown stane
  O' his restin' place to tell.

But fancy gangs back to my schule-boy days,
   When youth was in its prime,
An' we sought the Loan in our reivin' raids
   In the pleasant nestin' time :
For we kenned the spot where the robin bigged,
   The yorlin' an' katie wren,
An' the favourite spot where the shilfa built
   In the hedge by the Packman's Stane.

'Twas a' very weel i' the braid daylicht,
   'Mang the sunshine an' the flowers,
But wha alane wad hae cared to gang
   Thro' the loan i' mirk nicht hours ?
For the tales o' witches an' ghaists we heard
   Wad hae frozen your very bluid :
An' gin we had to gang near the spot,
   We but gang by anither road.

An' a' the same we kenned fu' weel
   There were ithers that were na feared :
For lovers went there—but owre much ta'en up
   To tak' tent gin' the ghaists appeared :
An' they raither liket the quiet road
   Where nae pryin' een cam' near,
Where the fond, endearin' words they spoke
   Wadna fa' on some listener's ear.

Aye, there's mony a wife in the village noo
   Wha's locks are gettin' grey,
Wha's heart will warm at the mention o'
   The scene o' their love's bricht day :
For 'twas there they met at the gloamin' hour,
   'Twas there that their hearts were won,
An' the word was gi'en that sealed their fate,
   In the shade o' the Packman's Loan.

It's travelled alike by the rich an' puir,
   By the village lad an' lass,
While the cottar's coo an' the cadger's horse
   Aft nibble the wayside grass :

It has been the scene o' love's young dream,
  O' hopes that were doomed to fade,
O' vows, alas! that were never kept
  By some faithless man or maid.

An' yet, when parted by time an' space
  Frae the scenes our childhood knew.
Fond memory clings to the dear auld hame,
  An' wad fain the auld joys renew ;
But tho' the glamour o' youth has gane,
  An' the spot seems no' the same,
A faint glow stirs i' the careworn heart
  When we visit the dear auld hame.

An' I aften think o' the Packman's Loan
  As a picture o' life itsel'—
What varied scenes o' love an' hate
  Its every foot could tell ;
It has seen baith solemn and tragic scenes,
  An' joys that the young hae shared ;
While the schule-hoose stands at the heid o' the brae,
  An' it leads to the auld kirk-yard.

THE AULD BARN-YAIRD.

Just where the wimplin' burnie
  Threads its pebble-bedded track,
The barn stan's by the roadside,
  That the auld folk ca' the "back" :
An' alangside where the thrissels
  Their jaggit tassels reared,
Was the play-ground o' oor childhood,
  In the auld barn-yaird.

To the struggles o' oor boyhood
  Oor memory ca's us back,
To days, when on the whinny,
  We toiled to gather rack ;
Tho' we wist nae that the acres
  By oor labour were prepared,
For the gatherin' o' the harvest
  To the auld barn-yaird.

Tho' we watched the clover bloomin',
   An' the grain to gowden turn,
Nae thocht o' play or profit
   E'er gied us much concern :
But we watched the time approachin'
   When the stacks wad sune be reared,
An' we'd play at tigg or bogley
   In the auld barn-yaird.

At the time o' schule vacation,
   Blithe an' barefit we wad rin,
To cheer the sturdy crofters
   At the glorious "leadin'-in" :
An' when the corn was dichtin',
   An' the whirr o't could be heard,
We smuggled i' the shelter
   O' the auld barn-yaird.

They were only bits o' kylies,
   But they looked sae nice an' snug,
As they stood securely theekit
   Wi' the rashes frae the bog ;
What enjoyment then we tasted
   As oor elders' toil we shared,
When we thrawed the rapes for theekin'
   I' the auld barn-yaird !

When the hairst was fairly ended
   An' secured was the corn,
There was pleasant merry-makin'
   At the lang projected kirn :
Oh ! the reels an' jigs they footit,
   As the lads an' lassies paired,
Wi' mony a sly kiss stolen
   By the auld barn-yaird.

Noo again the scene's before me,
   But nae stacks are to be seen,
The dyke is doon, an' dockens
   Grow the fa'in' stanes atween ;

The barn floor is silent,
  For the flail is never heard;
An' the yett is aff its hinges
  At the auld barn-yaird.

The spot presents a picture
  O' puirtith an' decay,
For the humble toilin' cottars
  Are deid, or far away;
An' ruined cots, ance cheery
  Wi' the joys their inmates shared,
Are deserted now and dreary
  Like the auld barn-yaird.

Wi' shame I tent the reason
  For the ruin that I see,
An' that drove my rustic playmates
  Frae these scenes o' infancy;
To the same auld shamefu' story
  O' a near or graspin' laird,
We maun trace the ruined homesteads
  An' the weed-grown barn-yaird.

I hope the day will come yet
  That will change this dreary scene,
Wi' the happy sports revivin'
  On that famed auld village Green;
When the honest thrifty rustics
  Share the wealth their toil has reared,
Wi' a cottage clean an' cheery,
  An' a weel-stocked barn-yaird.

PENNY'S BRAE.

'Mang a' the scenes where in my youth
  I wandered free o' care,
At morning's dawn, or sunset hour,
  To snuff the cauler air,
There's ae scene o' the langsyne days
  Still owre my heart hauds sway—
The shady paths an' quiet neuks
  Alang by Penny's Brae.

'Twas there my young friend Rab,[1] an' I,
　First sang oor sangs thegither,
Or lay beneath some spreadin' tree
　In sultry summer weather;
We little thocht that frae such scenes
　We'd wander far away,
To cherish but the memories o'
　Oor nichts by Penny's Brae.

There, aft when wandering alane,
　When simmer days were fair,
I used to meet my shopmate Bob,
　An' kenn'd what brocht him there:
For in some quiet gloaming hour
　He'd meet sweet Betty Gray
Their favourite tryst on Sunday nichts
　Was doon by Penny's Brae.

Still, as my memory wanders back,
　I seek that scene again,
To meet beneath the trystin' tree
　My first fond sweetheart, Jane;
I seem to press her hand again,
　An' vow I'll ne'er betray
The trustin' heart she plighted me
　Langsyne by Penny's Brae.

An' now while I, a stranger, roam
　O'er many a foreign part,
Some ither may have woo'd an' won
　Her young an' trustin' heart;
Tho' such may be, I'll ne'er forget,
　Until my dying day,
The memories o' the happy hours
　I spent by Penny's Brae.

JASPER'S MILL.

In sadness now I view the spot
　So dear to boyhood's happy days
The old mill-dam, the sluice, and race,
　So snug between the fir-clad braes.

[1] Robert Pringle; see *Minstrelsy of the Merse*, page 261.

The scene out o'er the Lammiebirks,
    Or up the waters to the Muir,
Recall the school-boy sports we shared,
    Or wayward rovings, free as air.

Again does fancy paint the scene
    Where Jasper sat to feed the flame—
The blazing kiln, the water-wheel,
    The dogs and cats we knew by name :
The troutlets jumping in the dam,
    The garden circled by the stream ;
The ripples by the stepping-stones,
    Are pictured now as in a dream.

Up on the Scaur we've climbed the trees,
    For cushie's or for squirrel's nest,
Roamed o'er the Birks till fairly tired,
    Then back to the old mill to rest ;
And there beside the old kiln door,
    When Jasper kept the fire ablaze,
We chatted to the kind old man :
    Ah ! those were pleasant, cheery days.

Now only, scattered here and there,
    Some straggling moss-clad stones remain
To mark where stood the dear old mill,
    Now viewed with thoughts akin to pain ;
We miss the splashing water-wheel,
    The whirr of stone and crank within,
The dusty miller's kindly words,
    Scarce heard above the clank and din.

Gone ere the mill had disappeared,
    Old Jasper sleeps beside his kin,
No relative had he to heir
    The land where his forebears had been ;
To stranger hands the old mill passed,
    In years when we were far away ;
Now they too rest from toil or care,
    And here we view the scene to-day.

No mill, no miller! both are gone,
  And silence reigns where all was stir ;
The ruined cottage by the stream
  Adds to the desolation there :
And now, where ruin's imprint marks
  What now is only but a name,
That stream, the source of wealth and power,
  Flows calmly murmuring on the same :

Fit emblem of a fleeting world,
  A world of changing joy or care :
We seek the old familiar spot
  To find but silent ruins there ;
So like our fates, a dreary scene
  Of ruined hopes of love or fame :
And while we mourn what might have been,
  The stream of life flows on the same.

THE QUARRY ON THE HILL.

WE sat upon the rustic seat
  That taps the Quarry Knowe,
Ae sunny autumn day, when roun'
  A' nature was a glow.
We'd wandered thro' the plantin's shade
  To find the trees that bore
The names we cut o' sel' an' mates
  Some thirty years before :
    An' noo, wi' minds attuned to thocht,
      We could reca' at will
    The happy hours we spent langsyne
      By the Quarry on the hill.

A garden fair lay at our feet,
  Far stretchin' to the sea,
Or southward, where the clouds sailed low,
  Owre Cheviot's hills sae hie ;
We saw Hume's ruined castle stan',
  Dark lined against the sky,
The Eildon's filling up the scene,
  Where Tweed rins rowin' by ;

An' yet, tho' grand the view thus spread
  O' mountain, moor, an' rill,
Oor thochts aye wandered back again
  To the Quarry on the hill.

What was the spell that held us here,
  An' changed the moorland scene
To ane o' beauty, that could draw
  The tear-draps frae oor een;
To mak' the heart-beats louder soun',
  The auld smile to come back,
An' keep us, as it were, enthralled
  Wi' memory's sunny track?
    Ah! here again, where aft as bairns
      We wandered at oor will,
    We met, auld frien'ships to renew
      By the Quarry on the hill.

Hoo sweet the sunny hours we spent,
  Nane but oorsel's can ken,
The scenes renewed o' boyhood's days,
  An' what we'd seen sin' then;
The griefs an' joys we baith had felt,
  Yet lived thro' a' to meet
True frien's as ever yet had sat
  Upon that rustic seat;
    While in oorsel's the change had been,
      We met as brithers still,
    Tho' there was little change to note
      By the Quarry on the hill.

An' yet the spot was different noo,
  Oor hearts had to confess,
Altho' the heather bloomed as fair
  To woo the breeze's kiss.
Noo silence reigned, where ance the soun'
  O' toilin' hands was heard;
As doon the Quarry's depths we gazed,
  No bird nor insect stirred.

Sae like oor lives ance stir an' strife,
    Noo smooth as yonder rill,
An' peacefu' as a Sabbath morn,
    By the Quarry on the hill.

Still in that Quarry's hidden depths
    May wealth untold yet be,
As in oor hearts by sufferin' seared,
    That worldlings canna see.
Some great upheaval yet to come
    May bare these treasures rare,
An' strengthen heart and soul again
    Oor joys an' griefs to share.
But for the present we're content
    To rest as calm an' still,
Reca'in' bygone pleasures spent
    By the Quarry on the hill.

BY FOGO BRAES.

On ! dear to me's my native hame,
    Far frae the busy haunts o' men,
Its gardens sma' where roses blaw,
    Its humble cots wi' but an' ben ;
Its stream, meandering in the dell,
    Where troutlets gleam in sunny rays,
Its pebbled strand, where aft as bairns
    We barefit played by Fogo braes.

I see the kirk upon the hill,
    The auld kirkyard where dear anes rest,
I think I hear the pastor's voice,
    In counsels grave or airy jest.
Sweet comfort to the auld he brocht,
    The young he taught o' wisdom's ways,
E'en joined the gleesome sportin' bairns
    In cheery romps by Fogo braes.

I've seen the giant rivers row
    Their swelling billows to the sea,
An' still the humble burns at hame
    Had dearer, fonder charms for me.

I've roamed the forest deep, where ne'er
    Had pierced the sun's maist searchin' rays,
An' still I longed to hae a glint
    O' simmer's charms by Fogo braes.

Sae ance again I fain wad roam
    Alang the mead or up the dell,
An' see the haunted Quarry Knowe,
    Where first I trysted wi' my Nell.
An' could the joys come back again
    That ance were mine in childhood's days.
I'd leave the baubles wealth an' fame
    For peace an' rest by Fogo braes.

But na, the fond enchantment's gane,
    Thae joys can never mair return:
An' yet, while nature smiles sae sweet,
    Why should I owre lost pleasures mourn?
I'd happy be if I could hae
    A faint reflection o' youth's days,
An' let life's ebbing years depart
    In happy dreams by Fogo braes.

THE KIRK ON THE BRAE.

Gang up the burn frae Cothill braes,
    Till it winds through Lounsdale haugh,
Where primrose an' bluebell slyly peep
    Frae the bowers o' hazel and saugh,
Each scene, each nook, brings back to me
    Faint echoes o' youth's bricht day,
But a sadness mingles wi' a' my joy,
    When I see the auld kirk on the brae:

For it's there, in that grass-grown auld kirkyard,
    The dearest an' truest lie,
Far frae the strife an' cares o' life,
    Till they meet again by an' by:
An' as years roll by, an' age creeps on,
    An' the locks get thin an' gray,
Still closer the heart clings to the scene
    O' the auld kirk on the brae.

Merry an' thochtless as bairns we played
  'Mang the mossy heid-stanes there,
An' gathered the gowans to weave in braids
  For our favourite lassie's hair;
It was only when daylicht, growin' faint,
  Merged to the gloamin' gray,
That we hurried awa' to the village Green,
  Frae the auld kirk on the brae.

The auld kirk has its history, too,
  O' the Covenantin' days,
When Sir Patrick hid in its darksome aisle,
  An' the troopers besieged Redbraes;
An' mony a time wi' curious een
  We hae marked, by the faintest ray,
The restin' place o' the great anes there,
  'Neath the auld kirk on the brae.

Yet 'mid a' its sad an' solemn scenes,
  Its memories dark an' drear,
A brichter fancy comes back to me
  My wanin' life to cheer;
It was there, by the bowers in Lounsdale haughs,
  An' beneath the spreadin' slae,
I first felt the glamour o' love's young dream,
  Near the auld kirk on the brae.

Noo when I visit the spot again,
  Each auld familiar nook,
I canna but picture our trystin' days
  An' reca' each word an' look;
Ah! me, but the place seems no' the same,
  An' the glamour is gane for aye,
An' a' thing is changed but the silent scene
  O' the auld kirk on the brae.

UP THE BURN.

In childhood's days, when a' was bricht
  An' we kenned nought o' care,
We had oor favourite haunts to roam
  By meadow, glen, an' muir;

UP THE BURN.

When free frae schule we laid our plans
  Where we wad spend the day,
Then up the burn, the muirland burn,
  We blithely hied away.

Oh! what a wealth o' sport was there
  In spring or summer days!
The search for heather-linties' nests,
  The rowin' doon the braes:
The hidin' in the ferny howes,
  The races owre the lea,
When up the burn, the wimplin' burn,
  We wandered wild and free.

Not many sounds broke on the air
  In that sweet, peacefu' glen,
But when our merry notes were heard,
  The echoes rang again:
We scared the muir-fowl frae its nest,
  The hare frae 'mang the bent,
When up the burn, the bonnie burn,
  Oor blithesome hours we spent.

We kenned where the primroses first
  Shone in their spring array,
An' foxgloves reared their purple bells
  Beside the scaurie brae:
We pleated wreaths o' varied hues,
  To bind our lassies' hair,
When up the burn, the windin' burn,
  They cam' to tryst us there.

When autumn's mellow tints were seen,
  An' hips were on the brier,
To gather haws an' hazel nuts
  We wandered here an' there:
Till laden wi' oor pooches crammed,
  An' bonnets heapit fu',
Then doon the burn we sauntered then,
  Fit-sair an' tired enoo.

The herd, wha had frae early morn
  Roamed owre the muir his lane,
Wad list oor stories an' oor sangs,
  An' wish them owre again;
We shared his bannocks an' his cheese
  Wi' appetites fu' keen,
When, up the burn, beside the brig,
  We rested on the green.

Aft dae I wonder, where are noo
  The schulemates o' the past;
Has fortune aye befriended, an'
  Its sunshine owre them cast?
Or dae they mourn in far-aff lands,
  Ance mair to tread the bent,
Where up the burn, the muirland burn,
  Their happiest hours were spent?

I canna speel the heather hills
  As I was wont to dae, -
My stiffened limbs feel sair eneuch
  Before I tap the brae;
Yet aften, on the slopin' vale,
  On couch o' tangled fern,
Beside the burn, the croodlin' burn,
  These youthfu' scenes return.

An' tho' I wander there alane,
  Wi' nae companion near,
A peacefu' calm comes owre my heart
  An' stops the ready tear.
Tho' faint the joys, compared wi' what
  As bairns we used to ken,
Still up the burn I seem to feel
  Youth's brightness back again.

DANCIN' IN THE BARN.

It's Hogmanay, the dark short day
  O' winter cauld an' drear,
Noo nicks the thread that helps to speed
  The auld departin' year:

But nae sad thocht to us is brocht
   At nicht or New Year's morn ;
We hail the year wi' blithesome cheer
   When dancin' in the Barn.

The neibour lads hae chanced the roads
   In spite o' frost an' snaw,
To share the sport, an' there consort
   Wi' lassies buskit braw :
For village queens, auld folks an' weans,
   Alike maun hae their turn,
To reel an' swing, or blithesome sing,
   While dancin' in the Barn.

The smith an' wricht are there fu' bricht
   To see the place redd up,
The seats set roun', the floor made soun'.
   Where younkers lithe may trip ;
The fiddler chap has had his drap,
   Prepared his fees to earn,
While couples mate, to celebrate
   Wi' dancin' in the Barn.

Frae onsteads near the lads appear,
   An' lassies, bloomin' fair,
Come here to see the auld year die,
   Wi' mirth devoid o' care ;
In reel an' set, auld frien's are met,
   Prepared to dae their turn ;
Wi' toast an' sang, the fleet hours gang
   While dancin' in the Barn.

Noo Davie's ta'en the floor his lane
   To dance the Hielan' fling :
Or Johnny Cope, wi' triplin' step,
   He's ready aye to sing :
Auld Jockie's there the fun to share,
   As, when at Davie's kirn,
He does his best to gie a zest
   To dancin' in the Barn.

The Yirl cam' east to grace the feast,
    Decked oot in Sunday braws;
Meanwhile the wricht sang a' his micht,
    Eneuch to fricht the craws.
Then tailor Will hands roun' the gill
    Wi' gracefu' swing an' turn,
An' Robin gabs wi' Smyrna Rab
    While dancin' in the Barn.

Lame Yiddie's there, the sport to share,
    Though dancin's no his forte,
While Spadie trips wi' gracefu' steps,
    Like laddie fu' o' sport;
An' Yappish, too, tho' auld an' gray,
    Aye does his best to earn
The smiles an' cheers o' village dears,
    When dancin' in the Barn.

I min' langsyne wi' mates o' mine
    Owre blate to tak' the floor,
When younger jauds brisked up to lads,
    An' tripped it by the hour;
But when we ance gat up to dance,
    An' step an' figure learn,
We ne'er were blate to fiel the set
    When dancin' in the Barn.

A' nicht they reeled, and taed, an' heeled,
    Till day began to dawn,
While pies an' sweets, an' ither treats,
    Regaled the inner man;
An' nae lad cam' withoot a dram,
    Glenlivet or Strathearn,
An' aft they took a quiet sook,
    While dancin' in the Barn.

Alas! owre sune the nicht is dune,
    An' partin's come at morn,
But ere they gang, they lilt a sang,
    An' trip it roun' the thorn;

Then hame they hie, wi' mony a sigh,
    To toil ance mair to turn,
Yet ne'er repent the hours they spent
    When dancin' in the Barn.

Noo, lookin' back owre life's rough track,
    Hoo few o' them we kent
Are here to share life's joy or care,
    Or join the merry rant.
An' silence reigns where aft the strains
    O' reel an' jig in turn
Set care aside, at New Year's tide,
    When dancin' in the Barn.

THE LEADIN' IN AT POLART.

I 'm lookin' back owre forty years,
That noo but like a span appears,
To youth, when a' thing charms and cheers—
    When blithe the seasons rin ;
To winter wi' its frost an' snaw,
To spring wi' its buddin' bank an' shaw,
Or simmer when the flowers are braw,
    To the hairst an' leadin' in.

What fun as bairns we used to hae,
Then 'mang the stooks we'd jouk an' play,
Frae mornin' till the gloamin' gray
    Barefitted we wad rin ;
We heeded na the stibble bare,
Or thistles that could jag fu' sair,
An' played the game o' "hunt the hare,"
    At the Polart leadin' in.

When the last sheaf at Clinkie's leas
Is cut an' boun'—auld Nell they seize,
An' gie the usual skyward heeze
    'Mang muckle fun an' din ;
The lassies then, revenge to hae,
Grip muckle Wull to hoist him tae :
Thus toil is sandwiched in wi' play.
    Before the leadin' in.

An mony a ride the bairnies had
When empty carts returned to lade,
They chattered to the driver lad,
   To mak' the horses rin ;
They watched the carts lade up ance mair,
Or chased the rabbit frae its lair ;
Gin noise were wark, they did their share
   At the Polart leadin' in.

When Yappish had his crop secure,
An' at the Mill the leadin' owre,
When a' the acres to the Muir
   Were lookin' bare an' thin,
We watched the laden carts return
To the mean-yaird beside the burn,
As blithe as lassies when the kirn
   Winds up the leadin' in'.

Noo Smyrna Rab, the cankered carl,
Talks owre the dyke to Jim the Yirl,
An' says his stack has sic a swirl,
   "Twill coup the first bit win' ;
The wright, the smith, an' tailor Wull,
Gie ilk a han' the stacks to pull,
An' lauch — ye'd hear them at the schule—
   At the Polart leadin' in.

The dominie comes yont the back,
Wi' lookers-on to hae a crack,
An' view the workers on the stack,
   Or langsyne yarns to spin ;
For news frae either far or near
But at rare intervals they hear,
While village gossip helps to cheer
   The guid folks leadin' in.

When a' the cottars' craps were stacked,
Wi' rapes an' rashes snugly thacked,
An' stragglin' pickles cleanly raked,
   An' a' thing redd up clean ;

Then while the auld folks tak' their ease,
An' talk o' craps, an' flowers, an' bees,
The barn-yaird games the younkers please,
　　At the Polart leadin' in.

These days are but a memory noo,
The frien's I used to ken are few,
An' tears will start, as noo I view
　　A change owre a' the scene;
For desolation marks the spot,
The thack-roofed barn has gane to rot,
An' puirtith noo the toiler's lot,
　　Nor sign o' leadin' in.

The auld thacked cots are crumblin' sair,
The barn-yaird noo weed-grown an' bare,
An' cottars' stacks are seen nae mair,
　　Where plenty ance has been;
For rack-rents keep the puir folk doon,
An' tho' they toil baith late an' sune,
The maist that's on the acres grown
　　Is scarce worth leadin' in.

Aye, aften has my heart been wae
To see them toil frae break o' day,
An' far ayont the gloamin' gray,
　　Exposed to weet an' win';
An' when the sair-won rent is paid,
The guissie an' the crummie fed,
There's little left o' ear or blade,
　　Far less a leadin' in.

Few, few of the auld folks remain,
Some langsyne to the mools hae gane,
Their bairns noo far across the main,
　　A brighter life to win;
While ane or twa still stan' the brunt,
Tho' sair wi' toil an' trouble bent,
Just waitin' till the ca' is sent,
　　For death's last leadin' in.

AROUN' THE VILLAGE THORN.

I'm lookin' back owre forty years,
  To boyhood's happy days,
When merry crowds met on the Green
  In rival sports an' plays;
When auld an' young were to be seen
  In frien'ly bouts by turn,
An' laughter, joke, an' sang were heard
  Aroun' the village thorn.

While grown-up chaps were busy wi'
  Their jumpin' or their quoits,
Wi' quiet interest we wad watch
  The rival sides' exploits;
Or else barefitted we wad rin
  Wi' mony a jouk an' turn,
Till, fairly fagged, we rested then
  Aroun' the village thorn.

E'en when the winter frosts had come,
  An' deep the snaw-drifts lay,
In cutty stools upturned, we sat
  An' skiddit doon the brae;
We rowed the snaw-ba's on the Green
  Until owre big to turn,
Or made snaw men an' hooses baith
  Aroun' the village thorn.

Tho' weddin's happened unco rare
  Among the lads an' queens,
They ne'er forgot the auld-time gift—
  A fitba' for the weans;
An' while we played wi' muckle din,
  The weddin' folks adjourn,
An' march wi' fiddler at their heid
  To dance aroun' the thorn.

At Hogmanay the village folks,
  Baith auld an' young, wad meet
To dance the New Year in, an' toast
  The Laird's health for the treat.

An' when the nicht was spent in mirth,
　　An' stars still blinked at morn,
They finished wi' the crowin' reel
　　Aroun' the village thorn.

Nae busier time was ever kenned,
　　Or raised sic hearty cheer,
As when the Burrlie met to hire
　　The herd anither year;
The business settled— to the Green
　　For pleasure they adjourn,
An' spend a jolly hour or twa
　　Aroun' the village thorn.

The muggers' camps were pitched at nicht
　　Upon the saft green swaird,
Till Sandy Malcolm drave them aff
　　By orders o' the Laird;
But camp-fires gleam nae mair at e'en,
　　Nae startin' oot at morn,
The gangrel folks noo seek their rest
　　Far frae the village thorn.

We laddies aye were pleased to see
　　The Gypsy folk an' weans,
Their cuddies, an' the snarlin' tykes
　　That quarrelled owre the banes;
We'd keek below the canvas beild,
　　Or watch the faggots burn,
An' envy them their roving life,
　　Aroun' the village thorn.

The Laird is gone, wha in his youth
　　Could foot it wi' the best,
An' mony a time wi' hamely folks
　　Enjoyed the sang an' jest;
An' when the Leddy cam' a bride
　　The Auld Hoose to adorn,
'Mid great rejoicin' auld an' young
　　Danced roun' the village thorn.

I picture 't noo, sae desolate
  Frae what it used to be;
Nae sport or play, nae trysts held there,
  Beside that sacred tree;
Yet I wad rather think o't as
  It was in life's fair morn,
For happy memories still cling
  Aroun' the village thorn.

ANE O' OORSEL'S.

Whenever I visit the hameland sae dear,
There's naething that cheers me sae much as to hear
The kind salutations frae auld and frae young,
That soun' kinder still in the saft Border tongue,
When the hearty hand-shake e'en the kind word excels,
"We're aye glad to see ye, you're ane o' oorsel's."

There's nae starched-up greetin', there's nae formal pride,
We're welcomed at ance to the hamely fireside,
An' frien's gather roun' us wi' welcome sae warm,
That life seems to wear quite a rosier charm
When the tone and the manner a' cauldness dispels:
"Dinna wait to be askit, you're ane o' oorsel's."

I canna put up wi' your stiffness ava,
I like to be frien'ly wherever I ca',
Tho' humble the cottage, tho' hamely the fare,
The welcome is a' thing when gi'en wi' an air
O' honest respect, and the kind look that tells,
"You're no' like the feck, you're just ane o' oorsel's."

When I ca' on the folk in the workshop or yaird,
They treat me as kindly as I were the laird;
A' shyness where met wi' is soon thrawn aside,
An' they mak' you to feel that your visit's enjoyed;
Tho' they say na the word, it's the manner that tells:
"We think a' the mair o' ye, you're ane o' oorsel's."

Ilk humble bit cot in the village I ken,
When I knock at the door, there's a kindly "come ben";
An' hoo couthie they'll crack owre the years that are bye,
Or the prospects they hae wi' their acres an' kye;
Sae free they confide a' their pleasures or ills:
"You're no' like a stranger, you're ane o' oorsel's."

Then lang may sic welcome be mine when I ca'
On frien's high or humble— in cottage or ha';
A welcome to share wi' them sic as they hae,
An' a kind word at partin' to cheer on the way:
Then cankering care frae oor pathway dispels,
Wi' the charm o' the greetin': "You're ane o' oorsel's."

IN DAYS GANE BYE.

Since first I knew the village Green,
   When but a toddlin' wean fu' wee,
What varied changes I hae seen—
   What wreck an' ruin' noo I see;
Few o' the village folks remain,
   While cottages in ruins lie,
That mak' me think that ne'er again
   'Twill thrive as in the days gane bye.

An odour o' romance clings roun'
   Ilk nook an' corner here and there
O' valiant deeds by heroes dune,
   Mayhap to free some maiden fair:
Or gallant stand for truth an' richt
   By those who did not fear to die,
Wha struggled 'gainst oppression's micht
   An' triumphed in the days gane bye.

I sing o' mair prosaic times,
   When Border feuds were past and gane,
When raidin' deeds were deemed as crimes,
   An' each could justly claim his ain;
When peace reigned o'er the Borderland,
   An' brought security an' joy,
When e'en the humblest took his stand
   For hearth an' hame in days gane bye.

When Laird an' Leddy frae the Ha'
   Their humbler neibours didna scorn,
But took their place amang them a'
   In sports aroun' the famous thorn:
When there was wark for a' to share,
   Wi' mutual trust 'tween low an' high,
An' time for sport to lessen care,
   An' mak' life smooth in days gane bye.

Aft when a laddie hae I sat
   An' listened by the ingle cheek
To hear the auld folks' hamely chat
   Aboot the times o' whilk I speak:
I've seen them shake their heids wi' grief,
   Or heave a mutual mournfu' sigh,
To think that in their time sae brief
   Sic change had been sin' days gane bye.

I've listened while some patriarch tauld
   O' village fairs held near the Green;
The spot still bears the name Hab's-Fauld—
   Nought but the name marks oot the scene;
I've heard them tell o' varied sport,
   When youths in trials o' strength wad try
To vanquish ithers wha'd resort
   For frien'ly bouts in days gane bye.

I've seen mysel', when but a wean,
   In simmer when the days were lang.
A crowd o' youths upon the Green,
   Nicht after nicht wi' games fu' thrang:
Till darkness put a stop to a',
   An' hame their several roads they'd hie—
Ah! mony a ane noo far awa'
   Still paints that scene o' days gane bye.

When toddlin' wee things, gaun to schule,
   We've heard the flail ring in the Barn,
Or watched at nicht the auld hand mill,
   When crofters met to dicht their corn;

IN DAYS GANE BYE.

We've listened by some wee thatched cot
    To hear the merry shuttle fly,
Or watched the smith's fire bleezin' hot,
    Where croods wad meet in days gane bye.

The busy souters plied their trade,
    By garret window 'neath the thatch :
The tailor hame-spun garments made,
    When fashions didna vex them much ;
An' when at e'en their wark was done
    The village band wad gather nigh,
To gie the folks a hearty tune,
    That cheered them in the days gane bye.

But picture noo that changèd scene,
    The ruined cots wi' roofs fa'en in,
No e'en a cuddie on the Green,
    Nor geese or ducks to mak' a din ;
The very weans speak laigh an' saft,
    The herd scarce needs to count his kye,
While mony a ane wha worked a croft
    Rack-rents keep doon, sin' days gane bye.

The thocht will aften come to me,—
    What means this ruin an' decay ?
An' can the spoiler wish to see
    That ancient hamlet swept away ?
It seems as if this was the aim,
    To heed not honest puirtith's cry,
But drive them to a stranger hame
    Frae that they kenned in days gane bye.

Still let us hope that dear auld spot
    Will flourish as it did before,
An' mony a rose-embowered cot
    Gie hamely comfort to the puir ;
When toil will reap its due reward,
    Wi' richts the rich dare no' deny,
Aye ready, hearth an' hame to guard,
    Like those wha lived in days gane bye.

MOORLAND MUSINGS.

O'er the moors I roving wander,
   'Mid the purple springing heath,
Where the breezes blow around me
   Like a maiden's fragrant breath ;
Where the sun in mid-day splendour
   Sheds its glorious rays around,
Over mountain, lake and valley,
   And the solitude profound.

Here I love to tread the valley
   Where the gurgling streamlet plays—
Where the leafy screen above me
   Shields me from the sun's fierce rays ;
Where the trout an' tiny minnow
   Wanton in the shaded streams,
Where the waving trees reflected—
   Like a fairy land it seems ;

Where the bright-eyed blooming flow'rets
   Waft their perfumed sweets along,
Where the heard but unseen cuckoo
   Sings her heart-refreshing song :
Where the cushat's mournful cooing
   From the forest greets my ear,
And the wild shrill-screaming pee-wit
   Sounds its pipe in upper air.

Or I wander down the meadow,
   Leading to the gray old mill,
Listening to the geese and peacocks
   Sound their clarions loud and shrill :
Or the mill-wheel, old and creaking,
   With its long familiar sound,
Breaks the stillness of the valley
   Wakes the echoes all around.

Or I roam where bees are humming
   Round the fragrant yellow broom,
In the daisy-dappled meadows
   Where the cup and clover bloom :

Where the perfumed milk-white blossom
    Of the hawthorn scents the gale,
And the myriad tinted daisies,
    Like a snow shower, clead the vale.

Where the blue-bell, and the thistle,
    And the fox-glove deck the glade,
To my memory recalling
    Spots where oft in youth we stray'd:
When our hearts were free and happy—
    When no cares sat on our brow;
Happy hours, alas! departed,
    Gone, and past recalling now.

Still I love to roam among them,—
    Still my fainting soul they cheer,
And my spirit, soaring upwards,
    Seeks to leave her sorrows drear;
To my soul they tell of pleasures
    I have never tasted yet,—
Of a land where all are happy,
    Where no shadows ever flit:

Where eternal summer reigneth,
    Clear and radiant, not a cloud;
Where no winter's snow descending
    Covers nature with a shroud;
Where the streams are ever flowing
    Stainless from the fount divine:
Where the sun, for ever beaming,
    Knows no fading, no decline;

Where the flow'rets, ever blooming,
    Sweetly scent the heavenly gale:
Where the balmy, soothing zephyrs
    Waft along no mourner's wail:
But the happy songs of thousands
    From the sins of earth made free,—
Where eternity rolls onward,
    Onward to eternity.

WHEN WE WERE A' AT HAME.

Ance mair I see the village Green,
   An' a' its scenes that please
Its auld thack't hooses here an' there
   Amang the spreadin' trees;
The wimplin' burn, the bonnie yairds,
   Its howes and knowes the same
As in the lang gane cheery days
   When we were a' at hame.

But here an' there are strongly marked
   Time's sair destroyin' tooth,
An' fell decay has left its trail
   Sin' oor blithe days o' youth;
Nae cheery voices reach us noo
   O' bairnies at their game—
The place is dreich an' dowie noo
   Since we were a' at hame.

I mark the cot where first I saw
   The licht o' love an' joy,
An' where within its humble wa's
   I played a blithesome boy;
Noo moss-grown is its dented roof,
   An' roun' the winnock frame
The rose an' jessmine nae mair nod
   As when we were at hame.

Yet thochts come back o' joyous days,
   When a' was bricht an' fair,
An' when we roamed the banks an' braes
   Wi' hearts devoid o' care;
An' I forget Time's blightin' change,
   An' picture a' the same
As when we gathered roun' the hearth
   When we were a' at hame.

I see the bricht peat fire a-bleeze,
   The kettle on the crook,
An' sang an' story cheer us as
   We snuggle i' the neuk;

My faither an' my mither baith
　　Had aye a constant aim
To mak' oor cot a cheery spot
　　When we were a' at hame.

Noo in the auld kirkyaird near by
　　Are dear anes laid at rest,
An' ithers hae left hame an' frien's
　　For new scenes i' the West:
Tho' noo 'mang strangers far they roam
　　In search o' wealth and fame,
My fancy paints the scene ance mair
　　When we were a' at hame.

An' maybe i' that ither warld,
　　When we are dune wi' this,
The sweetest drap that we shall fin'
　　In Heaven's cup of bliss,
Will be to meet ilk ither there,
　　Renewin' love's auld flame
In the hoose o' many mansions, where
　　We'll meet an' be at hame.

I LIKE MY AIN FIRESIDE.

What's a' your pomp an' wealth to me,
Or a' the honours State can gie?
They canna mak' the heart mair glad—
They canna cheer when life is sad.
In fact, the various cares they bring
Mak' peace an' comfort oft tak' wing;
They canna add to life's true zest:
I like my ain fireside the best.

It may be humble in its way,
A wee thatched cot beside the brae;
A garden plot wi' auld-time flowers,
The birds' sweet music 'mang the bowers:
A but an' ben, a' tosh an' snug,
Twa bonnie bairns, a cat an' doug;
My bonnie wife aye cleanly dressed:
I like my ain fireside the best.

Sae long as health is gi'en us a',
We envy nae the rich an' braw;
They seek their pleasures near an' far,
Wi' fashion as their guidin' star.
An' tho' we hae but simple joys,
Our hamely pleasure never cloys,
While honest toil brings welcome rest:
I like my ain fireside the best.

The scenes o' riot and debauch
May hearts o' thochtless votaries catch:
For me an' mine, we'd rather hae
The even tenor o' life's way:
We watch the pampered darlings pass
Wha deem us an inferior class:
Their jaded, worn-out lives attest
Our ain firside is aye the best.

The worldly proud in fashion's ranks
May hae their wealth in shares and banks,
Their stately mansions in the squares,
An' servants e'en that put on airs,
Where liveried flunkies flaunt aboot,
An' pass their wine at ball an' rout:
Sic empty pleasures time will test:
I like my ain fireside the best.

When winter comes wi' snaw an' drift,
An' storms careerin' owre the lift,
Our humble cot seems snug an' bien:
When, toil-worn, I get hame at e'en,
The couthie welcome that I meet
Frae thochtfu' wife an' bairnies sweet
Gie hamely comfort, peace, an' rest:
I like my ain fireside the best.

Then ne'er may I meet joy or care
Outside the hame my loved anes share;
Their smiles keep care outside the door,
Wi' them I'll share whate'er's in store.

An' should the pinch o' want appear,
  Wi' them life's struggles still I'll share ;
E'en then, wi' love's sweet heart-glints blest,
  I'll like my ain fireside the best.

THE AULD FOLKS O' THE VILLAGE.

In fancy aft I wander back
  To childhood's sunny days ;
Ance mair I'm in the meadows, or
  The burnie's banks an' braes :
An' tho' the feelin's o' my youth
  Revive wi' faintest glow,
I canna feel the same delight
  As in the lang ago :
    For 'mang the frien's I kent sae weel,
      An' trusted ane an' a',
    The auld folks o' the village noo
      Are wearin' fast awa'.

My faither's house was aye the howf
  Where couthie frien's wad meet
To tell their tales o' langsyne deeds,
  Or lilt their sangs sae sweet ;
The news frae far but seldom cam',
  Nor went they far frae hame ;
The parish an' some miles aboot
  Was a' the warl' to them :
    Let ithers gang to foreign lands,
      In search o' wealth or fame ;
    The auld folks o' the village were
      Content to bide at hame.

But hamely clad, an' plainly fed,
  Whiles burdensome their toil,
As lang as they were blessed wi' health
  They happy were the while.
Nor yet ambition had they e'er
  To rise aboon their lot ;
The palace wadna be sae dear
  As was the humble cot :

The auld thatched cot, the garden plot,
　　Their highest wishes ser'ed ;
The auld folks o' the village ne'er
　　Envied the wealthy laird.

They looked aye to the Sabbath day
　　For welcome peace an' rest,
When a' went decent to the kirk
　　In weel-hained Sunday's best ;
The preacher's words were lessons plain
　　That simple minds could learn,
An' doubts that loftier minds assailed
　　To them brought no concern :
　　　　To eat the fruit o' honest toil,
　　　　　　An' trust God for the rest,
　　　　The auld folks o' the village were
　　　　　　In calm contentment blest.

Noo things are changed ; the humble cots
　　Are half in ruins laid,
Wi' weed-grown yairds that never ken
　　The touch o' howe or spade ;
An' names for generations kent
　　Are never heard o' noo,
Exceptin' on the grave-yaird stanes,
　　Wi' moss half hid frae view :
　　　　Tho' time an' fate hae wrought sic change,
　　　　　　The place seems no' the same,
　　　　The auld folks o' the village still
　　　　　　Cling to the dear auld hame.

Whene'er my footsteps hameward turn,
　　On simmer pastime bent,
Aye fewer are the frien's I meet
　　Wi' whom I was acquent :
I note the changes time has wrought,
　　The gaps that death has made,
An' sorrow dark comes owre my heart
　　Where a' was ance sae glad :

I ken my years nae lichter feel,
   An' heavier weighs life's care.
While th' auld folks o' the village sune
   Will welcome me nae mair.

PUIR WULL'S AWA'.

Auld Jockie's frien', puir Wull, is gane,
An' noo he sighs an' grieves his lane :
While neibours roun' wi' waesome mane
    Let saut tears fa',
For death a faithfu' frien' has ta'en—
    Puir Wull's awa'.

He was a doug o' famous breed,
Wi' bushy flanks, an' noble heid,
Gifted wi' powers o' scent an' speed
    That few could show :
A wink or nod was a' he 'd need,
    An' aff he 'd go.

Wi' bairnies a' the clachan thro'
He was a frien' baith tried and true,
An' tho' his lugs an' tail they 'd pu',
    He ne'er let on,
While mony a "piece" he got, I trow,
    O' bread or scone.

The cat an' he were cronies guid,
An' shared ilk ither's plate o' food,
Their ways an' humours understood
    Like human folk,
An' smuggled close, as wooers would,
    By th' ingle neuk.

In a' the journeys Jockie gaed
Wull followed, tho' nae ca' was made ;
Whene'er he took his staff or plaid,
    He 'd youff wi' glee ;
An' when the hameward road seemed braid,
    A guide he 'd be.

When in the ditch Jock chanced to fa'
Amang the driftin' wreaths o' snaw,
Wull went to where a licht he saw
    An' brought relief,
Or else his chance to wake were sma'
    His time but brief.

But Jock the kindness paid him back;
When Wull, got auld an' scarce could walk,
Went to the well his drouth to slack,
    An' tum'led in,
Jock hauled him brinkwards in a crack,
    Wi' drookit skin.

When herdin' o' the cottar's kye,
By hill an' dale or wet or dry,
Beneath some beild the twa wad lie
    By moss or muir;
Yet runaways could ne'er get by,
    If Wull was there.

If rabbits started at his feet,
When gettin' stiff an' no' sae fleet,
To see Wull was a regular treat
    Start on the run,
While Puss, sune in a safe retreat,
    Just thought it fun.

When breakin' stanes on Chousley Brae,
On mony a sultry simmer day,
Close by the heap his dougship lay,
    Full at his ease:
Owre lazy e'en to drive away
    The wasps an' flees.

Noo a' his tricks an' plays are dune;
In Jock's auld plaid weel rappit roun',
Beneath yon tree he's sleeping soun'
    Beside the burn;
Where bairnies frae the schule at noon
    Come there to mourn.

"FASTEN'S E'EN."

The cat upon the hearthstane lies,
An' raises aft its heid an' sighs;
Here, where they slept as warm as pies,
    On rug or chair,
It gazes roun' wi' sad surprise,
    For Wull's nae mair.

The lads wha drap in there at e'en,
Where mony a time they've merry been,
Hae cause eneuch whiles to compleen
    O' bright times gane,
While Jockie noo wad just as sune
    Be left his lane.

Weel, folks maun dee as weel as dougs;
What need we then to hing oor lugs,
When death the life-thread rives an' rugs
    In cot or ha'?
Let's try to stan' Time's kicks an' tugs,
    Like Wull awa'.

Gin faithfu'ness an' patience here
Deserve reward beyond the bier,
These brutes, wha thro' a hard career
    Hae borne their yoke,
Should hae a chance o' yon bright sphere,
    Like ither folk.

"FASTEN'S E'EN."

'Mang the memories o' the langsyne days
O'er which my fancy aften strays,
That waft me back to the gowany braes,
    An' ilka lang-left scene,
I fondly lo'e that scene o' a',
When lads frae cottage an' frae ha'
Met ilka year to play the ba',
    An' haud their Fasten's E'en.

My puir auld heart will aften thrill
Wi' youth's bright recollections still—
O' hoo we played 'tween kirk an' mill
    Till the last prize was gi'en;

Hoo lads wi' neebour lads wad meet,
To spier for news, to crack, an' treat ;
An' hoo blithe lassies too wad greet
    The sports o' Fasten's E'en.

Even noo, my fancy still can trace
The crowd that thranged the market-place,
Where joy was seen in ilka face
    Baith auld an' young, I ween ;
For frail auld bodies then wad meet
To crack at corners o' the street,
An' drouthy cronies, too, wad weet
    Their gabs at Fasten's E'en.

The ba'-men, an' the fiddler loon,
Play "Never let the Gregor doon,"
'Till ilk shopkeeper in the toon
    His croon or shillin's gi'en ;
An' ere the sport at noon's begun
The 'prentice lads close up like fun,
Prepared to scramble, jouk, an' run,
    For the sports o' Fasten's E'en.

The laird comes doon frae his castle ha',
Wi' leddies, too, sae busk an' braw,
For he's aye the first to toss the ba',
    An' mak' the sport begin ;
The fiddler then, an' ba'-men chiel's,
Play round the toun-house, lichtsome reels,
Wi' callants shoutin' at their heels,
    For the fun o' Fasten's E'en.

Then frae before the toun-house steps,
'Mid shouts, an' tossing up o' caps,
The gowden ba' first upward pops
    An' owre their heads does spin ;
In earnest then begins the play,
While back an' fore they stragglin' sway,
An' lassies cheer an' shout hooray !
    For the sports o' Fasten's E'en.

Then comes the wrestling an' the sport;
'Mid yells an' cries o' every sort
They race pell-mell up lane an' court;
    The like was never seen:
They toss an' tumble, squeeze an' tear,
While hats an' bonnets skim the air,—
Nae fun at country hiring fair
    Beats this at Fasten's E'en.

The married men the ba' maun hail,
By ringin' wi't the auld kirk bell,
While single chaps rin for the mill
    To thraw't the happer in;
Sae there the wily lads keep guard
By yett an' dyke o' the auld kirk-yaird,
To win the laurels there prepared,
    For the fun o' Fasten's E'en.

Then here a squad o' country lads
Hae cast awa' their cumbrous duds,
Ready for ditches, slaps or wuds,
    An' for the mill to rin:
They stick at neither burns nor stiles,
Sae lang's they win the lassies' smiles,—
Nae money prize for them has wiles
    Like this at Fasten's E'en.

An' sae the fun's kept up until
The last ba's hailed at kirk or mill,
An' ilka ane has got his fill
    O' that day's sport, I ween;
Then to their hames at toun or stead
The lads an' lassies hameward speed,
Ilk Jock an' Jeanie as agreed
    Lang ere this Fasten's E'en.

An' then the ba'men wi' their frien's
Adjourn to some ane o' the inns,
Where langsyne yarns the landlord spins
    O' what he's dune an' seen;

An' when the noise an' din hae ceased
Then pork an' dumplin' crowns the feast,
Washed doon wi' toddy o' the best,
    To wind up Fasten's E'en.

HALLOWE'EN MEMORIES.

Come sit ye doon, my auld guidwife, an' let us hae a crack,
An' ance mair thro' the bygane years tread memory's
    storied track ;
The happy days o' auld langsyne, the cloudless an' the free,
Come ance mair back to cheer us wi' ilk hallowed memory :
For tho' 'tis lang sin' we, guidwife, left that hame far away,
Still a' her scenes o' hill an' dale are dear to us to-day,
An' wi' a schule-boy love I still think o' that happy scene,
When roun' oor cosy ingle-side we kept oor Hallowe'en.

Sic langsyne recollection aft yet my bosom thrills,
When thinkin' o' my dear auld hame amid the heather hills:
Wi' what licht heart I've sported o'er gowany bank an' brae,
When to the auld schule hoose we hied ilk sunny morn away :
But no' a happier day we spent, than when we roamed the
    glen,
To hunt for hazel nuts to burn, when hame we got again,
Or when, 'mid joke an' ringin' laugh, whilk ilk ane relished
    keen,
We joined the fun-provoking sports in the langsyne
    Hallowe'en.

What happy moments hae I spent on that all hallowed
    nicht,
When lads an' lasses gathered roun' the ingle burnin' bricht !
When mirth shone oot frae every face, an' a' were happy there,
For e'en the auld folks joined us wi' hearts devoid o' care :
They joined us in the merry laugh, the gossip an' the sang,
An' for ae nicht at least we drove awa' care's withering
    stang :
We blithely listened to their screeds o' what they'd dune
    and seen
On this same nicht, lang years ago,—the auld Scotch
    Hallowe'en.

An' Peggy, dae ye min' the time when I was courtin' you,
Those first fond years we aften met oor pledges to renew,
When owre the hills I gaily sped to the auld trysting tree,
My only thocht, to gain a look an' word o' love frae thee;
When there we wandered lang, an' talked o' days o' comin' joy—
For secretly I'd lo'ed thee, sin' a happy careless boy;
For ye maun min' that nicht, guidwife, some forty years I ween,
I drew thee as my valentine, that langsyne Hallowe'en?

Noo we are toddlin' doon the hill, an' sune maun reach the fit,
Still wi' a glow o' youthfu' fire my auld heart flutters yet,
When thinkin' o' that land I lo'e, far, far across the sea,
An' the happy days that hae been mine, my ain guidwife, wi' thee;
Noo bairns' bairns roun' us rin, an' pouk thee by the goun,
While, wi' the younkers on your knee, I like to hear ye croon
Some auld Scotch sang, that aft has brocht the saut tears to my een,
Or tell the frolics we hae had on the auld Scotch Hallowe'en.

Then let us haud oor Hallowe'en as we were wont to dae
Langsyne amang the schule-mates o' the auld hame far away;
We're nae sae soople's we hae been, an' canna join the fun,
But wi' the bairns aroun' us, we can tell hoo things were dune
When you an' I were bairns, too, as blithe as ony here,
Wi' burnin' nuts, an' pu'in' stocks, an' ither frolics queer;
An' let us hope, guidwife, that ere in death we close oor een,
We'll see a few mair winters come to bring us Hallowe'en.

HOGMANAY.

The year's noo hirplin' to its close,
　Seared, totterin', auld an' frail,
While we are watchin' for the hour
　The infant year to hail;

An' memory backward tak's a glint
  To youth's mair happy day,
When we enjoyed the sports an' plays
  We held on Hogmanay.

The best o' a' the Guizard time
  Was ance mair drawin' near,
An' mony nichts before, we'd aye
  Oor costumes to prepare;
While a' oor sangs we maun rehearse
  An' eke—the time-worn play,
O' "Here comes in Gilashon," wha
  Gets killed on Hogmanay.

Dressed in oor gaudy paper-hats,
  Wi' sarks ootside oor claes,
An' mimic swords hung by oor sides,
  At mirk we took oor ways;
An' first we took the Manse by storm,
  For there a welcome aye
Frae minister to maids we had
  On ilka Hogmanay.

Next to the laird's big-house we ca'ed,
  Where, in the servants' ha',
We were regaled wi' dainties, that
  But ance a year we saw.
We sang, an' danced, an' acted there,
  When, ance mair in the play,
A second time Gilashon fell
  To hansel Hogmanay.

To farm and cottar's hoose we gaed,
  An' aye a welcome gat,
An' when oor sangs an' plays were dune
  To hamely feast we sat;
An' e'en where pence they couldna gie
  We ne'er were turned away,
But aye got rowth o' scones an' cakes
  To cheer oor Hogmanay.

An' aft adventures, too, we met,
   As we gaed on oor roun',
Wi' muckle merry din we made
   The sharp nicht air resoun';
As when we tum'led in the burn
   When crossin' Cothill brae,
Till stiffened sarks like coats o' mail
   Decked us on Hogmanay.

Oor guizin' dune at stead an' toun,
   Where hoose to hoose we sang,
We turned oor faces hameward, yet
   Ne'er thocht the journey lang;
For joke an' story filled the time
   We speeled up Chousley brae,
An' hame owre Crummie Staps we went
   To finish Hogmanay.

For, ken ye that, for years gane bye,
   Oor village aye had been
A central spot, where lads an' queens,
   On that nicht did convene;
Where dancin' in the auld mein-barns
   Was held till break o' day,
When roun' the thorn we tripped a fit
   To wind up Hogmanay?

An' noo, far frae that happy scene,
   I still think o' the past,
An' picture scenes that ne'er shall fade
   While life itsel' shall last;
An' tho' I canna join the sports
   Wi' frien's noo far away,
I live, in memory, ance again
   The joys o' Hogmanay.

THE BLAEBERRY PLANTIN'.

ANCE mair I'm back to the village Green,
An' roam owre ilk weel remembered scene,
An' yet I canna just trust my een,
   For there's something seems awantin';

Where mony a spot looks just as before,
There are ithers I canna reca' as o' yore,
For there seems sic a wonderfu' change come o'er
    What we kenned as the Blaeberry Plantin'.

Yet this is the spot I ken fu' weel:
There's the Hunter's Well, an' the road by the fiel',
An' the hedges that aften we used to speel
    When the birds in the spring were nestin':
'Twas here that we sported when bairns at schule,
'Twas here that as wooers we played the fule,
An' trysted the lassies when a' was still,
    An' the mune was lang shadows castin'.

The gean-trees stand by the auld faile dyke,
An' the stunted scroggs seem familiar like,
Where we harried mony a bummie's byke,
    In the hairst when we watched the shearin':
There's the prickly clumps wi' the bonny red rasps,
A feast we shared wi' the birds an' wasps,
Familiar scenes that my memory grasps,
    An' yet 'mid the change, fu' cheerin'.

We kenned the nooks where the blaeberries grew,
Where we could just sit an' big handfu's pu',
An' feast till our hands and lips were blue,
    An' we stayed till the fa' o' the gloamin':
Or we hunted the squirrels frae tree to tree,
As lang as the daylicht wad let us see,
For nae care, nae fear, nae fatigue had we,
    Tho' frae mornin' we had been roamin'.

By the benty-knowes where the linties built
We rested whiles, an' our stories tell 't,
For time wi' our hearts then had lightly dealt,
    An' nae joy in our lives was wantin';
An' sae as the shadows began to fa',
An' an eerie stillness fell deep owre a',
We'd saunter hame by the Randy Raw,
    Frae the gloom o' the Blaeberry Plantin'.

But a change has come owre the dear auld scene.
Nae trees stan' noo where they aye had been,
An' the sunlight glints where it ne'er was seen,
   Where in simmer the shade was sae cheerin'.
For the villagers tell o' a fearfu' blast
That raged for hours oot the snell Nor-wast,
When the sturdy trees were like reeds owrecast,
   Till it looked like a Yankee clearin'.

Few blaeberries noo can be gathered there,
The raspberry clumps are stunted an' bare,
An' the branches that sheltered the timorous hare
   Miss the shade o' the spreadin' beeches :
The footpaths we trod are wi' grass owregrown,
As through the changed scene we wander alone,
An' try to reca' a' the landmarks gone,
   An' muse owre the lesson it teaches.

E'en the village itsel' is changed to me,
An' its moss-grown ruins I grieve to see,
The playmates I loved are far owre the sea,
   Or lie in the Kirkyard dreary ;
I miss the auld familiar scene
O' the youths at play on the village Green,
The sturdy bairns that were a' where seen,
   An' the voices that rang sae cheery.

The auld folks are gane to their lang last rest,
An' their children hae sought new hames in the West.
The pathways we loved are by feet unpressed,
   An' the stir an' the life are wantin' ;
Few, few are the kent folks, auld and grey,
Noo waitin' the ca' when they'll slip away,
Like the gnarled stumps that we watch decay,
   'Mid the wreck o' the Blaeberry Plantin'.

DAVY'S HA'.

It's only but a theekit house that stan's beside the byre,
A but an' ben, an' plenty room to snuggle roon' the fire ;
An' when the winter storms hae come an' wreathed the
   roads wi' snaw,
The cosiest place to spen' an' hour is up at Davy's Ha'.

The Laird himsel's a cantie chiel', an' trusty frien' forbye,
A skeilie sort o' body amang horses, sheep, an' kye;
Besides, he's got a kindly turn, weel liked by ane an' a',
For there's aye a smile an' cheery word for them at Davy's Ha'.

There's nae guidwife to fume an' scold if things shonld gang agee,
To lock up press an' cupboard an' appropriate the key;
There's rowth o' a' thing ane could want, an' sae, whae'er may ca',
There is nae hungry welcome ever gi'en at Davy's Ha'.

What hamely music I hae heard that made the rafters ring,
When ilka ane his turn aboot wad tell a tale or sing,
When eight-some reels, an'-heel-an'-toe made time flee fast awa',
An' we were laith to pairt, an' tak' the road frae Davy's Ha'.

When a' the chores were dune at e'en, an' Geordie played the flute,
An' guid auld neibour Timmer wi' the fiddle followed suit;
When Jockie sang his favourite sang, an' younkers ane an' a'
Joined in a rousin' chorus, only heard at Davy's Ha':

The farmer lads frae far an' near wad aften join us there,
An' speech an' sang gaed roun' fu' blithe when Davy took the chair;
When mirth an' fun 'mang auld an' young sune drave dull care awa',
Sae cantie aye the meetin's were we held at Davy's Ha'.

The rich may hae their pleasures that are far ayont oor reach,
But oor's were humbler joys that might a halesome lesson teach;
For there were nae regrets to come—nae after ills ava,
But a' was happiness supreme when up at Davy's Ha'.

As time rows roun' an' brings the siller glint to mony a pow,
We still look back wi' pleasure, an' auld memories fan the lowe;
We picture aft the cosie scene; an' noo, when far awa',
We ne'er forget the pleasant hours we spent at Davy's Ha'.

YIDDUM.

Never was there sic a loon
    As that laddie Yiddum ;
He's the terror o' the toun,
    Mischief-workin' Yiddum.
At the schule or on the Green,
At his pranks at morn an' e'en,
    A' the callants dread 'im ;
An' the games they play when there
He maun boss the whole affair,
    Nane daur nay-say Yiddum.

Gin a hen or duck gets lamed,
    Credit's gi'en to Yiddum ;
Right or wrang a' mischief's blamed
    On the heid o' Yiddum.
Is it divots on the lums,
Tammy-reekies stuffed wi' thrums—
    Guissies gi'en their freedom ;
Turnip-bogles in the dark,
Coupit carts, an' a' sic wark,
    Aye set doon to Yiddum.

Gin hard words wad break his banes,
    Sma' chance then for Yiddum :
But he heeds na a' their sayin's,
    Wasted breath on Yiddum.
Folks aboot the clachan say
He'll aye please himself an' dae
    As his ain deil bade 'im ;
That nae guid will be his end,
Gin he no' tak' thocht an' mend
    Puir, ill-dreaded Yiddum.

But beneath that ragged coat
    Beats a heart in Yiddum
Wadna harm a mouse or stoat—
    Puir, misca'd wee Yiddum.
Tho' deem'd ripe for ony ill,
Deep doon in his briest there's still
    Gin ye could but read 'em—

Kindly feelin's for the puir;
Sufferin' creatures everywhere
　　Find a frien' in Yiddum.

E'en the maister at the schule
　　Whiles will favour Yiddum,
For he sees he's no' a fule—
　　Rattlin', rompin' Yiddum.
When the schule's in, he's aye there
Eident at his books an' lear,
　　Showin' he's got smeddum;
An' the laddies there maun grind
Ear' an' late, to tak' the wind
　　Oot the sails o' Yiddum.

But his mither kens him best,
　　She has faith in Yiddum;
Noo his faither's gane to rest,
　　She has nane but Yiddum:
An' tho' wee an' barely clad—
No' owre weel or fairly fed
　　She will ne'er upbraid him;
An' by look or word he ne'er
Hurts the heart that lo'es sae dear
　　Her wee curly Yiddum.

Aften will she pray alane
　　For her bairnie Yiddum,
That he'll strength an' wisdom gain
　　When a man grows Yiddum:
For he's a' she has to lo'e,
An' tho' wild an' tho'tless noo,
　　Aye she tries to lead him
In the path that's free frae sin,
Seekin' council frae abune;
　　Then nae fear for Yiddum.

There, we'll let him rin an' play,
　　Merry, lauchin' Yiddum,
Sune enench will come the day
　　Bringin' care to Yiddum;

An' nae fear but when he grows,
Folks, wha owre him shake their pows
  At the ploys he 's led 'em,
Will respect him for his worth
Mair than them o' titled birth—
  Honest, manly Yiddum !

GAUN TO THE KIRK AT POLART.

A Sabbath morn an' a simmer sky,
  Wi' never a clud aboon us,—
Warblin' birds in the groves hard by,
  An' the wild flooers noddin' roun' us ;
Ne'er can ye find sic a peaceful scene
As comes to me noo at life's sombre e'en,
When the villagers step o'er the famous Green
  As they gang to the Kirk at Polart.

The kye are milkit an' aff to the muir,
  In the care o' the herd an' his collie,
An' there isna a soun' to be heard in the air,
  While mirth wad be waur than folly ;
The auld folks, douce in their Sunday rig,
The young folks a thocht mair braw an' trig,
Come doon the Back an' owre Jockey's Brig,
  As they gang to the Kirk at Polart.

At the schule, the farm folks meet them there,
  An' exchange their weekly greetin',
An' the same auld topics come up ance mair,
  As at mony a bygane meetin' ;
The weather an' crops are subjects dear,
An' the prices o' stock they 're aye pleased to hear,
An' it never varies richt thro' the year,
  As they gang to the Kirk at Polart.

They leisurely chat gaun doon the hill
  There 's Spadie as brisk as a laddie,
An' Wattie han's roun' his sneeshin'-mull
  For a pinch o' his famous Taddy ;

There's Canny Willie frae Vertie's Raw,
Auld John o' the Tafts, an' Dave frae the Ha',
An' ither auld folks—I could name them a'
   That gaed to the Kirk at Polart.

They dauner doon thro' the Packman's Loan,
   By the plantin' at Denham's Entry,
Past Murlie-rig road, an' farther on
   Where the big palm tree stan's sentry;
The gates are open, an' just by the stile,
On the kirk-yaird dyke they linger awhile,
Or saunter roun' by the ancient aisle,
   As they gang to the Kirk at Polart.

What a quiet spot is the auld kirk-yaird,
   That is a' thro' the week deserted,
Except when some mourner's wail is heard
   By the grave o' some dear departed!
E'en noo on this joyous Sabbath morn
Nae jarrin' noise to the ear is borne,
For the talk is as meek as the faces worn
   When they gang to the Kirk at Polart.

The bellman is heard wi' his ding, ding, dong,
   High up in the ivy turret,
An' they watch the manse folk comin' along,
   An' wait till they're nearly forrit;
Then the Laird, wha has driven his ain shanks pair
Doon Lounsdale's valley sae still an' fair,
Is seen at the steps - an' they a' repair
   To their seats in the Kirk at Polart.

If ye've never been into that famed auld place,
   It is worth your while to see it,
For tho' changed, there is many an ancient trace
   O' the past that will never lea' it:
There are tablets to mony a deid auld laird,
An' the guid Sir Patrick, wha's life was spared
In the vault, where sweet Grisell nichtly shared
   His watch, 'neath the Kirk at Polart.

POLWARTH CHURCH.

Photo by Geo. Bruce, Duns.

There's the white-washed cupples an' high-backed seats,
　　The same as langsyne I mind it,
Tho' the ivy's gane that ance hung in pleats
　　An' roun' the auld pu'pit they twined it;
I hae seen it sway in the simmer breeze
An' attract frae ootside the butterflies :
It was something oor boyish minds to please,
　　As we sat in the Kirk at Polart.

There's the seat where the beadle, auld John Grant,
　　Sat a' thro' the sermon dozin',
An' snored awa', wi' supreme content,
　　'Till the service was near the closin';
An' there was the square auld pew, select
For the elders an' deacons—the Kirk's elect,
Wham we younkers looked on wi' grave respect,
　　When we gaed to the Kirk at Polart.

An' weel I remember the lettergae's voice
　　As he gasped an' droned oot the singin',
An', when a' was dune, a skirlin' noise
　　Frae auld Leezie Hogg cam' ringin';
Nor can I forget the minister's style,
Wi' his hamely words an' his kindly smile,
An' his prayers that ilk ane kenned the while,
　　Aye the same, at the Kirk at Polart.

But the years bring changes amid their train,
　　New customs rise while the auld anes vanish,
And saddened feelings are mine again
　　'Mong scenes that my mem'ry ne'er can banish.
Of the haunts of that long-gone early day
I'll cherish through life this blessed house on the brae,
Where my fathers oft met to praise and to pray,
　　In the dear auld Kirk at Polart.

LOUNSDALE HAUGHS.

How oft in sunny summer days
　　We wandered down the silent dell
To gather scroggs, or geans, or slaes,
Or pull the primrose on the braes,
　　The foxglove and the pale bluebell.

Here, too, when hearts were tuned to love,
  And nature seemed to share our joy,
We trysted in the shady grove
To plight our vows, while fancy wove
  A dream of bliss without alloy.

Ah! that was bliss which could not last,
  For little then we knew of care;
We thought not that time's withering blast
Would wreck our hopes as on it passed,
  And leave our hearts all bleak and bare.

Yet, when I roam again the scene,
  And see it just as in my prime,
I crush the thought—what might have been—
And feel a glow of peace within
  That gilds once more my childhood's time.

Bright memories of the past come back,
  And dear companions round me play;
We seek the old familiar track,
While laughter light and boyish talk
  Beguile the sunlit woodland way.

And though the clouds of care may loom,
  Our fancy still will brighter glow:
Away with all despair and gloom,
When all our old loved flowerets bloom,
  And zephyrs whisper soft and low.

Who could be sad in such a spot,
  Where beauty smiles on every hand,
Where blooms the sweet forget-me-not,
Where lilies on the waters float,
  And pebbles glisten 'mid the sand?

It were unfitting I should bring
  A tear or sigh to such a spot;
Nay, round it still let memory cling
To brighten all, as time's fleet wing
  Brings age and sorrow as my lot.

Then fare-thee-well; and if denied
  To roam again thy banks and braes,
I'll cherish with a miser's pride
These flowers, when o'er the ocean wide;
  They'll bring me back my childhood days.

BYGONE DAYS.

Oft at evening when I wander
  Where the sun's last beams are shed,
And the twilight star is beaming
  With silvery rays o'erhead,
Then a sadness comes upon me
  As, in fancy's eye, I see
Those happy bygone days,
O'er which my memory strays,
When we sung our merry lays
  'Neath the greenwood tree.

In the sombre voiceless watches
  Of darkness and repose,
When my tired limbs are aching,
  And my weary eyelids close,
Then away in airy dreamland,
  'Neath brightest skies, I see
Those happy bygone days,
O'er which my memory strays,
When we sung our merry lays
  'Neath the greenwood tree.

In the city's noise and bustle,
  In its never-ceasing strife,
For my daily bread I wrestle
  In this battle-field of life;
Yet 'mid all its toil and turmoil
  My fancy oft would flee
Away to bygone days,
O'er which my memory strays,
When we sung our merry lays
  'Neath the greenwood tree.

'Mid the pleasure-seeking party
    And happy festal throng,
I have watch'd the whirling dancers
    Or listen'd to the song :
Yet oft there came this feeling
    'Mid all such revelry,
A longing for the days,
O'er which my memory strays,
When we sung our merry lays
    'Neath the greenwood tree.

Far from home and friends residing,
    Tho' enchanting be the scene,
It cannot this sad spirit
    From the by-past moments wean :
For they only keep reminding
    Of those scenes, where fain I'd be,
And those cloudless bygone days,
O'er which my memory strays,
When we sung our merry lays
    'Neath the greenwood tree.

When I seek to read the future
    By the cheering hope-lit beams
Of that blissful time that's coming
    Foretold in poets' dreams,
Then I cannot help recalling
    Those times so gay and free,
When in the bygone days,
O'er which my memory strays,
We sung our merry lays
    'Neath the greenwood tree.

But however bright the present,
    However full my joy,
I have not that airy buoyancy
    Of the careless laughing boy ;
My happiness is fleeting,
    And like that bursting glee

Of those sunny bygone days,
O'er which my memory strays,
When we sung our merry lays
   'Neath the greenwood tree.

Now, as alone I ponder
  Upon that sunny past,
There's a bright unclouded picture
  On fancy's vision cast;
In such my happiest moments,
  With throbbing heart, I see
Those scenes of bygone days,
O'er which my memory strays,
When we sung our merry lays
   'Neath the greenwood tree.

II.

Hame Sangs.

"It's hame, an' it's hame, hame fain wad I be,
An' it's hame, hame, hame to my ain countrie."
—*Allan Cunningham.*

"O! let us ne'er forget our hame,
   Auld Scotland's hills and cairns,
And let us a', where'er we be,
   Aye strive to be guid bairns.
We'll ne'er forget that glorious land
   Where Scott and Burns sung—
Their sangs are printed on our hearts—
   In our auld mither tongue."
—*Andrew Wanless.*

II.

HAME SANGS.

ST. ANDREW'S DAY.

Come, neebour Scots, ance mair forgather
To celebrate wi' ane anither
The memories o' the land o' heather,
     Tho' far away,
An' toast oor Patron's name together,—
     St. Andrew's Day.

Come, lassies, wi' your witchin' smiles,
Again to cheer wi' women's wiles;
Come, labourers, frae your cares an' toils,
     Ance mair be gay,
An' share the joy which aye beguiles
     St. Andrew's Day.

Here mony a son o' Scotia's hills,
Forgettin' a' his griefs an' ills,
This day will range the glens an' dells
     Far, far away;
For 'tis a time ilk bosom thrills,—
     St. Andrew's Day.

Nor dae we meet alane to think
O happy times, or toasts to drink;
A' ye wha mourn at poortith's brink
     Will find us aye
Prepared to honour wi' the chink,
     St. Andrew's Day.

We meet to talk o' what's been dune
The poor frae pinchin' want to win,
To keep the wolf, be't debt or dun,
    Frae's door away,
Till frae his heart he bless oor ain
    St. Andrew's Day.

We meet to wipe the widow's tear,
Wha mourns o'er husband's early bier ;
Her heart to lichten, she maun share
    Oor charity,
Till blessin' a' in heartfelt prayer,
    St. Andrew's Day.

Or she oppressed wi' poverty,
Wha langs her frien's ance mair to see ;
Make glad, when we can set her free,
    Her sea-bound way,
To thank, when hame across the sea,
    St. Andrew's Day.

Or they wha've suffered poortith's ills
Amang their native heather hills,
An' come amang us sturdy chiel's
    To push their way,
Will ne'er forget, when fortune smiles,
    St. Andrew's Day.

There's no' a day in a' the year
We greet wi' sic a hearty cheer ;
For Scotia's sons frae far an' near
    Their hearts obey,
To haud oor Patron saint aye dear,
    St. Andrew's Day.

Frae east to west, baith south an' north,
In ilka corner o' the earth,
Will Scotsmen gie in joyous mirth
    Their feelin's play,
To celebrate oor Patron's birth,
    St. Andrew's Day.

An' in oor ain Dominion land,
Frae forest wild to sea-girt strand,
Scotsmen will meet, a mighty band,
    Respect to pay,
When "chill November" brings to hand
    St. Andrew's Day.

Oor wives an' dochters, too, maun greet
This hallowed time wi' honours meet;
An' bairnies, too, maun hae their treat,
    An' grannies gray
Tell hoo they kept langsyne the great
    St. Andrew's Day.

Then let us hope that mony a year
We lang may meet ilk ither here,
Oor jokes to crack, oor questions spier,
    An', blithe an' gay,
To welcome wi' a joyous cheer
    St. Andrew's Day.

An' in this land for years to come,
While burnies rin, an' forests bloom,
When hearts are sad an' pooches toom,
    Let nae ane say
We failed to free frae grief an' gloom
    St. Andrew's Day.

THE THISTLE.

While memory backward tracks the time
Sin' first I trod a foreign clime,
In fancy aft the hills I climb
    Where waves proud Scotia's thistle;
By knowe an' cairn, by mead an' moor,
By linn an' loch, by glen an' shore,
My childhood's scenes I aft explore
    'Mang heather, fern, and thistle.

Hoo aft, in boyhood's sunny days.
I've skelpit barefit o'er the braes,
An' little cared tho' heels and taes
    Were tanglin' wi' the thistle;
Or when its summer bloom was past.
An' downy feathers wayward cast,
I've grieved that autumn's thieving blast
    Should bare the bonnie thistle.

I carena for your garden flowers,
Sae trim an' neat in ladies' bowers;
There's ane aboon them a' that towers,
    The stalwart bearded thistle:
Noo noddin' to the surly breeze,
Noo hid beneath the hazel trees,
Noo sunward baskin' where the bees
    Sip honey frae the thistle.

The flowers may languish in the field,
When simmer days nae showers may yield;
It needs nae plantin's shade or beild,
    The hardy, burly thistle:
Tho' sharp an' keen the blasts may blaw,
An' ither flowers may fade an' fa',
It rears its head aboon them a',
    The sturdy bearded thistle.

The sun may glint wi' a' its power,
An' clouds deny the fresh'ning shower;
Tho' dewdrops at the gloamin' hour
    Begem nae blade or thistle,
Still nourished by its native earth,
Defiantly it branches forth,
Tho' bendin' 'neath the biting north,
    Still bravely wags the thistle.

When warlike hordes cam' owre the main,
Wi' hopes o' conquest an' o' gain,
A city's slumberers wad been slain
    If 't hadna been the thistle.

While barefit, for surprise prepared,
They steal upon the drowsy guard,
A warnin' cry o' pain was heard—
　　Their curses on the thistle.

An' so the thistle proved to be
The guardian o' oor liberty ;
Then wha can ever doot that we
　　Are proud o' Scotia's thistle ?
On mountain heights it rears its head,
Proudly an' stern, as if it said,
"For Scotia's cause ye ne'er may dread,
　　Sae lang 's ye lo'e the thistle."

Sae when we see its sturdy form,
Aft bent an' toss'd before the storm,
Oor hearts to Scotia's heroes warm,
　　Sae like their native thistle :
Tho' aft assailed by war's rude blast,
When broadside Mars' red bolts were cast,
They cam' triumphant forth at last,
　　Unconquered, like the thistle.

What tho' oor hardy mountaineer
May rough and rugged still appear
To pamper'd fools wha scoff an' sneer
　　At Scotia's cherish'd thistle !
Tho' hearts that beat 'neath silken gown
Were saft as fleece or thistledoon,
Still warm as breath o' balmy June
　　Are hearts that lo'e the thistle.

Here, parted frae oor sea-girt hame
Still dotin' on auld Scotia's name,
Oor hearts leap up wi' boundin' flame
　　At mention o' the thistle.
Her name, her fame to us are dear,
Undimm'd by wealth an' fortune here ;
We'll teach oor children to revere
　　The land where wags the thistle.

At times my heart is often fain
To cross ance mair the trackless main
An' roam my native hills again,
   Where bonnie blooms the thistle,
If but a glint 'twere mine to see,
Ere death's cauld hand had closed my e'e,
That my last restin' place might be
   Beneath the waving thistle.

IT'S HARD TO LEAVE THE HAME.

It's hard to leave the hame
   Where sae mony years we've been,
It's hard to leave auld frien's,
   An' the pairtin' grief is keen;
Tho' the prospects may be bricht,
   An' the frien's we meet are dear,
We'll miss the kindly hearts
   We kenn'd for mony a year.
     It's hard to leave the hame
       Where we've sae happy been,
     An' wander far awa'
       Frae the auld hame on the Green.

The thochts o' ither scenes
   May lure us for awhile;
An' tho' to them we meet
   We wear a happy smile,
Deep down within our hearts
   A wae that rankles keen,
When fareweels maun be said
   To the auld hame on the Green.
     It's hard to leave the hame, etc.

We visit each dear spot
   When pairtin' time draws nigh,
An' each familiar nook
   We leave wi' mony a sigh;

When frien'ship's ties are rent,
   An' last farewcels are said,
The sunshine o' our life
   Seems then for ever fled.
     It's hard to leave the hame, etc.

But distance ne'er can keep
   Our thochts frae lingerin' here,
Nor time efface the bonds
   That made each scene sae dear;
An' tho' we ne'er return
   To view that hallowed spot,
The frien's we leave behind
   Will never be forgot.
     It's hard to leave the hame, etc.

I LOVE TO DREAM OF HOME.

I LOVE to dream of home,
   Of kind friends far away,
'Tis then sweet mem'ries come,
   Like morning's cheering ray,
Which from my drooping heart
   Dispel all care and gloom,
And soothin' joys impart;
    Oh! happy dreams of home.
      Oh! happy dreams of home,
        Around my pillow come,
      And tell me of the loving ones
        Who think of me at home.

I love to dream of home,
   In fancy's pleasing reign,
With loving friends to roam,
   And share their joys again;
Or sport in boyish glee
   By mead and sylvan scene,
As oft in days when we
   Roamed o'er the village Green.
     Oh! happy dreams of home, etc

I love to dream of home,
  Sweet home, oh! happy theme
When morning dawn is come,
  To tell me 'twas a dream:
I often wish 'twas more,
  That I indeed were there,
Within that cottage door,
  Their happiness to share.
    Oh! happy dreams of home, etc.

I love to dream of home,
  And though I never meet
Those friends of youth, or roam
  Those scenes so fair and sweet:
Yet, till my dying day,
  Whatever sorrows come,
Till memory's decay
  I'll love to dream of home.
    Oh! happy dreams of home, etc.

HAME SICK.

I'm wearin' doon the hill o' life, an' sune maun reach the fit
Wi' feeble step I toddle roun', or by the ingle sit:
While in sweet dreams o' langsyne days the time slips saftly by,
For my heart's awa' across the sea, 'mang scenes o' infancy;
An' tho' for mony years I've been a wanderer frae her shores,
Wi' stronger love as death draws near, I lo'e her glens an' moors,
An' my heart is often hame-sick for ae look owre fell an' flood,
Or a breath o' Scotland's mountain air that fires the patriot's blood.

Just five an' fifty years gane by sin' I left hame an' frien's;
A sonsy, brawny chiel' I was, tho' only in my teens;
I'd listened tales, an' conned owre buiks which fanned the youthfu' flame,
To see the wide warld for mysel' an' seek a foreign hame;

An' sin' that day owre mony lands my weary steps I've traced,
Yet still the love o' childhood's scenes has never been effaced,
But stronger grown ; wi' failin' years my ae desire has been
To see the hame I left langsyne ere death has closed my een.

The snaws o' age hae frosted owre my haffets thin an' bare,
An' my een grow dim an' feeble as the gloamin's drawin' near :
But my soul on wings o' fancy seems to break its bands o' clay,
An' to revel in the dreamland o' the auld hame far away ;
An' bonnie are the visions that licht my soul at times,
Far grander than the boasted scenes o' myrtle-scented climes :
They're the scenes o' childhood's cloudless years, my native banks an' braes,
Where I roved, a fair-haired laddie, wi' the frien's o' ither days.

In fancy's e'e I'm ance again a laddie 'mang the lave,
An' climb the mist-clad mountains where the ferns an' heather wave ;
Or listen to the music o' the bonnie wimplin' burns,
Or the sough o' simmer breezes amang the mossy cairns :
'Mang a' the favourite neuks we kenn'd, by meadow, hill an' glen,
Wi' lichtsome heart, an' boundin' step, I rove them ance again,
Or wi' a fond expectant heart I seek the trystin' tree
Where first I met my life's ae love, now lost to earth an' me.

Deep in my heart's most inward neuk wi' miser care I prize
Auld Scotland's hallowed scenes where famed historic memories rise,—
Her battlefields—dear cherished spots—where our forefathers bled,
Victorious owre their country's foes, by Bruce an' Wallace led,—

Or the lonely, wild, romantic spots, by mountain, glen or hill,
Where the Covenanters worshipp'd wi' Peden an' Cargill,—
Or waukenin' sadder memories by mony a lane hill-side,
The moss-clad cairns which mark the spot where Scotland's martyrs died.

While croonin' owre some auld Scotch sang, some lilt o' happier days,
I seem to be among the scenes where Burns ance tuned his lays
Those deathless sangs which find a chord in ilka Scotchman's briest,
Whene'er wi' joy elated, or e'er wi' grief oppress'd ;
Or I wander, sad and pensive, by mony a grove an' rill,
The scenes o' plaintive melody—the haunts o' Tannahill,—
Or by the banks o' bonnie Tweed, wi' pilgrim steps, I hie,
Where sang the Border Minstrel, Scott,—high priest o' chivalry.

At times I'm dow an' dreary, an' the tear-drap dims my e'e,
Wi' the thocht that this, my last desire, may be denied to me :
Gin sic the will o' heaven be, I'll humbly bow my heid,
Contented, in a foreign land, to lay me wi' the deid :
But while I'm to the fore, I'll ne'er forget the langsyne days,
When I roamed amang the heather, or speeled the gowany braes ;
Nor cease to hae a Scotchman's pride in ilka honoured name,
That frae the path o' puirtith rose to win a lastin' fame.

My weary life has been as fu' o' crosses as my plaid,
An' welcome will be rest at last when 'mang the mools I'm laid ;
But oh ! gin I could hae my wish, how peacefu' could I die !
Tho' there were nane to drap a tear, or heave a sigh for me:
For I think I'd sleep sae sweetly wi' the heather owre my heid,
An' the bluebells droopin' lowly as if to mourn me deid,
Could my last desire be granted ere the thread o' life is riven ;
For ae sicht o' bonnie Scotland were like a glint o' heaven.

MY BOYHOOD'S HAME.

My boyhood's hame, how dear to me !
    My heart enshrines each sacred scene :
Ance mair I see the hawthorn tree,
    Ance mair I roam the village green :
An' dear companions roun' me play
    As happy as in the days o' yore,
An' auld frien's noo beneath the clay,
    I see beside the cottage door.
        My boyhood's hame, my boyhood's hame,
            Oh ! a' its scenes are dear to me :
        Where'er my lot, to that dear spot
            My fancy wanders o'er the sea.

I conjure up the hallowed scenes,
    Bricht wi' the sunshine o' youth's prime,
I converse wi' the langsyne frien's,
    Still young to me tho' scaured wi' time.
We roam ance mair the whinny knowes,
    We speel ance mair the gowany braes,
Wi' ne'er a care to cloud oor brows,
    Or storm to mar oor sunny days.
        My boyhood's hame, etc.

What's a' the gear that years hae brocht !
    Or a' the honours we hae won !
Can they bestow the cheery thocht
    When doon life's brae oor course has run ?
Na, na ; we willingly wad gie
    Oor hoarded pelf, or hard won prize,
Oor boyhood's hame ance mair to see,
    An' feel again youth's cloudless joys.
        My boyhood's hame, etc.

MY HAME ACROSS THE SEA.

I've heard you speak o' sunny lands
    An' far-aff Southern bowers,
I've heard you sing in loyal strains
    "This Canada of ours" ;

But there's a land 'boon a' the lave
    That's dearer far to me,
Scene o' my happy childhood's hours,
    My hame across the sea.

Tho' lang an' mony a day since I
    Bade hame an' frien's fareweel,
Yet aften dearest memories
    Will fondly o'er me steal :
An' bring me back the loved o' youth,
    The happy an' the free,
Wha aft my joys an' sorrows shared
    In my hame across the sea.

I canna stop the tear that fa's
    When thinkin' o' the past,
An' youth's dear frien's noo scattered wide
    Like leaves in winter's blast :
Or they wha sleep their lang last rest
    Beneath some kirkyard tree,
Yet link my heart still closer to
    My hame across the sea.

Tho' here I've found a happy hame,
    An' frien's baith leal an' true,
Yet noo when wearin' doon the hill,
    An' sune maun bid adieu
To a' I dearly lo'e on earth,
    My only wish would be,
To rest beneath my native sod
    In my hame across the sea.

FAR FRAE HAME.

Far awa' in mony lands,
    Frien's we kenn'd in bygane days,
Hameward turn to happier times
    Spent amang their native braes :
A' the pleasures life may bring,
    Be it honour, wealth, or fame,
Canna fill the void they feel
    In their hearts when far frae hame.

Chorus— Far frae hame the dear anes wander
    In bright lands across the faem,
  And our thochts are wi' them ever,
    Dearer noo when far frae hame.

Think they o' the humble cot,
    Meadows where as bairns they played,
Flowery glens, and wimplin' burns,
    Muirland hills wi' heather clad ;
Pictured in their fancy's e'e
    A' thing just remains the same,
Only that these scenes sae dear
    Grow still dearer far frae hame.

Scotia's sons, wherever met,
    Love to ponder owre the past,
And reca' the sunny days
    When nae cloud o' care owrecast ;
A' was sweet contentment then,
    Present joys compared are tame,
Even the dreams o' bygane days
    Bring them comfort far frae hame.

Can we wonder when they meet,
    Auld-time thochts come back sae clear,
Memories o' the youthfu' days
    Spent 'mid scenes for aye held dear !
Hazel bower, an' flowery nook,
    Lichted wi' their love's first flame,
Fancy pictures bonnier still,
    Noo when pairted far frae hame.

SANGS O' HAME.

Far frae the land I lo'e sae weel,
    Across the ocean's faem,
A soothin' sense o' joy I feel
    At pictured scenes o' hame ;
The hallowed spots where martyrs fell,
    For freedom and for right,
The ruined towers that yet can tell
    O' mony a gallant fight.

  Then sing to me the sangs o' hame
   That tell auld Scotland's story,
  O' gleamin' blades, in Border raids,
   For country, hame, and glory.

Noo wanderin' on a foreign strand,
 My heart turns back wi' pride
To hours spent in that dear hameland
 By glen or burnie side ;
Or by the ingle gathered aft,
 Wi' kindly hearts we'd meet,
An' lilt wi' glee, whiles loud or saft,
 Auld Scotia's sangs sae sweet.
  Then sing to me the sangs o' hame
   That mak' my auld een glisten,
  O' gloamin' hours by hazel bowers,
   Where wooers held their trystin'.

I like to hear the dear auld lays
 O' Tannahill or Burns ;
They bring me back my youthfu' days
 I laugh an' cry by turns.
While dear young voices round me ring,
 I bless them ane an' a',
For memories wauken as they sing
 O' days lang, lang awa'.
  Then sing to me the sangs o' hame,
   O' them I never weary ;
  They gild the page o' toil-worn age,
   An' mak' my life mair cheery.

MY HAME AMANG THE HILLS.

Where burnies wimple doon the howes,
 'Mid banks o' wavin' fern,
An' heather glints on benty knowes
 Where'er the e'e can turn :
Where 'boon the scaurs the heather-bells
 Hing noddin' to the rills,
I see again in fancy's spells
 My hame amang the hills.

'Mid foreign scenes my lot is cast,
　　Far, far frae hame an' frien's,
Yet memory aft reca's the past
　　Wi' youth's unclouded scenes ;
Wi' joys renewed my heart beats free,
　　An' sorrow's gloom dispels,
As ance again in dreams I see
　　My hame amang the hills.

Let ithers seek their joys in gear,
　　It canna fill the heart :
Or Fortune sketch a grand career
　　An' dootfu' joys impart ;
I'd part wi' a' to feel again
　　My boyhood's pure heart-thrills,
An' see ance mair across the main
　　My hame amang the hills.

MY HEART IS HAME IN SCOTLAND.

My heart is hame in Scotland,
　　My heart it isna here ;
Tho' skies are fair, an' flowers are rare,
　　An' nature smiles to cheer,
This land is no' my ain land,
　　Whatever charms it hae ;
There's naething here sae hamely dear
　　As the auld land far away.
　　　My heart is hame in Scotland,
　　　　Beside its wimplin' rills,
　　　In dear auld bonnie Scotland,
　　　　Amang her heather hills.

I've kind frien's here in plenty,
　　I've mair than I can name ;
I'm free frae care, I've wealth to spare,
　　I hae a cheerfu' hame :
An' yet I'm aften yearnin'
　　To cross the surgin' main,
Wi' pleasure rare to tread ance mair
　　My native hills again.

My heart is hame in Scotland,
　An' I'll ne'er be content
Till ance mair I am roamin'
　Where youth's bricht days were spent.

Oh! could my prayer be granted,
　I'd lea' this land behind,
An' a' that's here, for scenes mair dear,
　Wi' childhood's days entwined;
The very thocht is cheerin',
　Tho' faint the hope may be,
But I will pray, that come what may,
　I'll see 't before I die.
　　My heart is hame in Scotland,
　　　Beside her gowany braes,
　　An' there in dear auld Scotland
　　　I'd peacefu' end my days.

SCOTIA'S SANGS.

Aft I think on bygane days,
　When my heart was blithe an' gay;
When I joined the canty thrang
　In the auld hame far away.
Noo I'm gettin' auld an' stiff,
　Canna join the merry fling;
A' the better I enjoy
　Hearin' sweet young voices sing
　　"Scots wha hae" or "Afton Water,"
　　　"Banks o' Doon" or "Craigielea";
　　When I hear them lilted sweetly,
　　　Childhood's days come back to me.

Mony a time when care an' dool
　Fling their shadow owre the heart,
A' the cheery sunshine gane,
　A' the simmer frien's depart,
Dark an' dreary seems the gate
　We maun be resigned to gang;
But the sunshine a' comes back
　When we hear a canty sang.

"Duncan Gray" or "Kate Dalrymple."
"Tibbie Fowler o' the glen":
Auld-time lilts sae dear to boyhood.
Mak' me think I'm young again.

Can we wonder Scotia's sons,
  Wha hae wandered owre the faem,
Like to hear their mither tongue,
  Or the cherished sangs o' hame?
Aft I've seen the exile's joy,
  When some word or note was heard,
Movin' him to smiles or tears,
  As his soul the music stirred.
"Scotland yet" or "Dainty Davie,"
"Lassie, lay thy loof in mine,"
Banish a' the present sorrows
In the joys o' "Auld Langsyne."

WHERE THE HEATHER IS IN BLOOM.

When the summer sun is shining
  Sweetly over land and sea,
Then my heart, for Scotland pining,
  Longs for mountain, mead, and lea.
Far my ardent feet would wander
  From the city's strife and gloom,
Where the crystal streams meander
  And the heather is in bloom.

Chorus— Sweetly blooming, breeze perfuming,
    Wood notes wild, from brier and broom,
Sunlight glancing, streamlets dancing,
    Where the heather is in bloom.

Far in distant lands, the wand'rer
  Backward looks across the foam,
For the fairest scenes of grandeur
  Cannot dim his love of home.
Proudly he will tell the story
  To the children at his knee,
Of his country's pride and glory,
  Of her struggles to be free.—*Chorus.*

Deep within my bosom dwelling
  Is the love of childhood's scenes,
And my heart with rapture swelling
  Beats responsive to the strains
Of the love songs true and tender,
  Treasured in my memory's store;
Then, in fancy oft I wander
  O'er the heath-clad hills once more.—*Chorus.*

ANCE MAIR AMANG THE HEATHER.

Ance mair amang the heather
  Fain wad I like to be,
Awa' frae a' the city's din,
  Its vice an' misery:
To where the fresh'nin' breezes blaw,
  Where flow the limpid streams,
That thro' the winter's gloomy hours
  I've visited in dreams.

Ance mair amang the heather,
  A' carkin' cares forgot,
I'd sing as blithe 's the woodland birds,
  An' just sic hamely note;
Nae foreign lilts could charm me there
  Like Scotia's sangs sae dear,
Or Nature's music, wafted on
  To please the listenin' ear.

Ance mair amang the heather
  I'd wander withoot aim,
Wherever fancy led me on,
  For there I'd be at hame:
The bluebells noddin' 'mang my feet,
  The brackens on the braes,
By moorland glens where in oor youth
  We gathered nuts an' slaes.

Ance mair amang the heather,
  I'd seek nae happier state,
Nor wad I envy rich or hie,
  The titled or the great;

I'd lea' a' warldly thochts aside,
  An' wi' contentment see
Nae object but the fleecy clouds
  Between heaven's blue an' me.

I MUST COME BACK.

Far though I wander away from the spot
  Dear to my heart as the home of my youth,
Not one dear nook have I ever forgot,
  Nor friends who once plighted their honour and truth
And though those dear ones have wandered afar,
  Or lie calm at rest near the sweet hallowed scene,
My heart fondly yearns for the dear home once more,
  And I must come back to the old village green.
    It does my heart good, as the years go by,
    To visit the spot I loved as a boy ;
    Sunshine once more lights up the fair scene
      Of the dear old village green.

Fortune has favoured, and fortune has frowned ;
  Sadness and joy have been mine in the past ;
Sometimes my lot with prosperity crowned,
  Or again with the dark clouds of failure o'ercast ;
But through it all has my heart, ever true,
  Clung to the memories that welcomely come,
Bringing me only life's rosiest hue,
  As backward I turn to the dear old home.
    So, sweetly again let me taste of the joy
    That gilded my life when an innocent boy :
    With light step again I would willingly roam
      By the dear old cottage home.

Let me forget all the sorrow and tears
  That well might have blighted my heart once so gay,
If it were not the glamour of youth's sunny years
  That still can dispel the dark shadows away ;
Let me drive back all the falsehood and shame
  That over life's pathway stern destiny wove ;
To feel once again friendship more than a name,
  I must come back to old friends that I love.

Then, let me meet with the friends I once knew,
Faithful and loving, kind-hearted and true:
Nor will I seek from that haven to rove,
From the dear old friends I love.

WE HAE BEEN LANG ACQUENT!

Oh! sad's the pairtin' ony day
   When frien's maun say fareweel,
Maybe to meet nae mair, wha kens,
   As time rows aff the reel.
An' sadder still gin pairtin's come
   When they've ilk ither kent
Sin' they were bairns, an' can wi' pride
   Say, we've been lang acquent.

When far frae hame in ither lands
   My heart wad hameward turn,
While fancy wad reca' ilk scene,
   O' gowan, brae, or burn;
An' when a frien'ly letter came,
   By some auld cronie sent,
The tears wad fa' as tho'ts reca'
   That we'd been lang acquent.

When simmer comes wi' smilin' scenes
   O' bloomin' hill an' glen,
I'm fain to seek auld Scotia's shores,
   An' wander there again;
An' when lang-pairted frien's we meet,
   Wha's lives afar are spent,
We grasp the kindly han', an' say,
   We hae been lang acquent.

An' noo, when time has left its mark,
   An' we've owre-tapped the brae,
The dear auld frien's we lo'ed sae weel
   Are slippin' fast away;
An' as the saut tears tricklin' fa'
   Owre heart-ties rudely rent,
Our grief is deeper at the thocht
   That we've been lang acquent.

HOME OF YOUTH, I LEAVE THEE.

Home of youth, I leave thee,
    To wander far away;
And, though sad to say farewell
To each stream and flowery dell,
    I cannot stay.

No! though starts the bitter tears,
    Still I must depart;
And those scenes so fair and glad,
With emotions strange and sad
    Fill my heart.

I must leave you, friends of youth,
    Though we've sported oft together,
And have ever happy been,
By the mead or moorland scene,
    'Mid the heather.

Father, mother, all, good-bye!
    Loved of home, where'er I be,
Look upon my vacant chair,
Think of him who once sat there—
    Pray for me.

Thus cheer'd on in life's rough way,
    Never shall I once repine;
Though misfortune's clouds surround me,
Though the darts of sorrow wound me,
    Hope is mine.

On I'll wander, hoping ever,
    Seeking help from God above;
He will hear my humble prayer,
He will be my guide where'er
    I may rove.

Home of youth, I leave thee!
    Now each shady dell,
Purling streamlets, flowery dales,
Hazel bowers, and winding vales,
    All, farewell!

WE WERE A' BROCHT UP TOGETHER.

My auld frien' Dick, ance mair we meet:
  I fin' ye just the same,
Tho' I hae roved 'neath foreign skies
  An' ye've been here at hame;
We've had oor share o' ups an' doons,
  Like them that's gane before,
But still I fin' your heart is true,
  As in the days of yore.
    An' as we meet, an' kindly greet,
      When social frien's foregather,
    Ye turn aside, an' say wi' pride,
      "We were a' brocht up together."

My childhood's days come back again,
  An' mem'ry fondly dwells
On days gane bye, when you and I
  Roamed thro' the bosky dells:
Or, aulder grown, wi' lassies baith,
  Oot owre the Staney-muir,
We wandered at the gloamin' hour
  Wi' hearts devoid o' care.
    Then we'll renew oor frien'ship true,
      Just like a lang-lost brither;
    An' pledge the glass to ilk ane's lass,
      "We were a' brocht up together."

Whate'er the future has in store
  For either you or me,
We'll cherish still the guileless hours,
  When life was fair and free.
Whatever cares the days may bring
  We'll cast ahint oor backs,
An' lilt again the auld refrain,
  When owre our social cracks.
    Ilk joy an' care we'll freely share,
      An' pledge to ane anither,
    That trust and faith may bind us baith,
      "We were a' brocht up together."

WE WERE CRONIES AT THE SCHULE.

[DEDICATED TO MR GEORGE ELDER, GLASGOW.]

My guid auld frien', ance mair we meet
   An' kindly greet ilk ither,
Tho' mony years hae passed sin' we
   Roamed o'er these scenes together;
Your locks are getting thin like mine,
   Your step is no' sae jaunty,
But still I ken your heart's as warm,
   Your nature blithe an' canty :
      An' tho' we've had oor ups an' doons,
        Oor share o' care an' dool,
      In frien'ship fast, we in the past
        Were cronies at the schule.

Oh! dae ye mind o' boyhood's days,
   We wandered oot to gather
The brier an' bluebell frae the lane,
   The rowan red, an' heather?
What reivin' splores at nestin' time,
   By whinny knowe an' plantin';
We bore oor treasures carefu' hame,
   Like kings owre conquests vauntin'.

Oh! dae ye mind the hours we roamed,
   When Lounsdale's trees were buddin',
Or joyous sports o' winter's days,
   The green where we went skiddin';
An' dae ye mind the schule itsel'—
   Oor ink-bespattered places;
The laddies wha oor lessons shared,
   Or swapped oor scones an' pieces?

Noo ilka place seems changed to me,
   The scenes are dull and dreary:
Or is it in oorselves alane
   Oor hearts are no' sae cheery?
I care na, when we meet as noo
   To croon owre sang an' story,
Sae we forget the darksome years
   Wi' a' their grief or glory.

An' tho' we've had oor ups an' dooms,
   Oor share o' care an' dool,
We in the past, in frien'ship fast,
   Were cronies at the schule.

WHEN THE KETTLE'S ON THE SWEE.

There isna sic a cheery hour,
   In a' the lee-lang day,
As that, when at the gloamin' tide,
   I hameward tak' my way:
My care an' toil are a' forgot,
   When 'neath my cot I see
A warm an' cheery ingle-side,
   An' the kettle on the swee.

I like to see the dancin' lowe,
   Wi' mony a merry blink,
Licht up the snaw-white delfin ware
   That stands upon the bink:
When at the shadows on the wa'
   The bairnies laugh wi' glee,
An' dance to hear the kettle sing
   That's hingin' on the swee.

Let lordlings seek the noisy rout,
   Wi' a' its grand display;
They haena half the quiet joy
   That honest puir folk hae.
Gie me a cantie hour at e'en
   Wi' bairnies on my knee,
A fond guidwife, a clean hearthstane,
   An' the kettle on the swee.

An' when the bairnies say their prayers,
   An' cuddle 'mang the claes,
The wife an' I will aften sit
   An' plan for comin' days;
Tho' darklin' thochts will come at times,
   Our cares an' sorrows flee
When listenin' to the cheery sang
   O' the kettle on the swee.

WHEN THE BAIRNIES SAY GUID-NICHT.

My hame is but a humble cot,
　　Where puirtith aft intrudes,
An' Fortune froons wi' jaundiced e'e
　　When in her fickle moods:
But bless'd wi' lovin' wife an' weans,
　　My worries a' tak' flicht
When, roun' oor cosy neuk at e'en,
　　The bairnies say guid-nicht.

My toil is hard, my earnin's sma',
　　Tho' stirrin' late an' sune,
Wi' weary tramps owre hill an' muir,
　　When a' the dargs are dune:
When black despair weighs doon my heart,
　　An' there's nae blink o' licht,
The load is lifted when I hear
　　The bairnies say guid-nicht.

Oor cares are mony thro' the day,
　　Oor trials aften sair,
Altho' oor hearts gang aften oot
　　To ask a Faither's care:
'Tis then a soothin' calm ensues,
　　An' hope again gleams bricht,
When, 'neath their mither's sheltering wing,
　　The bairnies say guid-nicht.

I wadna gie that e'enin' hour
　　Amang the bairns at hame
For a' the pleasures wealth can boast,
　　For honours, place, or fame:
An' e'en tho' darker days may come,
　　Nor cheerin' ray in sicht,
Oor faith is strengthened when we hear
　　The bairnies say guid-nicht.

WHEN AULD FRIEN'S MEET.

AFTER lang years o' toil an' care,
An' sundered wanderin's here an' there,
What joy in life will e'er compare
    Wi' moments sweet,
As hands are kindly clasped ance mair,
    When auld frien's meet?

The past may hae its share o' gloom,
An' storm-tried thro' the blasts we've come,
The joy-strings o' oor hearts be dumb,
    Yet chords fu' sweet
Will in oor withered hearts find room,
    When auld frien's meet.

We'll skip the intervening time
To days when, in oor youth an' prime,
Again the gowany braes we'll climb,
    Wi' tireless feet,
While fancy conjures scenes sublime,
    When auld frien's meet.

An' tho' the scaurs o' age we bear,
The wrinkled broo, the scanty hair,
We'll banish tho'ts o' dool an' care
    Frae memory's seat,
An' nurse oor present joys the mair,
    When auld frien's meet.

We'll con owre a' the bygane days
When we ran bare-fit doon the braes,
As simmer sun or autumn haze
    Made life complete:
Nae clouds shall dim life's cherished rays
    When auld frien's meet.

We'll banish tho'ts o' winter drear,
Or gloomy way-gaun o' the year,
When woods were bare an' leaves lay sear
    'Neath snaw an' sleet,
An' picture only scenes that cheer,
    When auld frien's meet.

Nae time is this for cauldrife wae,
Black blasts o' grief to chill oor day;
I'd rather think o' sunny May,
    An' flowerets greet,
That come to deck the leafy spray,
    When auld frien's meet.

Tho' we hae climbed life's rugged hill
Since days when we were mates at schule,
An' gained a place we try to fill
    In ways discreet,
Ance mair we'll just be Rab an' Will,
    When auld frien's meet.

Tho' thou hast gained an honoured place,
That baith your worth an' learnin' grace,
While I was hampered in the race
    An' met defeat,
As equals still noo face to face,
    When auld frien's meet.

An' aye, at least when met as noo
The auld-time memories to renew,
We'll wipe the intervening view
    Frae aff life's slate,
An' firmly cling to joys too few,
    When auld frien's meet.

Again we part, perhaps nae mair
To meet for mony a weary year;
But should kind Heaven oor lives but spare,
    We may repeat
These soul-communings, aft owre rare,
    When auld frien's meet.

THE WEE ANES AT HAME.

'MANG a' life's enjoyment there's naething can cheer
Sae weel as the love o' our bairnies sae dear;
Tho' humble the cottage that shelters us a',
We're happier, maybe, than them at the Ha':
They hae wealth that we haena, are prood o' their name;
But our riches we count in the wee anes at hame.

Chorus —The wee anes at hame,
    The dear anes at hame,
    Aye blithe are we there wi'
    The wee anes at hame.

Far doon in the depths o' our hearts there's a spot
Kept free frae the gross things that darken our lot :
Nae rank weeds are there, but the fairest o' flowers,
An' the sunshine o' hame-love illumines the bowers :
But the sunshine wad be but a puir cauldrife flame
That waukened nae joy for the wee anes at hame.

The sodger wha fechts for his country an' Queen
In lands far awa' frae his ain hills sae green,
When dangers surround him, an' death may be near,
His thochts aften turn to the hame-land sae dear :
He seeks na the guerdon o' honour or fame,
But is nerved to the strife for the wee anes at hame.

The sailor wha faces the storms o' the deep,
In lang weary vigils his watch has to keep,
'Tis then that the stars peepin' out frae the lift
Remind o' the dear native hame he has left :
For the same stars that glint on the crest o' the faem
Watch owre the dear forms o' the wee anes at hame.

The cottar wha toils thro' the rain an' the snaw,
In lang weary days has this comfort thro' a' ;
It's no' for himsel' that he struggles sae sair,
But the hame-ties that cheer him, an' drive off despair,
Are the nestlin's sae helpless, wha rightly lay claim
To the bread he maun win for the wee anes at hame.

Oh ! what wad this life be to mony wha toil,
That the rich may enjoy a' the fruits o' the soil,
Wha thro' the lang year drudge the same dreary roun',
An' grudged e'en the bite that their sair toil has won !
A' the buffets o' fortune, the cankered auld dame,
Canna weaken their care for the wee anes at hame.

HAME AT E'EN.

The birds may flit on wanton wing,
  An' chirp the lee-lang day;
The bees intent on gatherin'
  Their sweets amang the hay:
But when the gloamin' draws its veil
  O'er mead an' muirland scene,
Baith bird an' bee wi' fleetest wing
  Seek aye their hames at e'en.

The frail auld cottar in the fields,
  Wha toils baith late an' ear',
An' aften when a scrimpit pay
  Leaves puirtith pinchin' sair:
Few o' the joys o' life he kens,
  Sma' glints an' seldom seen:
His greatest pleasure is the tho't
  O' rest when hame at e'en.

The bairns may rove o'er bank an' brae,
  An' sport the hours away,
While tho'ts o' hame ne'er fash their heids
  Till comes the gloamin' gray;
'Tis then the anxious mither asks,
  "Guid sakes, where hae ye been?"
But noo her fears are set at rest
  When nestlin' hame at e'en.

The traveller o'er the muirland road
  Where dangerous sloughs aboun',
Tho' fit-sair, hurries on his pace,
  Ere darkness settles doon;
For he may tint his gate, an' stray
  Where dangers lurk unseen,
But yonder light wi' joy he hails,
  That guides him hame at e'en.

The wanderer far in foreign lands,
  Tho' bright his lot may be,
Aft hame-sick, to the land he left
  Will turn a wistfu' e'e:

Oh! could he ance mair cross the sea,
　To boyhood's cherished scene,
An' there, contented, wait life's close
　'Mang loved anes hame at e'en.

An' ye, wha've wandered frae the hame
　Where peace an' virtue reigned,
Allured by glitterin' vice to roam,
　While lovin' hearts were pained ;
Aft, when the still sma' voice appeals,
　Or tho'ts o' joys unseen
Come back, the wanderer returns
　Repentant hame at e'en.

An' sae in life's long pilgrimage,
　When strength an' spirit fail,
Hoo bless'd are they wha's faith has fixed
　Their hopes within the veil ;
The aged Christian calmly waits
　His ca' to that Unseen,
For death is but a change that brings
　A welcome hame at e'en.

AN AULD SETTLER.

She left her hame in youth's fair morn,
　An' crossed the boundin' main ;
But aft her heart wad yearn to roam
　Her native hills again :
To wander wi' her playmates dear
　Adoon the bosky dells,
Where 'mang the nooks the violets bloomed,
　The primrose, an' bluebells.

As age crept on, her memory seemed
　To cling to langsyne days,
An' she wad tell o' pranks an' ploys
　Amang the gowany braes :
Hoo aft she climbed the Harden's hill,
　Or roamed thro' Langton wood,
An' waded bare-fit i' the burn
　That thro' the meadow flowed.

She talked wi' pride o' famed Duns Law,
   Where stood the Covenant Stane,
Where heroes vowed to do or die
   Their freedom to maintain:
She aft described the Castle woods,
   The Hen-poo's placid lake,
The spots where geans an' brambles grew,
   By glen or tangled brake.

From a Sketch.

SITE OF THE OLD CASTLE OF POLWARTH.

Hoo aft to me she has recalled
   The quiet sylvan scene,
By Marchmont's bonnie woods an' braes,
   Or Polwarth-on-the-Green:
The auld kirkyard by Lounsdale's haughs,
   The bonnie wimplin' burn;
The hills an' howes, the glens an' knowes,
   To which her heart wad turn:

Hoo mony times she wished ance mair
 To tread the heath-clad braes,
Ance mair to hae a glint o' hame,
 An' there to end her days:
An' while her heart wad dwell on this,
 An' saut tears dim her e'e,
She'd say: "I'm owre auld noo for that:
 Na, na! it canna be."

Yet while the lamp held on to burn,
 An' memory held its sway,
Wi' fondest love she aft recalled
 The auld hame far away:
She gloried in its spotless fame,
 Its fights in freedom's cause,
Its martyr heroes wha laid doon
 Their lives for righteous laws.

Alas! that wish was ne'er attained:
 Death cut the vital thread;
An' noo beneath the maple boughs
 She rests amang the dead.
But while oor memory aft recalls
 That humble, honoured name,
We'll think o' her in youth renewed,
 In a brighter, fairer hame.

THE GLOAMIN' HOUR.

At the witchin' hour o' nicht
 I hae watched wi' strange delight
The twinklin' stars that stud the lift sae hie:
 I hae listened to the cry
 O' the howlets far an' nigh,
Or the wind's weird sough in leafy bush an' tree;
 I hae seen the rosy dawn,
 When the gowan-dotted lawn
Showed dewy gems on ilka blade and flower:
 But I've felt a sweeter spell
 In Lounsdale's leafy dell,
When wanderin' at the fairy gloamin' hour.

In childhood's happy days,
   'Mid primrose-speckled braes,
We'd wander there an' sport the hale day lang :
   We heeded na time's flicht,
   Until the shades o' nicht
Reminded o' the hameward road to gang ;
   E'en then the day seemed short
   For our pleasure an' oor sport,
An' sweir were we to lea' oor fairy bower ;
   Tho' warned ere we went there,
   An' cautioned to be sure
To be hame afore the shadowed gloamin' hour.

But the happiest days o' a'
   That oor memory can reca',
Were when as lovers aft we wandered there,
   An' whispered vows were made
   Beneath the hazel's shade,
An' love's first kiss was bliss beyond compare.
   E'en noo, when youth has gane,
   An' we wander there alane,
Oor fancy can reca', wi' soothin' power,
   The blissfu' times noo gane,
   When, as lover or as wean,
We dreamed or sported thro' the gloamin' hour.

BY THE BURNIE SIDE.

There's a little cottage stands
   By the burnie side,
An' the droopin' willow bends
   Where its pure waters glide ;
It is but a humble cot
Wi' a bonnie garden plot,
An' I've aye a welcome got
   By the burnie side.

The folk are leal an' true
   By the burnie side,
While we fin' true frien's sae few
   As we roam the warl' wide ;

But it's there I aye repair,
Ilka day that I can spare,
For there's aye a kind word there,
   By the burnie side.

They mak' nae pretence to show
   By the burnie side,
An' they may be reckoned slow
   By the crowds that past them ride;
Their speech may be uncouth
To the warl's ears forsooth,
But it has the ring o' truth
   By the burnie side.

They haena wealth, I own,
   By the burnie side;
But the Queen upon the throne
   Has less cause for honest pride;
For the helpless and the poor
Find a welcome at their door,
An' a share o' what's in store
   By the burnie side.

Frae the warl's cares I'd flee
   To the burnie side;
An' frae frien's baith proud an' hie
   I wad be content to bide,
Gin I could but hae a share
O' the peace that's reignin' there,
Free frae fashion's pomp an' glare,
   By the burnie side.

Then my blessin' on that cot
   By the burnie side;
Ever happy be their lot,
   Whatever may betide;
An' when ca'd this earth to lea',
May their welcome yonder be
As kind as that to me
   By the burnie side.

ON THE ROAD HAME.

After the wearisome toils o' the day,
When mirk nicht sets in, and a lang road to gae,
Tho' bleak the surroundin's, my heart's in a flame;
For the love-licht's afore me, I'm on the road hame.

Hard tho' my toil be, an' scanty my fare,
Wi' health an' guid spirits, I whistle at care;
The joys o' the city to me a' seem tame
When the wife an' the weans ken I'm on the road hame.

Oot in the mornin' aft ere the day breaks,
I think na o' hardships when dune for their sakes;
Tho' while shafts o' care seem to mak' me their aim,
I shake off the load when I'm on the road hame.

In the mornin' o' life, like the laddies to schule,
Sae sweir to start oot, an' owre late as a rule;
When schule tasks are owre, o'd, they no' seem the same,
They're sae frisky an' cheery, when on the road hame.

Aft in life's journey we'll find a stey brae,
That tries us gey sair wi' the burdens we hae;
Yet thro' mirk an' mud, tho' we gang tired an' lame,
We hae this consolation—we're on the road hame.

Auld age creeps on us, the winter draws near;
But why should we think o' death's comin' wi' fear?
If back owre the past we can look withoot shame,
We'll be welcomed wi' joy when at last we get hame.

COME AGAIN.

These are cheery words of welcome,
 Like some sweet old song's refrain,
And we love to hear them uttered
 By some loved voice: Come again.

Chorus—Welcome ever will you be
 While your friendship we retain,
These our parting words to thee—
 Come again, come again.

A BERWICKSHIRE BARD.

There are memories that we cherish
  Which the heart loves to retain,
With the hand-clasp of affection,
  And the kindly : Come again.

What though distance now may sever
  Friends we left across the main,
Oft in fancy's ear we listen
  To the dear words : Come again.

While amid our joys and sorrows,
  Hours of pleasure or of pain,
This fond memory still delights us,
  Fare-thee-well, but Come again.

Though the years bring many changes,
  Days we ne'er shall see again,
This remains on memory's tablet,
  Graven deeply : Come again.

Oh ! we may be sad and dreary,
  And our hearts be chilled with pain,
But there's sunshine in the welcome
  Of the kindly : Come again.

III.

Songs Set to Music.

"Music, the tender child of rudest times,
The gentle native of all lands and climes;
Who hymns alike man's cradle and his grave,
Lulls the low cot, or peals along the nave."
—*Mrs Norton.*

Many of the songs that follow have been very popular both in this country and in Canada. Several well-known vocalists have been attracted to them, and through their delightful renderings of them have charmed not a few of patriotic spirit.

III.

SONGS SET TO MUSIC.

WAIT A-WEE AN' DINNA WEARY.

WAIT a-wee an' dinna weary:
  Tho' your heart be sad an' sair,
An' your youthfu' dreams hae vanished,
  Leavin' nocht but grief an' care;
Tho' the clouds be dark an' lowerin',
  Faded flowers lie 'neath the snaw,
Simmer suns wi' bricht hopes burnin',
  Sune the mists will clear awa'.
    Wait a-wee an' dinna weary:
      Tho' the winter's lang an' dreary,
    Simmer days will come to cheer ye,
      Gin ye'll only wait a-wee.

Wait a-wee an' dinna weary:
  Tho' ye're maybe crossed in love,
An' your springhood's hopes lie withered,
  Time will yet your cares remove:
Tho' the joys that langsyne perished
  Left a wound baith deep and sair,
Maybe some true heart has cherished
  Love for you, deep an' sincere.
    Wait a-wee an' dinna weary, etc.

Wait a-wee an' dinna weary:
  There are ithers sad an' wae;
Sufferin' puir, wi' heavy burthens,
  Strugglin' 'gainst adversity:

For awhile forget your sorrows,
　　Sune a' cankerin' cares will flee,
Gin ye'll soothe the broken-hearted,
　　Wipe the tear frae puirtith's e'e.
　　　　Wait a-wee an' dinna weary, etc.

MY HEART WARMS TO THE TARTAN.

Is there a land like Scotland,
　　Wi' sons sae brave and free,
Can show sae fair a record
　　O' dauntless chivalry?
I love her cloud-capped mountains,
　　Her glens and wimplin' rills,
While my heart warms to the tartan
　　An' my native heather hills.
　　　　I love thee, dear auld Scotland,
　　　　　　Thy mountains heather clad,
　　　　For my heart warms to the tartan,
　　　　　　An' the lads that wear the plaid.

We'll ne'er forget her heroes,
　　Wha fought in freedom's cause,
An' laid the grand foundation
　　O' a' her righteous laws;
I listen to the lyrics
　　By deathless poets sung,
While my heart warms to the tartan
　　An' my native mither tongue.
　　　　I love thee, dear auld Scotland, etc.

I hear the pibroch soundin'
　　A rousin' martial blast,
Wi' shattered pennons flyin'
　　The troops are marchin' past;
A hearty loyal welcome
　　Sounds in that loud hurrah,
An' my heart warms to the tartan
　　And the gallant forty-twa.
　　　　I love thee, dear auld Scotland, etc.

In mony lands I've wandered,
  Far, far across the sea,
But aften hameward turnin',
  My thochts wad wander free ;
An' noo I tread the heather,
  I fain would be at rest,
For my heart warms to the tartan,
  An' the land I lo'e the best.
    I love thee, dear auld Scotland, etc.

WHEN THE BAIRNIES ARE FRAE HAME.

THE house is dowf an' dreary
  When the bairnies are frae hame,
An' ilka 'oor I weary
  When the bairnies are frae hame :
I miss their merry lauchin',
  Their friskin' an' their daffin',
Their shouts an' sangs sae cheery,
  When the bairnies are frae hame.

When John comes hame at e'enin',
  When the bairnies are frae hame,
Tho' ne'er a word compleenin'
  When the bairnies are frae hame :
Tho' he seeks to hide his feelin',
  His thochts there's nae concealin',
For his looks confess his meanin'
  When the bairnies are frae hame.

Noo, John, just write to granny
  To bring the bairnies hame,
For withoot they're here we canna
  Feel the hoose to be the same ;
An' ilka day she'll see them,
  For when she comes here wi' them,
We'll just keep her, for we maunna
  Let the bairnies gang frae hame.

An' sae ance mair thegither,
  When the bairnies are at hame,
Fu' blithe will be their mither
  When the bairnies are at hame.
We'll just keep them aye beside us,
  An' what joy or grief betide us,
We maun share wi' ane anither,
  When the bairnies are at hame.

HEAVEN IS WHERE OUR FATHER IS.

LITTLE hearts which throb with pain,
  Little eyes which swim in tears,
Let me take you to my heart,
  Let me quiet all your fears.
I will teach you of that home
  Where our loved ones rest in bliss ;
All our troubled hearts need know—
  Heaven is where our Father is.

Yes, there is heaven, calm, peaceful heaven,
  There are the dear ones happy and blest,
  There with the Father they loved while on earth,
There, in His presence only, is heaven :
  Yes, there is heaven.

Hearts may cling to earthly ties ;
  These, alas! will pass away ;
Idols that we worship now,
  We will find are only clay.
All is fleeting here below ;
  One by one our friends we miss ;
But this truth should calm our woe—
  Heaven is where our Father is.
    Yes, there is heaven, etc.

Sweet the thought that those we miss
  Sympathise with all our care,
And rejoice to know we seek,
  After life, to join them there ;

And though doubts and fears assail,
  We will cling in faith to this,
That at last we may unite
  In that heaven where Father is.
    Yes, there is heaven, etc.

KISS THE BAIRNS FOR ME

My guidman's far awa' frae hame,
  An' oh! I miss him sair;
But, still, I ken that he is leal,
  An' lo'es me a' the mair;
For when his tender letters come
  Frae far across the sea,
He ne'er forgets the weans, but says,
  "Just kiss the bairns for me."

Oh! dool an' dark wad be my lot
  If 'twere na for the weans:
I've aye their love to cheer me on,
  Tho' far may be my frien's.
An' weel I ken the faither's heart,
  Wherever he may be,
Gangs oot in kindly words o' love:
  "Just kiss the bairns for me."

I hear their lauchin' voices ring,
  I see ilk rosy cheek;
An' when my thochts are far awa',
  My heart's owre fu' to speak.
But when at nicht they cuddle doon,
  An' close ilk rougish e'e,
I ne'er forget their faither's wish:
  "Just kiss the bairns for me."

My prayers are aye that we ere lang
  May meet, an' part nae mair:
Tho' puir oor lot, wi' him we'll a'
  Our joys an' sorrows share.
But while he roams in distant lands,
  Tho' lang oor partin' be,
I'll ne'er forget his lovin' words:
  "Just kiss the bairns for me."

UNDER THE ORCHARD TREES.

As amid the silent sadness
   Of winter's gloomy days,
We dwell on bygone pleasures
   Of the summer's sunny haze ;
So in my heart's lone sadness
   Comes memory's passing breeze,
To tell the hours of gladness
   Under the orchard trees.

'Twas in the days of summer
   When first we wandered there,
When the blossoms lent their fragrance
   To the balmy twilight air ;
And my hopes were young and blooming,
   As when fancy only sees
The future bright with sunshine
   Under the orchard trees.

My heart went out in rapture
   To the song-birds in their glee ;
The flowers bedecked my pathway,
   My sky from clouds was free ;
The hours brought only sweetness,
   As the flowers repaid the bees ;
And we reckoned not their fleetness
   Under the orchard trees.

Each look, each word, and promise,
   I stored within my heart,
Till her image, there engraven,
   Became of me a part ;
Wherever fortune called me,
   O'er foreign lands or seas,
I fed on dreams of wooing
   Under the orchard trees.

The orchard trees are leafless,
   Their branches, gaunt and bare,
Keep time to the winds of winter
   In a low funereal air ;

The leaves are lowly lying
  Where the biting wintry breeze
Has left them sear and mouldering,
  Under the orchard trees.

So are my life's hopes faded
  And mingled with the dust;
So has my dream departed
  Of a life of love and trust:
And all that's left to cheer me,
  This sad heart only sees
That summer gleam of wooing
  Under the orchard trees.

THE LAND OF THE MAPLE FOR ME.

Here's a health to the land of the forest and flood,
  And the Queen who rules over the free;
While united we stand, as our forefathers stood,
  In liberty's van we will be.
Though our hearts fondly cherish the memories of old,
  And the homes we have left o'er the sea,
Our love for old Canada ne'er shall grow cold;
  Oh! the land of the maple for me.

If invasion should threaten our lake-sheltered land,
  And the war-cloud be thundering near,
We will stand, a true-hearted and vigorous band,
  To strike for our country so dear;
While the memories of those who fought not in vain
  To bequeath us the rights of the free,
Shall nerve us to deeds of true valour again;
  Oh! the land of the maple for me.

Then hurrah! for old Canada, home of the free;
  May heaven still over her smile,
And may plenty and peace the true blessings still be
  Of our hard-handed heroes of toil!
From her ocean-girt coast to her wild forest shades,
  Where the hall or the homestead may be,
Ever brave be her sons, and devoted her maids;
  Oh! the land of the maple for me.

CONSTANT STILL.

We have loved, and we have parted,
    And my life is sadly changed
Since I find thee fickle-hearted,
    And thy love from me estranged:
Though thou gav'st me many a token,
    Time nor change my hopes would kill.
Yet thy ardent vows are broken,
    While my heart is constant still.

Oh! how fondly memory lingers
    On the days, when, void of care,
Love had touched with fairy fingers
    Future scenes, serene and fair.
Now the sky is darkly clouded,
    Storms of sadness work their will;
Though despair my life has shrouded,
    Yet my heart is constant still.

How I thought of thee when severed,
    For I deemed thy heart was true,
And my trust in thee ne'er wavered,
    Anxious cares I never knew;
Yet there came a sad awaking,
    Future years with grief to fill;
Silently my heart was breaking,
    Yet I loved thee constant still.

Though you wed for wealth and station
    And despise my humble love,
Though time brings no consolation
    And my life a burden prove;
Still the bygone joys I'll cherish,
    Faintly though the void they fill.
And, till life or memory perish,
    I will suffer, constant still.

"LOVE WILL BIDE WHEN SIMMER'S GANE."

    Winter's frost has nipp'd the roses,
        Winter's wind in sadness grieves,
    Yet a perfume sweet reposes
        'Mang the dry an' wither'd leaves;
    So the heart when sear'd wi' sadness,
        Blasted wi' the frosts o' pain,
    Clings to bygane scenes o' gladness;
        "Love will bide when simmer's gane."

    When the years, nae pleasure bringin',
        Keenly blaw their scarin' blast,
    Still a heart-shine, brightly clingin',
        Sheds a radiance o'er the past;
    A' the fond endearments tasted,
        Loves we cherish'd, tho' in vain;
    Tho' our hopes were rudely blasted,
        "Love will bide when simmer's gane."

    Tho' the clouds are darkly loomin'
        O'er the scenes awhile sae fair,
    An' the flowers ance sweetly bloomin'
        Deck the woodland scene nae mair,
    Spring will come again, invitin'
        To the flower-deck'd mead an' plain,
    A' our bygane griefs requitin';
        "Love will bide when simmer's gane."

    An' when years creep on an' age us,
        An' the broo is bent wi' care,
    Shall we scan life's written pages
        For a time mair bright and fair?
    Needless to regret our losses,
        Grieve o'er ilka blot an' stain;
    Tho' ere lang our journey closes,
        "Love will bide when simmer's gane."

LITTLE BLUEBELL.

Down in the dell, where the streamlet glides cheery,
   Now in the sunshine, and now in the shade,
Where bees humming blithely seem never to weary,
   Gleaning their sweets from the flowers in the glade :
Glancing so modestly out from the shadows,
   Nodding its head to the zephyrs' faint swell,
Brightly reflecting the sky's cloudless azure,
   Pride of the valley, the little bluebell.
      Little bluebell, waving bluebell,
      List to the fairy chimes rung in the moonlight ;
      Little bluebell, modest bluebell,
      Pride of the valley is little bluebell.

Down in the valley, as modest and winning
   As the fair flow'rets that dapple the glade,
Blithe as a fairy, with steps light and airy,
   Blooms in her spring-hood, my dear little maid ;
Often I sing of her charms to the breezes,
   Oft to the song-bird her graces I tell,
Often compare her to flowers of the meadow,
   Dear to my heart is my little bluebell.
      Little bluebell, charming bluebell,
      List to its fairy chimes rung in the moonlight
      Little bluebell, modest bluebell,
      Pride of the valley is little bluebell.

Never may winter blasts come near her dwelling,
   Never chill night-dews wither the bloom,
Safe in her home from the storm and the tempest,
   Ever the same when a-wooing I come ;
Soon may the hour come, when, claiming her promise,
   Safe in my home and my bosom to dwell ;
Years may roll o'er us, as happy and joyous
   As when I first met my little bluebell.
      Little bluebell, winsome bluebell,
      List to the fairy chimes rung in the moonlight ;
      Little bluebell, modest bluebell,
      Pride of the valley is little bluebell.

THE LITTLE PATCH OF SUNSHINE.

In my quiet little cottage I am working all the day,
  While the autumn mists and fogs are in the air,
When now and then the sun glints out with sickly feeble ray,
  Like hope-gleams 'mid the darkness of despair;
I have my cares and troubles, and my heart will often sink
  At the gloomy prospect looming where the mists so thickly fall;
When through my kitchen window comes a cheery golden blink,
  And a little patch of sunshine on the wall.

'Tis only just a little patch, no bigger than a hand,
  But 'tis welcome for the cheerfulness it brings;
It seems to bring a message from some brighter, better land,
  And clears my heart from grosser, meaner things;
The caged-bird seeks the corner where it feels the warm gleam,
  And trills its note of thankfulness that summer days recall,
And memory goes back again to youth's unclouded dream.
  Through the little patch of sunshine on the wall.

'Mong all the clouds and sorrows that afflict us in our path,
  There's a golden stream that glistens now and then,
And the wildest storms of winter, that are charged with murkiest wrath,
  But prepare the way for brighter scenes again;
So, too, in life's declining years, when strength and spirits fail,
  As in age's sombre evening the depressing shadows fall,
There's a comfort for the weary when they look beyond the veil,
  From a little patch of sunshine on the wall.

HAND IN HAND.

We have lived and loved together
  Through the years, 'mid joy and care;
Sorrow's trials have closer bound us
  Than the smiles of fortune fair;

Sweethearts yet as in the bygone,
  When our prospects all were bright,
May our love be still enduring,
  As we near the darkling night.

Chorus Hand in hand we'll go together
    Through the chequered vale of life:
  And in dark or sunny weather
    I'll be near thee, darling wife.

Hand in hand we roamed as children
  By the hill-side and the vale,
Gathering flowerets by the wayside,
  Weaving many a fairy tale;
Then as sweethearts, in the gloaming,
  When the lights and shadows blend,
Whispering words of fond endearment,
  We have wandered hand in hand.

Now our limbs are growing feeble,
  And our locks are thin and grey;
We can not be long together,
  For the end's not far away.
But, till death shall come to part us,
  We will journey hand in hand,
Parting—but to be united
  In that brighter, better land.

THE BORDER LADS.

Air "The Battle of Stirling."

From Berwick's ancient town
  A band of Borderers came,
And met with speech and song to fan
  The patriotic flame:
In stirring tones the Chairman said:
" Breathes there a man with soul so dead,
  Who does not love the heather?
He is no credit to his race;
Such recreant Scot shall find no place
  Where Border lads foregather."

With song and toast, the hours
  Went all too swiftly by,
While pictured scenes of glens and bowers
  Shone bright in memory's eye;
And no uncertain sound went forth
To that dear home-land in the north,
  The land of hill and heather;
Sweet recollections warmed the heart,
As each spoke of his native part
  Where Border lads foregather.

Then let us hope that we
  Ere long may meet again
To speak of Scotland's glories, we
  With pride will aye maintain;
And should it be our lot to roam
To other lands across the foam,
  We'll toast the kilt and feather;
Thus aye may social mirth abound,
And trusty friendship shall be found
  Where Border lads foregather.

LASSIE DEAR!

When the mornin' sun is shinin' owre the hills,
  Lassie dear,
An' glistenin' in the crystal murmurin' rills,
  Lassie dear,
  Let the hours sae swiftly flee,
  What is time to you or me?
  When we thus ilk ither see,
    Lassie dear, lassie dear.

When the sheep hae sought a coolin' shade at noon,
  Lassie dear,
An' the burnie sings a quiet languid tune,
  Lassie dear,
  I wad meet thee there an' then,
  Where the wild flowers deck the glen,
  An' the joyous hours we'd spen',
    Lassie dear, lassie dear.

A bonnie mune is shinin' in the lift,
    Lassie dear,
Its glints break thro' the cloudlet's fleecy rift,
    Lassie dear :
E'en then when shadows fa',
An' a stillness reigns owre a',
I wad meet thee doon the shaw,
    Lassie dear, lassie dear.

When a' the village seems to be at rest,
    Lassie dear,
The hour that wooers aye enjoy the best,
    Lassie dear,
Thro' the fairy glen we'll rove,
Where the rustlin' leaves above
Whisper messages o' love,
    Lassie dear, lassie dear.

For at mornin', noon, or at the twinklin' nicht,
    Lassie dear,
Thy ever welcome presence brings delicht,
    Lassie dear :
An' sae, whate'er betide,
Ye maun say ye'll be my bride,
For I'm happiest by thy side,
    Lassie dear, lassie dear.

WHEN THE SUMMER BUDS UNFOLD.

When the summer buds unfold
  To the wooing summer sun,
And the charm of wood and wold
  Tells that winter's course is run ;
When a gladsome smile is spread
  Over nature's beaming face :
Shall the hopes we deemed as fled
  Bloom again with sweeter grace ?
    When the doves are gently cooing,
    When the birds begin their wooing,
    What should we, my love, be doing
    When the summer buds unfold ?

When the summer buds unfold,
    And the flow'rets deck the vale,
We will whisper, as of old,
    Love's enchanting oft-told tale;
And our hearts will feel the glow
    Of our childhood's sunny hours,
As when balmy zephyrs blow
    'Mid the fragrant blooming flowers.
        When the doves are gently cooing, etc.

When the summer buds unfold
    'Neath the sunshine and the rain,
All our hopes, once seared and cold,
    Will revive to bloom again;
And tho' winter's blight may come,
    And the flowers may droop and die,
Love's bright beams will light our home
    With a pure and lasting joy.
        When the doves are gently cooing, etc.

"SHOUTHER TO SHOUTHER."

(ADDRESSED TO THE ST. ANDREW'S SOCIETY OF MEMPHIS, TENN., DURING THE YELLOW-FEVER SCOURGE.)

When oor forefaithers foucht by land or by sea,
Prepared for their richts aye to do or to dee,
'Twas then that they made their prood foemen to feel
In vain was their charge 'gainst a phalanx o' steel;
Or as forward they sprang at their chieftain's word,
Dealing death at each blow wi' the bayonet an' sword,
As they fell dead or wounded, an' front ranks were thinned,
Still closer pressed forward the heroes behind,
    "Shouther to shouther."

When the enemy's force cam' sweeping alang,
Wi' the wail an' the dirge, for the lauch an' the sang;
When thousands were fa'ing, like leaves in the blast,
Leaving sair desolation wherever they passed,

A brave band o' Scots, like their faithers o' yore,
Stood firm to their posts for the nameless an' poor;
They flinched na tho' ithers were weak wi' despair;
Tho' death's shafts micht reach them, their duty was there,
    "Shouther to shouther."

Where'er in the land o' the stranger are met
The sons o' auld Scotia, they're brethren yet:
They're proud o' the fact that they're clannish an' leal,
An' hae aye a true heart for puirtith to feel;
Their love has na dimmed for their hame o'er the sea,
The land o' the heather, the land o' the free:
That the honour o' Scotland may ne'er bear a blot
Is the heart-wish o' every true, loyal brither Scot.
    "Shouther to shouther."

This life's a sair fecht 'mid its puirtith an' pain,
But the wail o' the sad, Scotchmen hear na in vain,
An' they wha wi' plenty or little are blessed,
Are ready, aye ready, to help the distressed.
Go bravely on, brithers; the scourge now has passed,
An' the prayer o' the stricken is answered at last;
And should in the future new troubles appear,
Ye can aye count on help frae your brethren here.
    "Shouther to shouther."

THE MUIRLAND GLEN.

Oh! bonnie rows the burnie in the Muirland Glen;
There's nae a spot I lo'e sae weel in a' the scenes I ken,
    Where the haws an' hazels hing,
    An' the birds sae sweetly sing,
An' the gloamin' breeze blaws saftly in the Muirland Glen.

It was there in days o' childhood, in the Muirland Glen,
Ere youth's bright glamour faded an' its joys cam' to an en',
    I hae roved the lee-lang day
    Wi' the frien's noo far away,
An' oor hearts kenned nought but simmer in the Muirland
    Glen.

Gin ye ask me why I lo'e sae weel the Muirland Glen,
I'd maybe blush an' falter, an' say I dinna ken ;
   But if further ye should spier,
   I might maybe hint that here
Lives the lassie I lo'e dearly in the Muirland Glen.

But there's anither reason why I lo'e the Muirland Glen :
There's a wee thatched cottage near it wi' a cosy but an'
     ben,
   An' it's here I'd wish to bide
   When I win my winsome bride,
Where nae warld's cares can reach us in the Muirland Glen.

THE LITTLE WHITE COT IN THE CLEARING.

Down in yon little white cot in the clearing,
Where the bright summer roses encircle the door,
   Dwells a sweet maiden
   With eyes beauty laden,
And dark raven tresses her brow streaming o'er.
Soft is her glance as the bright summer dawning,
Ere the fierce sun sheds his fire-piercing dart ;
   Gentle and airy,
   Like light flitting fairy,
   Sweet winsome Mary,
     The maid of my heart.

Down by yon little white cot in the clearing
Often I roam at the close of the day,
   List'ning her singing,
   Like silver bells ringing
Borne on the soft twilight zephyrs away ;
Then will a feeling steal over my spirit,
Wafting me backward to childhood's bright day,
     Years when no sadness
     Darkened our gladness,
     Nor yet love's madness
       Held me in sway.

Down in yon little white cot in the clearing
Gladly I'd linger till life's closing scene,
    No more to wander,
      Though scenes of bright grandeur
Tempted my wild roving footsteps again ;
But in that cottage, though ever so humble,
Blithe would I be as a bird on the wing,
    Never to weary,
    Though others are dreary,
    But with my dearie
      A light-hearted king.

MY BONNIE BORDER LASSIE.

WHERE rivers row to meet the sea,
    An' hills their crests are rearin',
Where verdant valleys tempt oor feet,
    Wi' birds an' flowers sae cheerin' ;
By gentle slopes where bluebells gleam,
    On gowaned meadows grassy,
The fairest flower that blossoms there's
    My bonnie Border Lassie.

As snaw on Cheviot's hoary crest,
    Sae pure's my winsome Mary,
Like zephyrs saft in Bowmont vale,
    Her step is light an' airy ;
An' tho' she treats me wi' disdain,
    An' looks sae proud an' saucy,
She's mair to me than tongue can tell,
    My bonnie Border Lassie.

I kenna if her heart may turn
    An' think o' me wi' favour,
Yet I wad guard her wi' my life
    Frae him wha wad deceive her ;
But whae'er wins her, time will prove,
    Tho' warldly cares harass ye,
They'll a' dispel before the smile
    O' my dear Border Lassie.

OUR COORTIN' DAYS.

Oh! Maggie, dae ye mind
    O' our coortin' days,
When in simmer we reclined
    On the mossy braes,
An' the gowans braw I'd pu',
Wi' the wavin' bells sae blue,
To bind aroun' your broo,
    In our coortin' days?

Oh! the mavis sang sae sweet
    In our coortin' days,
Where the wimplin' burnies meet,
    'Mang the hazels an' the slaes;
When the gloamin' shadows fell,
An' we felt their soothin' spell,
We hae trysted in the dell,
    In our coortin' days.

Dae ye mind the sangs we'd sing
    In our coortin' days,
When we made the valley ring
    Wi' our cheery lays;
Or we'd whisper o'er an' o'er,
As we'd aften dune before,
O' the joys we had in store,
    In our coortin' days?

When the moon lit up the vales,
    In our coortin' days,
I hae tauld thee eerie tales
    O' the midnicht fays;
For I kenn'd ye'd closer press
To my side, my bonnie lass,
An' I cheered thee wi' a kiss,
    In our coortin' days.

We hae journeyed side by side
    Sin' our coortin' days,
A' our bairns we see wi' pride
    Takin' after our ways;

An' tho' noo we're gettin' auld,
An' we're wrinkled, grey, an' bald,
Our love has ne'er grown cauld
    Sin' our coortin' days.

Let lovers aye mak' sure,
    In their coortin' days,
Their affection's warm an' pure,
    As the sun's bricht rays;
For that love is but a name,
An' a fitfu' cauldrife flame,
If in age is no' the same
    As in coortin' days.

WHEN THE KYE GANG TO THE MUIR.

Oh! hae ye seen my lassie,
Oh! hae ye seen my queen,
    On simmer days,
    By mossy braes,
At Polwart-on-the-Green?
I'm sure ye'd ken my lassie,
Gin e'er ye twasome met,
    At early morn
    Beside the thorn
When flowers wi' dew are wet.
    Her cheeks are aye sae rosy,
    Her broo is aye sae fair,
    When I meet my ain dear lassie
    As the kye gang to the muir.

At milkin' in the morning,
There's no' a lassie there,
    Tho' buxom queens,
    Just in their teens,
That can wi' her compare:
And, oh! I feel sae happy
Whene'er my lassie's by:
    The herd himsel'
    Seems in a spell,
An' thinks na o' his kye.

      The time sae quickly passes,
        Wi' merry daffin' there,
      Among the lads an' lassies
        When the kye gang to the muir.
Oh! shall I win my charmer,
An' ca' her aye my ain?
    I'd rather hae
    Her smile for aye
Than a' the warld's gain;
I'd rather hae a cottage,
Be hamely clad an' a',
    Wi' her to share
    Love's pleasure there,
Than wealth an' housin' braw.
      I ken na gin she lo'es me,
        But just to ease my care,
      I'll spier her in the mornin'
        When the kye gang to the muir.

WHERE DUTY CALLS.

WHERE duty calls to daring deeds,
The British soldier onward speeds;
No fear unnerves the stalwart arm,
No fearful odds can cause alarm:
He goes to fight for Britain's cause,
He goes defending freedom's laws;
For home and country proud to go
To meet the stern unsparing foe.
    On to the front when the bugle calls;
      What though like hail the red shot falls,
    On through the smoke and din, fearing no foe,
      Where duty calls, they go.

Where duty calls when the sea runs high,
And heard is the shipwrecked sailor's cry,
No thought of danger unnerves the hand
When the lifeboat shoots from the surf-beat strand;
Over the crests of the surging wave,
With only one thought—of the lives to save,
They seek no reward for the deeds they do—
No heroes so brave as the lifeboat crew.

What though death looks in the sailor's eyes,
Sturdy and strong the oar he plies ;
Nerved by the cries of despair and woe,
    Where duty calls, they go.

When duty calls to the flaming fire,
Where the scorching tongues mount higher and higher,
When the flames shoot out over roof and wall
And the tottering pile seems about to fall,
The fireman mounts 'mid the red-hot blaze,
Nor thought of danger his progress stays,
Till the helpless victims are saved at last ;
No rest they seek till the danger's past.
    Through the burning blaze, through the smoke and
    To save from the jaws of a fiery tomb,   [fume,
    Fearless they mount where the red flames glow
        Where duty calls, they go.

KEEP A CORNER IN YOUR HEART FOR ME.

You have many friends who love you,
And who pray the Power above you
    To guard and guide wherever you may be :
Yet though they love sincerely,
And seek your welfare dearly,
    Keep a corner in your heart for me.

Chorus — I ask not all your heart,
    I'm content to share a part ;
        Only keep a little corner in your heart for me.

Tho' you may have lovers many,
Yet not plighted vows with any,
    And art still a maiden young and fancy free,
Don't forget me altogether,
Do not let old friendships wither ;
    Keep a corner in your heart for me.—*Chorus.*

In the happy days of childhood
We together roamed the wildwood,
    When skies were bright and life was full of glee ;
Then whatever fate betide us,
Tho' distant seas divide us,
    Keep a corner in your heart for me.—*Chorus.*

IV.

Poems founded on familiar Scottish Proverbs and Sayings.

"The wisdom of many and the wit of one."—*Earl Russell.*

"The short expression of a long experience."—*Cervantes.*

"Proverbs preserve the genius, wit, and spirit of a nation."
Bacon.

"Jewels five words long,
That on the stretch'd forefinger of all Time
Sparkle for ever." –*Tennyson.*

IV.

POEMS FOUNDED ON FAMILIAR SCOTTISH PROVERBS AND SAYINGS.

CREEP BEFORE YE GANG.

Ye chiel's wha spend your brichtest hours
   On "trifles licht as air,"
Build towering castles in the clouds
   That end but in despair.
Ne'er seek to jump owre far at first;
   For tho' the roads be lang,
The slowest's aye the surest gate;
   Sae creep before you gang.

Ye see that toddlin' fair-haired wean
   That crousely gi'es his craw;
Oh! hoo he struggles sair to reach
   The pictures on the wa'.
By chair and table-fit he hauds,
   As slow he crawls alang;
He's learning noo the lesson,—he
   Maun creep before he'll gang.

In mony o' the walks o' life
   We bigger bairns here
May learn a lesson fraught wi' truth,
   Hoo we our course should steer:
The race is no' gi'en to the swift,
   Nor battle to the strang,
An' rich an' puir alike maun learn
   To creep before they gang.

If routh o' riches be your wish,
　　Ye maunna end wi' wishes ;
The gowd will slip your fingers thro'
　　Like sma' fish thro' the meshes.
Just tak' as muckle care to keep
　　The pennies frae gaun wrang,
Nor grumble that they're hard to get,
　　But creep before ye gang.

If ye want knowledge, ye will find
　　'Tis hard to get the same ;
There's nae royal road to learnin',
　　Ye maun *climb* the hill o' fame.
But be na frichten'd at the thocht
　　O' strugglin' sair an' lang ;
The first blow's half the battle, sae
　　Just creep before ye gang.

'Tis richt to seek for honest fame,
　　If ye wad only mind
Ne'er to get puff'd wi' warldly pride
　　When honour's path ye find.
Aye keep bricht honour's star in view
　　As ye press thro' the thrang ;
Ye'll gain the summit some fine day,
　　Sae creep before ye gang.

But trust na fame or wealth to bring
　　Ye joy an' peace o' mind ;
It isna every wealthy chiel'
　　Can true enjoyment find.
The simplest joys are aye the best,
　　They leave nae bitter stang ;
Sae cultivate a cheerfu' mind,
　　An' creep before ye gang.

An' trust na ilka sleepy cove
　　Wha seeks your confidence ;
Aye keep your weather eye awake,
　　An' lippen Providence ;

Else ye will surely miss your way,
    Till thieves ye fa' amang,
An' learn, by sad experience,
    To creep before ye gang.

But think na the chief end o' man
    Is to find happiness,
An' seek in wealth, or lear, or fame
    Ae drap o' lasting bliss.
Na, na : just dae the thing that 's richt,
    An' ye will find, ere lang,
A conscience clear will smooth your way :
    Sae creep before you gang.

Oor younkers noo-a-days, I find,
    Talk big, an' boast like men ;
There's naething ye can teach them, for
    What is 't they dinna ken ?
They 're lookin' owre sune oot the nest,
    But they maun learn, ere lang,
To tak' advice frae aulder heads,
    An' creep before they gang.

An' there are chiel's wha swagger fine,
    A' dress'd in borrow'd plumes,
Rin lang accounts wi' *snip* an' *snob*,
    But think na o' the sums ;
When some day, up the donkey goes
    An' down they come slap-bang,
Till on their knees they spell the creed,
    To creep before they gang.

Noo a' you coves wi' empty heads
    Wha hae a wish to learn,
An' you puir chiel's wi' pooches toom
    Gin honest wealth ye 'd earn,
Think na the goal is owre far aff,—
    The road owre steep an' lang ;
Tak' tent,—ye 'll gain the prize, gin ye
    Will creep before ye gang.

COME OOT FRAE 'MANG THE NEEPS.

Eh! callants, dae ye mind the time when youth was in its
    prime,
Oor schuleboy days—oor brichtest days—life's cheery,
    cloudless time?
What pranks we played, what rievin' raids we planned baith
    nicht an' morn,
As thochtless as the maukins that were nibblin' 'mang the
    corn;
When baigies were just at their best, we've ventured
    'mang the shaws,
Nor thocht for sic misdeeds we yet should feel the maister's
    tawse;
Until a runkled face appears—a voice oor paikment
    threeps—
"Ye deevils, buckies, that ye are, come oot frae 'mang the
    neeps."

Aye mony happy days we had at Polwarth-on-the-Green,
When thochtlessly we ventured where we kenn'd we
    sudna been;
Thro' slaps an' stiles, owre bank an' burn, to hunt for
    scroggs an' slaes,
Or maybe harry lav'rocks' nests by Marchmont's woods an'
    braes;
We catched the mennents i' the burn, or chased the startled
    hare,
Nor thocht oor voices could be heard, or ocht to fricht us
    there;
But see us rin for life or death when thro' the bushes creeps
The keeper's doug, an' shouts are heard, "Get oot frae
    'mang the neeps."

When aulder grown, like a' the chiel's, I'd but to hae a lass,
An' mony a winnin' glance I cuist aroun' oor singin' class;
For there were sonsy lassies there wi' pawky rougish een,
An' ane I took a fancy till—the miller's dochter, Jean;
But whether I was rather slow, or no, I dinna ken;
But when I just was spierin'—"could I see her up the
    glen"—

Her lad— I ne'er jaloused she'd ane—between us canny creeps,
An' wi' a dunch he says to me, "Get oot frae 'mang the neeps."

When oot I steer'd into the warl' to warsle for mysel',
Wi' mony pitfa's 'mang my feet where thochtless comrades fell,
I didna aye steer clear o' them, but still I kept my grip,
An' managed to get thro' the mire whene'er I made a slip;
An' then I'd aften think o' what my faither used to say,
"Gin wicked, drinkin' comrades seek to wile your feet astray,
You're sure to get yoursel' defiled gin ye consort wi' sweeps;
Sae when you're like to tint your gate, come oot frae 'mang the neeps."

In business, too, I ventured whiles a wee thocht aff the road,
When no' content to save by sma's an' cautiously to plod:
I took a dab in railway shares, or else in minin' stock,
An' used to dream o' wealth secured, until the bubble broke,
Then, wi' a pooch as toom as when a laddie at the schule,
I groaned o'er a' my bawbees gane, an' ca'd mysel' a fule;
But when the cloud o' ruin breaks, an' daylicht ance mair peeps,
I learned a lesson that wad last when oot frae 'mang the neeps.

I've no' forgot the lesson yet, an' aftentimes sinsyne,
Whene'er I strayed frae duty's path, an' crossed the boundary line,—
When sinfu' pleasures tempted me, and lured me into ill,
I've wavered—left the narrow road—but yet, when a' was still,
When nicht cam' on wi' gruesome gloom, an' a' was dark an' drear,
I've kent the sweat come o'er my broo, my heart to quake wi' fear;
An' whispered chidin's, frae the wee sma' voice that never sleeps,
Rang i' my ears as i' the past—"Come oot frae 'mang the neeps."

DOON AT THE HEEL.

This life is a warsle at best, ye'll alloo,
An' we hae mony back-sets before we win thro';
But sic things we could thole gin it were na the way
Your frien's look asklent when ye tint what ye hae.
When ye need na their help—oh! it's a' very weel,
But their sang seems to change when you're doon at the heel.

It's a garment o' shoddy—a fabric o' thrums,
The frien'ship that cools when adversity comes;
Ye'll hae plenty o' frien's in your bricht simmer hours,
When your pathway is cheery wi' sunlicht an' flowers;
But let a bit frost come, their feelin's congeal,
An' their hearts turn like ice when you're doon at the heel.

When ye needna their help, oh! they'll mak' sic a phraise;
But ance ye get scanty o' meat an' o' claes,
What tho' at your table they've eaten an' drank
When they kenn'd ye'd a balance a' safe at the bank,
As ye bricsted the brae they wad help ye to speel;
But they'll shove ye aside when you're doon at the heel.

If in manners and speech you're as rude as a cad,
Your fau'ts they'll o'erlook; but you're a' thing that's bad
Gin ye hae a come-doon, thro' nae faut o' your ain;
Ye'll fin' ye'll be left just to toddle your lane;
Ye may die in a ditch, ye may beg or may steal;
It's nae business o' theirs when you're doon at the heel.

Ne'er min' hoo ye got it, if siller ye hae,
Ye'll be flattered an' praised ilka hour o' the day;
At kirk ye'll be welcomed, sae lang's ye donate
A share o' your ill-gotten wealth to the plate;
Gin they dinna just brand ye a limb o' the deil,
Ye'll get the cauld shouther when doon at the heel.

I'm sweer to believe that a' mankind's the same,
But it's best gin ye needna their praise or their blame;
Just steer your ain path, an' ne'er trust to the reed
That's sure to gie way when assistance ye need;
Keep your frien' i' your pooch—hae a heart that can feel,
An' a han' that will help them that's doon at the heel.

BE AS GUID AS YE CAN.

It's no' gi'en to men to attain to perfection,
   Tho' whiles they rax oot an' get weel up the brae ;
But because o' the fac', ne'er gie way to dejection,
   An' say, "It's nae use, let us strive as we may";
There's naebody asks ye to try it, my man,
But this ye can dae—be as guid as ye can.

We a' hae oor failin's, it's nae use denyin't,
   Tho' whiles we are laith to alloo it's the fac',
An' when taxed wi' the same, then we birse up defiant,
   An' try to mak' everything white, when it's black :
Far better to boo to the verdic' aff-han',
An' to square the account—be as guid as ye can.

Hoo often we see the bit bairns, like their aulders,
   Wi' nieves ready doubl't, just likely to fecht,
For the hate o' the man in the wee briestie smothers,
   An' it's just in degree gin the differ is aucht ;
An' the words o' advice come wi' truth to the man,
"Noo gree, bairnies, gree—be as guid as ye can."

An' the lassies—the joy o' existence—God bless them,
   We ken they've their fau'ts like their auld mither Eve :
But, just as they are, we are fain to embrace them,
   An' vow an' protest mair than's safe to believe :
Noo, lassies, ye hae a great poo'er in your han',
For weel or for wae—be as guid as ye can.

We ken there is muckle to mak' us dejected,
   When lookin' aroun' on life's folly an' sin ;
We see wealthy rogues a' sae highly respected,
   Wi' cuffs for the puir folk wha labour an' spin ;
Yet to grumble at fortune, or foolishly ban,
Is to mak' maitters waur—be as guid as ye can.

We've a' muckle need the advice to be takin',
   An' no' look on ithers as only to blame—
At oor neibours' shortcomin's eternally craikin',
   When we, mair mensefu'-like, should be lookin' at hame :
Gin ye get aff the straucht, just own up like a man,
An' in deed or in word—be as guid as ye can.

IT MICHT HAE BEEN WAUR.

There isna an ill that owretak's us in life,
  Tho' just at the time rather grievous to bear,
But what, when we look roun' where trouble is rife,
  Will no' seem sae bad gin we'll only compare
What ithers endure ; an' wherever we are,
We'll hae this consolation — it micht hae been waur.

Success disna aye croon oor efforts, ye'll fin',
  But o' losses an' crosses oor life is made up :
Aften serious eneuch to unbalance the min',
  When frae oor parched lips fate has dashed doon the cup;
An' we think we've been born 'neath some ill-omened star,
An' it's nae use to strive — yet it micht hae been waur.

The hopes o' oor youth rarely come to fruition,
  Tho' that is nae reason for ceasin' to strive ;
An' tho' we ne'er reach the exalted position
  We longed for, yet guid may reward us belyve ;
We maun ever be ready to dae an' to daur,
An' meet life's rebuffs wi' " It micht hae been waur."

Is it losses in business, the fruits o' lang years
  O' labour an' thrift that hae suddenly gone ?
An' we mak' a sad molliegrunt mingled wi' tears,
  As waesome's a coo in an unco lang loan :
Hoots ! man, dinna sit doon an' nurse your despair ; [waur.
Gin ye've health yet, an' strength, weel — it micht hae been

Or you're pinin' awa'— are ye blighted in life,
  When some lassie has played wi' a love that was true ?
An' ye see her anither's— a fair, bloomin' wife,
  Wi' the smiles an' caresses ance plighted to you ;
What tho' on your heart there's a deep painfu' scaur,
Time will heal it, an' show ye it micht hae been waur.

In fac', there's nae ill that can come to us here
  That hasna its use, gin we only could see't ;
Behin' the black clouds there's a sun ever clear,
  That shall yet thrill wi' joy the wee flowers at oor feet ;
Let us look 'yont the clouds to the sunshine afar,
An' shut oot life's gloom wi' " It micht hae been waur."

WHUSTLE ON YOUR DOUG.

There's nae mistak' aboot it,
  That we aften gang astray,
An' funny things we say at times,
  An' daft-like things we dae;
An' aft we fin', when rather late,
  Far better wad it be
Gin we could just restrain oorsels
  When like to gang agee.
    Sae just a wee bit soun' advice
      I'll whisper i' your lug,
    Whene'er ye tint yer gate, haud up,
      An' whustle on your doug.

See yonder cummers gossipin'
  'Boot ither folk's concerns,
An' a' the while neglectin' to
  Look after their ain bairns;
Gin they wad only look at hame,
  An' min' their ain affairs,
They'd be a hantle better aff,
  An' free frae vexin' cares.
    Sae just a wee bit soun' advice
      I'll whisper i' your lug,
    Your duty's plain, look to your ain,
      An' whustle on your doug.

The bairns will no' gang far astray,
  An' gie ye cause to fret,
Gin ye will dae your pairt, an' aye
  A guid example set;
An' should they gang a wee thocht wrang,
  An' chum wi' orra weans,
Wi' canny han' just guide them back
  To hame an' lovin' frien's.
    Sae just a wee bit soun' advice
      I'll whisper i' your lug,
    Keep i' the straucht road aye yoursel',
      An' whustle on your doug.

When ony thing gangs wrang wi' us,
  We're sure to shift the blame,
Or hae excuses ready-made,
  An' lee to hide oor shame ;
But fairer, manlier wad it be
  To own the fau't's oor ain.
Then after-thochts wad never come
  To cause us grief an' pain.
    Sae just a wee bit soun' advice
      I'll whisper i' your lug,
    Just put the blame where it should licht,
      An' whustle on your doug.

WHEN THE PAT RINS OWRE.

WE'RE aye owre wise ahint the han',
  I've heard my faither say,
An' gie advice to ither folk
  When ony wrang they dae ;
We tell them what they should hae dune
  Ere this or that occurred,
But when we come to think awhile
  It's aften-times absurd.
    Your afterwut is oot o' place,
      Prevention past your power,
    Gin ye wait to seek the ladle
      Till the pat rins owre.

When i' oor bairns a fau't we fin'
  It should at ance be checked,
For tiny fau'ts, like weeds, will grow
  Till innocence is wrecked ;
Wi' precept an' example baith
  Encourage them i' guid,
An' ne'er owrelook the wee-est fau't,
  But nip it i' the bud.
    For human nature sune will warp
      The sweetest temper sour,
    Gin you wait to seek the ladle
      Till the pat rins owre.

Gin business troubles loom afar,
    It winna dae ava
To shut your een to comin' cares,
    Till storms aroun' you blaw ;
Get up an' pit your hoose to richts
    To meet the comin' blast,
An' tak' i' sail, as Jack wad say,
    Until the storm is past.
        In sunshine we maun be prepared
            For times when tempests lower ;
        For ye needna seek the ladle
            When the pat rins owre.

E'en i' the truest love affairs
    Whiles something gangs agley,
Sae dinna fail to own your faut
    When there's a chance to gree :
For hate may grow where love has been,
    An' hearts grow cauld an' sear :
Sae speak the word, an' mak' it up
    Before you tint your dear.
        For should she tak' anither han',
            Hoo like a fule you'd glower,
        An' vainly seek the ladle
            When the pat rins owre.

SPIT ON YOUR HANDS.

In a leisurely, thochtfu' kind o' way
    I was takin' a quiet walk,
When I sat me doon near some bairns at play,
    An' listened a while to their talk :
They were tryin' to loup owre a glaury hole,
    An' the biggest anes took it clear,
But a wee ane wavered, an' wadna jump
    Till they gied him a word o' cheer.
        "Noo, Johnny," they said, "it's easy eneuch :
            We'll see that ye dinna coup ;
        Ye needna be feared for a jaup o' glaur ;
            Just spit on your hands, an' loup."

An' I said to mysel', there's a lesson here
   For men as weel as for weans ;
If there's ony thing worth tryin' to dae,
   We shouldna spare effort or pains ;
Be na feared tho' obstacles stan' in your way,
   Press on wi' an object in view ;
Gin ye be determined to gain your end,
   Ten chances to ane ye'll won through.
      Ye may be shoved back mony times in a day,
         An' declare that it's no worth a rush ;
      Brace up, man, determined to carry your point ;
         Just spit on your hands, an' push.

I've seen mony men wi' the struggles they've had
   Gie themsel's clean up to despair,
Lose a' regard as to what ithers thocht,
   An' the future ne'er cost them a care.
Could they hae been moved a brave effort to mak',
   Sic obstacles quickly wad flee,
An' wi' strength to endure, success wad be sure,
   Till they gained the tap o' the tree.
      Then dinna sit doon to glunch an' gloom,
         Only cowards their duty will shirk ;
      Look up ! there's a future a-heid o' ye yet ;
         Just spit on your hands, an' work.

Look back owre the past to the guid an' the great,
   Wha hae made their mark in the warl' ;
Hoo bravely they've struggled to speel the brae
   'Gainst mony a dunt an' dirl.
Auld Scotia's sons in far-awa' lands
   Hae gained mony places o' trust,
Because they resolved, as the Yankees wad say,
   To gain what they aimed at, or "bust."
      A stoot heart will climb up the steepest o' braes,
         While the timid will sit doon an' sigh ;
      But, if aucht is worth daein', it's worth daein' weel,
         Sae spit on your hands, an' try.

DINNA DROON THE MILLER.

It's no' alane when brewin' o'
  A bowl o' whisky toddy
That ane is apt to stint the maut,
  Until it has nae body ;
Gae me nae brash o' water wi'
  A wee tate sugar sweetened,
A mixture fushionless an' wairsh,
  We 're better far withooten 't.
    Just mak' the reamin' usquebae
    A dose to drive dull care away ;
    Ne'er stint the generous barley bree,
    An' dinna droon the miller.

While some their pleasures grudgin' tak'
  In homeopathic doses,
An' seem to hug their bed o' thorns
  In preference to the roses ;
Sae ithers, whase life's problem seems
  To taste its full enjoyment,
Ne'er let the whirligig be stopped
  For usefu' wise employment.
    A better way to me it seems
    Is to avoid these mad extremes,
    Drink wi' a zest when pleasure brims,
    An' dinna droon the miller.

E'en love itsel', that sweetens a'
  Oor youth an' manhood's dreamin',
Should be encouraged wisely, lest
  It curdles in the creamin' ;
The lowe o' love maun burn slow
  To be in age a solace,
Else we 'll hae nocht in life's decline
  But memories o' youth's follies.
    Tak' tent then, bairns, an' wisely use
    Life's sweetest gift, an' ne'er abuse ;
    Let love be honest, kindly, douce,
    An' dinna droon the miller.

E'en frae the pu'pit ye will hear
　　Puir sinners aft admonished,
While frae his text the preacher roams,
　　Till point an' sense hae vanished;
See hoo he 'll beat aboot the bush,
　　Till a' his admonitions
Are just sae muckle empty chaff
　　O' pithless repetitions.
　　　　Then dinna mak' sae muckle din,
　　　　Launch forth the truth an' drive it in;
　　　　A stalwart foe to vice an' sin
　　　　Will never droon the miller.

Some ane has wisely said, there's but
　　A step 'tween pain an' pleasure,
An' sure the latter aften cloys
　　When folly heaps the measure;
An' sae there is a quiet sense
　　O' joy when pain is lessened;
When violent pangs awee subside,
　　'Tis bearable an' pleasant.
　　　　Then let us pray that we may sup
　　　　The richt ingredients frae life's cup,
　　　　An' see that when we fill it up
　　　　We dinna droon the miller.

AYE A SOMETHING.

This life is a queer kind o' mixture at best,
　　O' pleasure an' sorrow, o' sunshine an' rain;
For when we 're enjoyin 't wi' happiest zest,
　　There 's aye a something to gie us pain.

In youth, what bricht dreams o' the future we hae,
　　O' a life fu' o' cheeriest laughter an' sang;
But ere manhood, oor dreams hae a' faded away,
　　For there 's aye a something to put us wrang.

In the race that we rin, aft oor hopes we renew,
　　An' we mak' pretty speed owre a well-beaten track;
We put on a spurt, for the prize is in view,
　　But there 's aye a something to keep us back.

Be it honour or wealth as the goal we desire,
  Wi' honest endeavour we strive late an' sune;
But when nearin' the object to which we aspire,
  There's aye a something to pu' us doon.

We ploo an' we harrow an' seed the lan',
  An' dream o' fu' bickers an' bowies o' meal;
When we think that the crap is just ripe to oor han',
  There's aye a something to coup the creel.

The love o' oor life may seem smooth as a stream,
  No' a ripple o' care its pure tide to alloy;
While o' constancy sure as the seasons we dream,
  There's aye a something to mar oor joy.

We may strive a' we can in the straucht road to walk,
  An' shun the temptations that lurk in the cup,
To be honest an' upright in deed an' in talk,
  But there's aye a something to trip us up.

But the dullest o' lives has its fair sunny spot;
  Gin we nurse wi' contentment the glints that we hae,
We'll find, 'mid the storm-clouds that darken oor lot,
  There's aye a something to licht up oor way.

THAT'S ANITHER SANG.

What's weel eneuch in precept, aft
  In practice gangs agley;
We dinna dae the thing oorsel's,
  Tho' guid advice we gie:
We point the straucht road to oor frien's,
  An' tell them where to gang,
But when it comes to lead the way—
  Oh! that's anither sang.
    An' sae it is the warl' owre,
      Wherever ye may gang;
    To preach an' pray, an' lead the way,
      Is quite anither sang.

I daursay ye'll admit it's true,
　　You've seen the thing yoursel's,
Hoo the precept o' the pu'pit a'
　　Oor duty clearly tells;
Gin the practice o' the preachers wi'
　　Their teachings dinna gree,
There's some excuse for mortals wha
　　Get aff the straucht a-wee.
　　　　An' sae you'll see't, where caste an' creed
　　　　　　Are preached with fervour strang,
　　　　To square accounts in word an' deed
　　　　　　Is quite anither sang.

Hoo aften ye will meet wi' folk
　　Aye gleg at findin' fault,
An' e'en the wee-est slip ye mak'
　　They're sair astonished at;
They'll magnify it ten times owre,
　　That a' the warl' may see,
Until ye aften wonder what
　　A monster ye maun be.
　　　　Altho' the mote be e'er sae sma',
　　　　　　They'll search it oot ere lang;
　　　　But tak' the beam frae their ain een
　　　　　　Oh! that's anither sang.

In cheery days o' coortin' time,
　　When life is bricht wi' smiles,
Ye'll hae lasses vow to lo'e ye, but
　　Be wary o' their wiles;
For should a doon-come be your lot,
　　An' puirtith at your door,
Hoo sune they'll see fau'ts in you that
　　They never saw before!
　　　　For when you tint your wealth, you'll hae
　　　　　　Your leesome road to gang;
　　　　For love an' puirtith winna gree—
　　　　　　Na! that's anither sang.

The maist o' us can hardly count
　　Oor hosts o' simmer frien's,
Wha 'll stick to us as close as burrs
　　Sae lang 's we hae the means
To treat them weel ; but gin we 're doon,
　　Their help 's nae to be had ;
While for past favours dune by us—
　　Their memories are bad.
　　　　It isna every ane wha threeps
　　　　　　His frien'ship loud an' lang,
　　　　That 's like to be a frien' in need—
　　　　　　Na ! that 's anither sang.

What bonnie resolutions aft
　　Come to us ilka morn,
When comin' owre oor past misdeeds,
　　An' conscience plies its thorn :
We think o' what we 'll dae an' say
　　Should sair temptations come ;
But oor intentions are like reek
　　That 's whirlin' up the lum.
　　　　For when the day has passed away,
　　　　　　And brings reflection's stang,
　　　　Oor vows and actions winna square—
　　　　　　Na ! that 's anither sang.

KEEP THE CHAIN ON THE DOOR.

An Englishman's house is his castle, 'tis said,
It may be a mansion, or cottage, or shed ;
The saying holds good whether humble or high,
So prepare to defend it when danger is nigh ;
And when thieves lurk around you 'll be doubly secure
If you take the advice—" Keep the chain on the door."

In many more ways will the saying hold good
As a watchword through life, when 'tis well understood ;
For a man's inner self, like the house where he dwells,
May oft be beset by peace-banishing ills ;
Foes wiry and cunning we shun and abhor ;
So, as proof 'gainst their arts, " Keep the chain on the door."

When listening to those who can "draw the long bow,"
We feel just like giving advice to go slow ;
"Least said, soonest mended,"– a good wholesome rule
For the braggart, who's only a step from the fool :
And 'tis better to err on the safe side for sure,
With a silence discreet, and the "chain on the door."

We can't shut our eyes to the suffering near,
And the poor who deserve both our comfort and cheer ;
But beware of impostors, who ply as a trade
All sorts of devices for charity's aid :
There is no need to shut up your hearts to the poor,
But, 'gainst deep-scheming rogues, "Keep the chain on the
    door."

We are destined by heaven to enjoy what is good,
And to take our enjoyments like good wholesome food ;
But in all things, when tempted to run to excess,
Lest amusement should cloy, this maxim embrace :
In the pursuit of pleasure, its true joys secure,
In a moderate way, with the "chain on the door."

Now, love is a beautiful thing in its way,
And at some time or other we've all felt its sway :
Yet even in this we'll be wise to take heed,
Lest it blossom too quickly, and run all to seed :
And if we would have this sweet joy to endure,
We must nurse it with care, and the "chain on the door."

In pursuit of wealth, oh! how eager we run,
And are never content while there's aught to be won :
But the race has its dangers—the prize we abuse
When we yearn for more than we need for our use ;
Let us crush out that vain senseless crying for more,
And enjoy its true zest with the "chain on the door."

If doubt should assail you in matters of faith,
Prepare to defend the old truths "to the death" :
Not blindly to grope, but with reason to test
All systems and creeds, and to cling to the best ;
Lest false comforters fail you in life's trying hour,
Hold the citadel fast with the "chain on the door'

MAK' YOURSEL' AT HAME.

Our cot is but a humble beild,
   A hamely but an' ben,
We're humbly clad, we're humbly fed,
   As a' our neibours ken:
To uppish style, or fashion's smile,
   We scorn to mak' a claim;
Yet welcome a', whene'er they ca',
   To mak' themsel's at hame.
      Then let your frien'ship show itsel'
        'Thout fashion's phraise or fetter,
      An' kindly mak' yoursel' at hame;
        Your frien's will like ye better.

The rich folks in their lordly ha's
   Hae favours to dispense,
But seldom wealth does guid by stealth
   And nae tho't o' recompense:
It's aye the puir that help the puir
   In deed as weel as name;
At puirtith's ca' they welcome a'
   To mak' themsel's at hame.

I hate to see folk, when they ca',
   Sae unco proud and hie,
I canna thole your formal folk,
   Sae stiff wi' what they gie;
I like the couthy, honest hearts
   Wha treat ye aye the same,
An' gie a canty welcome aye
   To mak' yoursel's at hame.

We're only hamely folks oorsel's,
   An' tho' our haudin's sma',
Our neibours, wha will tak' pat-luck,
   Are welcome aye to ca':
We'll share wi' them the best we hae,
   An' greet them aye the same;
As aften as they care to come
   We'll mak' them feel at hame.

CA' YOUR GIRD.

LIFE for a' the warl' is just
   Like a game we callants played,
Ready wi' oor girds to birl,
   Startin' fair, the mark we tae'd ;
Kennin' that we 'd hae to rin
Fast an' straucht the game to win,
As the startin' word was gi'en,
              Ca' your gird.

Aye, but there was sure to be
   Some ane gettin' a' the straucht,
Ithers, fairly losin' hope,
   Sune gied up to strive for aught ;
An' the lesson a' were learnin',
Gin life's prize was worth the earnin',
Was to keep the wheel aye turnin',
              Ca' your gird.

Never slacken in your purpose,
   Keep the goal aye in your e'e,
Like the channel stane in curlin',
   Straucht goes birlin' for the tee :
Ever heed the frien'ly warnin',
A' temptations stoutly spurnin',
Keep the wheel o' evidence turnin',
              Ca' your gird.

Let your aim in life be single,
   Never waverin' frae the richt,
An' tho' darklin' days oppress ye,
   Times will yet be clear an' bricht :
Gin ye 'll but wi' zeal endeavour
To keep pushin', movin' ever,
No' frae this ae object waver,
              Ca' your gird.

Ne'er in fitfu' spurts engagin',
   Constancy be aye your law ;
Slowly tho' the gird be turnin'
   Keep it movin', or 'twill fa'.

Sae in time, gin we keep ploddin',
Nae rebuffs or back-sets bodin',
We may yet redeem life's Flodden,
            Ca' your gird.

Nor, tho' rocks an' ruts we meet,
   Maun we gie up in despair:
Gin we bravely face the warst,
   Obstacles will disappear:
Up the hill tho' toilin', strivin',
Breathless at the broo arrivin',
Owre the brae we'll sune gang skivin',
            Ca' your gird.

If the goal be wealth or fame,
   Love or learnin', place or power.
There's nae favoured road to them,
   Work we maun to win the dower;
An' it maun be work unceasin',
Ne'er abatin', but increasin'—
A' great triumphs point the lesson,
            Ca' your gird.

Nor when we hae gained oor end
   Shall we be content to rest;
Life withoot some noble aim
   Soon wad lose its joy an' zest:
While the lamp o' life is burnin'
We should aye new truths be learnin',
Ever for new triumphs yearnin',
            Ca' your gird.

CA' CANNY.

If at times ye're discontented wi' the present,
            Just ca' canny;
Tak' tent,—the future mayna turn sae pleasant,
            Eh! my manny.
Ye'll find that on a sudden
Your wings are fairly laden,
An' ye'll flounder in the midden;
            Sae ca' canny.

If your heart in love's fond mesh is fairly neckled.
    Just ca' canny ;
Ye'll get time to rue when ance you're fairly buckled,
    Eh! my manny.
Tho' noo ye think your treasure
Will bring ye nocht but pleasure,
Eh! man, there's luck in leisure :
    Sae ca' canny.

Gin it's wealth, wi' a' it brings, for which ye hanker,
    Just ca' canny ;
Mind that greed eats in the heart just like a canker ;
    Sae, my manny.
They that hasten to be rich
Sometimes whommle in the ditch,
While conscience plies her switch ;
    Sae ca' canny.

There is nae near cut to knowledge or to learnin',
    Sae ca' canny :
Set your face toward the goal, an' ne'er be turnin'.
    Eh! my manny.
Gin ye plod on day by day,
Learning something by the way,
Ye will some time tap the brae ;
    Sae ca' canny.

My laddie, gin ye want to learn a trade,
    Just ca' canny :
Skilled mechanics dinna rise up ready made,
    Eh! my manny.
Never think that sma' details
Are just fit for ploddin' snails ;
Slow but certain, seldom fails ;
    Sae ca' canny.

Never sigh for things ye scorn to earn by labour,
    Just ca' canny,
Nor cast an envious look toward your neighbour,
    Eh! my manny.

Honest work can ne'er degrade,
Be it handlin' pen or spade;
Never be abune your trade;
    Just ca' canny.

A KIND WELCOME HAME.

When the wearisome toils o' the day are past,
 An' hameward we trudge owre the road or the field.
Sometimes gey ill happit to keep oot the blast,
 Wi' neither a hedge or a plantin' to beild,
Aft darksome an' dreich wad the road seem to be,
 An' oor life, day or nicht, wad be joyless an' tame,
Gin it were na the scene that we fancy we see,
 An' the surety o' gettin' a kind welcome hame.

When fickle Dame Fortune, sae sly wi' her tricks,
 Aft leads us a dance we wad rather no hae,
An' fit-sair, as gin we'd been treadin' hot bricks,
 Noo limpin', noo pechin', we briest up the brae.
Hoo often we'd hae to gie way to despair,
 An' shauchle alang withoot object or aim,
If it were na the love-ties that lichten oor care,
 An' the thocht o' what waits us— a kind welcome hame!

The rich an' the puir baith alike hae their care;
 Tho' wealth proves a solace to mony an ill,
Yet hard, strugglin' toilers aft happily share
 True heart-glints that puirtith can never dispel;
Hoo aften the canker o' care wad tak' root
 An' crowd oot the joy-glints that ne'er reach a flame.
The warld's scorn or cauldness can ne'er mak' us doot
 The warmth o' the welcome that waits us at hame.

A' thro' oor life journey we warsle alang,
 Noo tired wi' oor burdens sae weary to bear,—
Noo cheered wi' some heart-stirrin' music or sang,
 That brings back the past when oor pathway was fair;
An' tho' for the present oor sky may be dark,
 An' the prospects ahead are just muckle the same,
Beyond a' we ken that, when dune wi' life's wark,
 There's a joy in the hope o' a kind welcome hame.

LOOK IN I' THE BY GAUN.

Auld Dod o' the Mill is a canty auld chiel',
His heid an' his heart are as richt as his meal;
Tho' noo he's weel on for the threescore an' ten,
He's cheerier an' chirper than mony young men.
He aye has a welcome sae hamely an' kind;
An', tak' him a' thro', there are few ye will find
Gie a warmer hand-shake, an' a kind welcome back,
Wi'— "Look in i' the by-gaun, an' gie us your crack."

I travel the kintra the hale o' the year,
In summer sae cheery, in winter sae drear,
An' mony a time, as I trudge thro' the Merse,
It's wearisome wark when the siller is scarce:
Yet aften, when dooncast wi' want o' success,
My troubles a' flee as I near the auld place,
An' think on the pairtin' when last by the track—
"Look in i' the by-gaun, an' gie us your crack."

Noo the wife's just as cheery an' couthy as him,
An' her heart o' guid nature is fu' to the brim;
She's aye clean an' tosh in her looks an' attire,
An' the same can be said o' the neuk by the fire:
There's the cosy broon teapat the clean shiny cup
For she's no' ane o' them that wad grudge bite or sup,
Wi' a—"Draw in your stool na, an' hae a bit snack;
For we're aye glad to hae ye ca' in for a crack."

Ye hae frien's wha's guid-word ye'd no' mourn should ye tine,
Nae doot your experience is muckle like mine;
An' ithers, tho' nae bluid-relations at a',
Wad ne'er see ye set wi' your back to the wa';
Their hearty han'-grip, an' a word o' guid cheer,
Send a warm thrill o' joy thro' your veins to career:
"Ne'er wait for the askin', ye're aye welcome back;
Aye look in i' the by-gaun, an' gie us your crack."

Like the green grassy spots in the wide dreary muir,
Like the sun-glints in winter, this warl' o' care
Has its bright cheery neuks, its sweet wayside flowers,
Its frien'ships an' favours, in life's darkest hours;

An' cheerier far than the clear simmer's day
Are the smiles an' kind words that we share on life's way,
When guid-byes are joined wi' a true welcome back ;
" Aye look in i' the by-gaun, an' gie us your crack."

COLLIE, WILL YE LICK ?

Awa' wi' a' the scurvy loons
   Devoid o' generous pairts,
Where self has gained the upper han',
   An' wizened up their hearts :
What cauldrife comfort meets ye there
   When, may-be faint or sick,
They haena mense eneuch to ask
   Gin, Collie, will ye lick ?

I hate these mean, tight-fisted folks
   Wha scrape, an' save, an' hoard,
Wha's kist-neuk or auld stockin'-fit
   Is wi' the bawbees stored ;
They grudge themsel's their meat an' claes,
   While to the puir an' sick
They ne'er were kenned to say as much
   As, Collie, will ye lick ?

Again, there is a class o' folk,
   Wi' hearts no 's big 's a midge,
Wha, if they dae a kindly turn,
   They dae it wi' a grudge ;
The puir they treat as lepers, wha
   They 'd touch na wi' a stick,
An' if a bite or sup they gie,
   It 's— Collie, will ye lick ?

Far be 't frae me to lichtlie them
   That dinna weel deserve 't,
Wha's charity is dune by stealth,
   An' may-be no' observed :
Gin dune at a' wi' honest aim,
   I 'll recognise, fu' quick,
A heart that winna staw puir folks
   Wi'—Collie, will ye lick ?

Then when ye dae a kindly turn,
  Or gie a kindly word,
Hooever little ye can spare
  Frae your ain stinted board,
Gie't wi' guidwill tho' dry the crust,
  Instead o' buttered thick
'Twill cheer far mair than gowpens gi'en
  Wi' Collie, will ye lick?

PUT OUT HAND AN' HELP YOURSEL'.

What's the use o' sittin' grumblin'
  When there's duties to be dune,
Like a lot o' bairns greetin'
  'Cause they canna get the mune?
Cast that peevish spirit frae ye,
  Buckle up, an' try a spell
O' hard wark; let this be your motto
  Put out hand an' help yoursel'.

Mony a man has got it in him
  To mak' heidway in the warl',
But distrusts his powers, an' wavers
  Like a chicken-hearted churl.
Mak' nae boastin' resolution,
  But determine that ye shall
Make or mar by honest action;
  Put out hand an' help yoursel'.

There are loiterers aroun' us
  For their keep to ithers look,
Think the warl' owes them livin',
  An' they'll hae't by hook or crook.
Gie nae heed to siccan havers,
  Patient toil will ere lang tell;
An' wi' health, you're independent;
  Put out hand an' help yoursel'.

It is peetifu' to see folk
  Lifeless, listless, morn an' noon,
Idly waitin' an' expectin'
  To step in some deid man's shoon;

Better far to buckle at it,
  Try hard honest wark a spell,
There's less chance o' disappointment;
  Put out hand an' help yoursel'.

E'en then, losses sair may thwart ye,
  An' your life seem naught but gloom,
Dinna sit an' nurse your sorrows,
  Rax yoursel' for elbow room ;
Care may kill a cat, but guidsakes,
  Gin ye'll warsle, time will tell,
There's nae charm like push an' courage ;
  Put out hand an' help yoursel'.

Let them mump an' grieve wha like it,
  They are just like bairns at best,
Cast your troubles a' ahint ye,
  Dae your pairt an' trust the rest ;
An' ye'll find that sturdy action
  Sune will banish every ill,
Bringin' peace an' solid comfort ;
  Put out hand an' help yoursel'.

WHAT'S THE GUID?

Life is fu' o' toils an' troubles,
  Thorns an' thistles 'mang the flowers ;
Joys an' waes—like April sunshine
  Blinkin' oot atween the showers.
But hoo apt we are to grunt,
Keepin' aye oor griefs in front,
Shuttin' oot the sun's warm glint,
            What's the guid ?

Hech ! we hae eneuch o' trouble
  Withoot makin' things the waur ;
A' the grainin' an' the worry
  Winna mak' our troubles sma'er.
Owre life's wearies never froon,
Chase them aff wi' cheery croon,
Never let your spirits doon,
            What's the guid ?

Things may a' gang wrang in business,
   Can we mend them gin we mourn ?
Better far keep up the struggle,
   Maybe things will tak' a turn.
Just keep workin' on an' wait,
Lilt your song an' laugh at fate,
While ye've health ne'er own you're beat,
                What's the guid !

Ane will meet wi' disappointments
   Every mile alang life's road :
An' when fain ye'd shift your burden,
   Find ye've got a heavier load.
Ne'er like coward sit an' fret,
Up an' at it toil an' sweat,
Show ye've got some smeddum yet,
                What's the guid !

If ye've loved an' lost your lassie,
   Just be thankfu' ye survive :
For there's mony ane wad end it
   Wi' a rape-end, or a dive ;
Aye, tho' lang an' fond ye wooed,
Till at last "the swine ran thro't,"
There'd been broken hearts about,
                What's the guid ?

Frae experience mony a lesson
   Has been learnt an' laid to heart :
For when our hopes hae flourished,
   Something cam' to "coup the cairt."
But tho' mony a clyte we got,
We were up an' on the stot ;
Let wha like grieve owre their lot,
                What's the guid ?

Na ! I'd rather seek the sunshine
   Ony day, than haunt the shade ;
Gin it's but a blink, the bonnier
   Will I think the faint ray shed ;

An' when storms blaw keen an' snell,
Ithers may despair wha will,
I'll just yammer to mysel',
    What's the guid?

HAUD YOUR WHEESHT!

It's a plan that's aften safest,
 Not to blab owre loud or lang,
Nor wi' frien's to be faut-findin',
 Should they gang a wee thocht wrang,
Else they're apt to get offended,
When there's nae offence intended,
Sae the least said soonest mended :
    Haud your wheesht!

Gin ye canna say a guid word
 For your neibour or your frien',
Dinna say ought that will wrang them,
 An' to mild fau'ts shut your een ;
For gin we oorsel's were noted,
A' oor fau'ts an' failin's quoted,
By the "unco" we'd be spotted ;
    Haud your wheesht!

Aboot ither folk's shortcomin's
 There is muckle we could say,
We're sae ready to add to them
 Mair than what we tak' away ;
Yet oor neibours may discover
Fau'ts mair black in us whatever ;
Gie the deil his due— or ever
    Haud your wheesht!

Owre their ain guid deeds or sayin's
 Nane but fules wad mak' a phraise ;
Gin ye've points that's worth commendin',
 Let the warl' bestow the praise :
Dae your part whate'er may happen,
Never waverin', never trippin',
An' the warl's just verdict lippen ;
    Haud your wheesht!

We may think oor troubles mony,
　　Few oppressed wi' siccan care,
An' we conjure up the shadows,
　　Shuttin' oot the sunshine fair ;
Look aroun', ye'll see grief's traces,
Stoopin' forms an' careworn faces,
E'en the rich wad swap ye places :
　　　　　　　Haud your wheesht !

Weel ye ken the guid auld sayin',
　　That self-praise comes stinkin' ben ;
An' if ye hae points o' guidness
　　That your neibours dinna ken,
Dinna blaw owre loud your horn,
For ye'll fin', as sure 's you 're born,
Ye'll but earn the warl's scorn ;
　　　　　　　Haud your wheesht !

UP IN YEARS.

In youth we dream of future fame
　　An' paint a grand career,
Where a' is roseate sunshine, an'
　　Without a care or tear ;
But ony picture we may paint
　　That then sae braw appears,
Its glamour loses in the strife
　　As we get up in years.

In childhood's sunny laughin' days
　　Our troubles are but sma',
Wi' cheery hearts hoo sune they 're gane,
　　An' we forget them a' ;
But later on when sorrows come,
　　An' grief our spirit sears,
Dae what we will, they come to stay
　　When we get up in years.

We little think in youth's gay hours
　　The pleasures that we hae
Will leave us dowf an' dreary, ere
　　We 're half-way up the brae :

UP IN YEARS.

Wi' wastefu' han' we pluck the flowers
   When simmer's plenty cheers,
Nocht but the nettle stangs are left
   When we get up in years.

The frien'ships that we formed in youth
   We thought wad last thro' life,
But there's a weedin' time gangs on
   When after-cares are rife :
An' ane by ane they drap awa',
   Till blank our way appears,
But where they're true we're closer knit
   As we get up in years.

Gin ye hae suffered love's collapse,
   Wi' pangs an' sighs it brought,
An' pictured life a blighted scene
   Without a sunny spot ;
Yet time brought healin' on its wings
   To dry up a' your tears,
An' left nae after-scaurs to wound
   As ye got up in years.

Faith, time will hae its sweet revenge
   Whatever we can dae,
We canna keep our youthfu' charms
   When we've owre-tapped the brae ;
Where ance we'd routh o' flowin' locks
   The siller streak appears,
An' care sets wrinkles in the broo
   When we get up in years.

Weel is 't gin we can bow to Fate,
   An' tak' what Time may bring,
Nor mourn owre joys for ever gane,
   But aye contented sing :
We've had our day, an' yet can say
   This thought our e'enin' cheers,
The comfort o' a weel-spent life,
   When we get up in years.

IT'S MAYBE JUST AS WEEL.

'Mang a' the ups an' doons o' life,
   There's lots o' things gae wrang,
To disappoint us in our aims,
   And put us aff our gang;
But could we see the goal we seek,
   That's yont the hill we speel,
We'd think our failure to get there
   Was maybe just as weel.

We've routh o' disappointments as
   We spranchle up the brae,
We dinna get the things we want,
   We lose the things we hae ;
An' yet 'mid a' that comes an' gangs,
   As time rows aff the reel,
We're forced to this conclusion, that
   It's maybe just as weel.

We deem events that loom afar
   Will prove to be a curse,
Yet when they happen—o'd, hoo sune
   We think them the reverse ;
In fact, we never can foresee
   What may prove wae or weel,
An' tho' we mourn owre blasted hopes,
   It's maybe just as weel.

Hoo aft we set our hearts to win
   Some place or thing we crave,
An' never heedin' wha may fa',
   We'd fain oot-step the lave ;
An' then when failure marks our course
   We'd fain our grief conceal,
An' try contentedly to say
   It's maybe just as weel.

In youth, what rosy dreams we hae,
   An' airy castles raise,
O' what we're gaun to dae when men,
   To win the warl's praise !

But poetry gies place to prose ;
    The fame by flood or fiel'
Ends up in moleskin an' kail-brose,
    An' maybe just as weel.

In puirtith hoo we aim an' strive
    To win a higher place,
Whiles no' owre scrup'lous o' the means
    By which we'd win the race :
We'd wear braid-claith, an' snaw-white sarks,
    An' everything genteel,
While yet the hame-spun suits us best,
    An' maybe just as weel.

Like maist young fules, we've had our share
    O' joys that coortin' brings,
But jilted love dashed a' the flowers
    An' left the nettle stings :
We thought the cut the fause ane left
    A wound that wadna heal,
But noo we ken her worth, we lilt
    It's maybe just as weel.

The road we seek owre aften proves
    A pitfa' for our feet ;
But what's the sense of mourning owre
    Our failure or defeat ;
Let's bide the warst that Fate may bring,
    Till comin' days reveal
Our course was shaped without our ken,
    An' maybe just as weel.

AULD FRIEN'S.

Hoo lanely wad oor pathway be,
    Hoo dreich life's sky wad seem,
Gin we were left to gang oor lane,
Tho' we had wealth to ca' oor ain,
    An' basked in pleasure's beam !
Gin frien'ship's joys frae us had fled,
    Gane wad be life's true zest ;
New frien's or auld, I like them a',
    But I like auld frien's the best.

True frien'ships in this warl', I fear,
    Are rather hard to find,
The best o' them are unco wauf;
To sift the corn frae 'mang the chaff
    Aft needs misfortune's wind:
An' this experience I hae learned,
    That growin' years attest,
The best frien's are the auld frien's,
    An' the auld frien's are the best.

The schuleboy frien'ships that I made
    Hae lasted a' thro' life,
An' I can count those best o' a'
That helped at dire misfortune's ca',
    When ills an' cares were rife;
An' tho' new frien's I fand where'er
    My lot o' life was cast,
This truth through a' was made mair clear,
    That auld frien's are the best.

A frien' in need ah! there indeed's
    The test that proves their worth;
It's no' the ane that mak's a phraise
That helps ye in the darksome days
    O' puirtith an' o' dearth:
My crust wi' them I'd gladly share,
    Where guidwill crowns the feast,
An' elbows oot life's cankerin' care,
    Where auld frien's are the best.

Thro' thick an' thin, thro' rain an' shine,
    They've stood by me an' mine,
An' I ungratefu' sure wad be
Gin I forget the days that we
    Spent happier far langsyne;
An' noo gin life a burden seems,
    Wi' darklin' clouds opprest,
Thro' change an' scene we've brithers been;
    I like auld frien's the best.

The mair the years begin to tell,
   An' mak' oor steps mair slow,
Thin oot the locks noo siller grey,
Mak' burdens o' what ance was play,
   An' wrinkle owre the broo;
When by the hand o' death bereft
   O' them I lo'ed the maist,
I closer cling to them that's left;
   I like auld frien's the best.

A LIFT ON THE ROAD.

We a' hae oor troubles in joggin' thro' life,
Wi' some they are few, but wi' ithers they're rife,
An' we're apt to mak' muckle o' a' oor bit ills,
While roun' us are mony waur aff that oorsel's;
An' tho' ony comfort or help we can gie
May be very sma', in the world's jaundiced e'e,
Yet a kind word or smile may aft lighten a load,
An' gie some puir neibour a lift on the road.

When the road we maun gang is baith hilly an' rough,
Whilk burdenless e'en wad be weary enough;
When mirkness comes on an' we've still far to gang,
An' fitsair an' trauchled we stumble alang,
Hoo welcome the sight o' some neibour we ken,
Wha offers his service as far as he's gaun,
Tak's half o' the burden, thus easin' the load,
An' quickens oor pace wi' a lift on the road.

When a task is on hand, or a journey to foot,
We're aften gey sweer at the first to set oot;
For we dread the lang travel owre hill an' owre muir,
Wi' the bog-holes an' pitfa's that aft meet us there:
But it's a' in the start; for, ance fair on the way,
We jog on serenely up hill an' doon brae;
For tho' owre rough roads an' steep hills we maun plod,
There's aye the off-chance o' a lift on the road.

It ne'er was intended, like snails in their shells,
We should be entirely wrapt up in oorsel's;
That oor rise in the warl' aye should be owre the backs
O' oor brithers an' sisters who fa' in their tracks.
For hoo aften a hand gi'en to help them alang
Wad start them afresh on the road they maun gang,
Till safe, thro' the succour thus timely bestowed,
Their thanks will reward for a lift on the road.

If the puir folk for help had to trust to the rich,
I'm inclined to believe that it wadna be much,
An' e'en what they gie, is aft gi'en, I observe,
As much as "It's far aboon what ye deserve."
It's the puir help the puir wi' what little they hae,
Nor look for reward for the kindness they dae:
For they ken by experience hoo weary 's the load,
An' hoo gratefu' the aid o' a lift on the road.

Auld age will come on us before we're aware,
Wi' neglect frae near frien's wha ance promised sae fair:
Sae let us be guid to the auld folks we meet,
For a kind word or act mak's life's journey mair sweet:
The bitter will come, let us strive as we may,
But at least we can help to drive sadness away;
For oorsel's yet, when eild comes, may look far abroad
In vain for a kind welcome lift on the road.

An' whiles, when the dark clouds o' care aft assail
The heart o' the Christian, an' doubtin's prevail,
Hoo sune they wad sink in the slough o' despair,
Convinced that for them there was hope never mair,
Gin it were na that some ane wi' far-seein' e'e,
Wha had struggled thro' doubts to the goal o' the free,
Can point to the siller-glint 'yond the dark cloud,
An' heavenward ance mair gie a lift on the road!

Like the Maister when doon on this warl' o' care,
Aye ready the burdens o' puirtith to bear,
The needy an' sufferin' to help oot the mire,
Wi' a purpose that nae opposition could tire;

Gang ye in His footsteps, an' dae what ye can
To brichten the life o' your puir fellow-man,
An' ye'll win the approval an' smile o' your God,
That ye gied some puir pilgrim a lift on the road.

KISS AN' GREE.

Eh! it disna mak' ye bonnie
   When your faces wear a froon;
I wad raither see ye smilin',
   Cheery, chirpin' a' in tune.
What means a' the sulks an' glunchin'
   When ye should be fu' o' glee?
Stop your angry words an' glances;
   Like guid bairnies, kiss an' gree.

Lovers, wooin' in the gloamin',
   Happy, thochtless, free frae care,
May your path be aye as pleasant,
   May your sky be aye as fair;
But gin jealous tifts an' quarrels
   Part ye only for a wee,
Ere it prove a life-lang sorrow,
   Better far to kiss an' gree.

Frien's wha lang hae kent ilk ither,
   Kindly, helpfu' thro' the years,
Hidin' fau'ts that flare oot sometimes
   In the best o' folk's careers;
Ere the shadow o' a rupture
   Parts ye like the surgin' sea,
Clasp the hand held oot in frien'ship,
   An' in spirit kiss an' gree.

Young an' auld alike, aye mind ye,
   Trusty, faithfu' frien's are few:
Cherish them ye hae, an' never
   Seek to wound a heart that's true:
Tho' ye think it may be childish
   Thus the same advice to gie,
Heart-aches cease, an' life's made brichter,
   When, like bairns, ye kiss an' gree.

OOR SIDE YET.

Oh! weel I mind oor boyhood's days,
    In winter's snaw-clad scene,
What mimic battles we hae fought
    Upon the village green:
Wi' charge, an' storm, or bold assault,
    We garred oor foes retreat,
An' raised a shout o' victory
    For oor side yet.

In simmer days, wi' shinties armed,
    We made the knurr to flee,
An' never heeded clours or fa's
    Sae lang's we hailed the tee:
We played determined we should win,
    An' tho'tna o' defeat,
While aye we raised the bantam cry –
    For oor side yet.

The warld's just fu' o' muckle bairns
    A' busy at their games,
Whiles honourable, or otherwise,
    Wi' guid or selfish aims:
It's a' the same—they blaw their horns
    The public ear to get,
An' rally followers to their camps
    For oor side yet.

This game o' war, whilk nations play,
    No' for their people's guid,
But greed an' grab—fresh lands annexed,
    Bought wi' oor heroes' bluid:
We deprecate these cruel wars
    As needless, base; an' yet
This jingo spirit blinds us a'
    For oor side yet.

Even politics are aft a game
    Amang the oots an' ins,
A tug-o'-war for place an' power,
    Nor aye the best that wins:

They promise fair : but, lack-a-day !
   Their words they sune forget,
While puir deluded followers cheer—
   For oor side yet.

The sects are at it, tooth an' nail,
   Wi' shibboleth an' creed,
While aft, amid the din, the puir's
   Neglected in their need :
The kirks will dae nae guid, while they
   This spite an' spleen beget,
Rin doon a' ither creeds, an' shout—
   For oor side yet.

We look abroad on ither lands,
   An' sometimes look wi' scorn,
An' thank kind Heaven, wi' pridefu' voice,
   That we are British born ;
What better are we than the lave,
   Gin oor deserts we get ?
That we should boast, an' crousely craw—
   For oor side yet.

Na ! let us simmer doon a bit,
   An' ken oor proper place,
Sae lang as we dae naething wrang
   To bring deserved disgrace :
Let ignorance boast, let pride exult,
   As men let us admit
The senselessness o' a' this cry—
   For oor side yet.

COME AWA' BEN.

It's a plain, hamely sayin', but couthie it soun's,
When ye gang in the kintra awa' frae the toons ;
Ye ca' at some auld thackit cot on the way,
An' spier—"Hoo the guid folks are fettlin' the day ?"
Nae cauldness or stiffness their manner betrays,
Aye kindly at heart though unlearned in their ways ·
"Oh ! thank ye for spierin' ; we're geylies, ye ken ;
Nae doot ye 'll be weary't, sae come awa' ben."

Wi' the hungry or feeble that ca' at their door
They'll aye share their wallet, tho' scanty their store.
There's a seat in the neuk by the glint o' the fire,
You're welcome to rest, gin rest ye require ;
A tap at the door, an' the guidwife will say,
"We're no' wantin' onything, thank ye, the day" ;
But a second glance tells them it's some ane they ken,
An' it's, "Hoo 're ye the day?" an' a "Come awa' ben."

Oh ! weel dae I mind when I courted my Jean,
As bonnie a lassie as tripped owre the green ;
Tho' aften we'd met by the auld trystin' tree,
To whisper oor love vows where nae ane could see :
I tho't it was time at the auld folks to spier
For the hand o' my lassie my fortune to share :
Sae wi' mony misgivin's I gaed up the glen,
An' sune was invited to "Come awa' ben."

I blushed an' I stammered, but I managed to tell
"I was thinkin' o' settin' up hoose for mysel' ;
That I'd fixed on their lass as my helpmate for life,"
When the auld man consented, an' sae the guidwife :
Then I turned to my lassie an' vowed to be true,
"My heart an' my hoose are baith waitin' for you,
An' gin ye like to share them, there's nae lassie I ken
Wad be made half as welcome, sae come awa' ben."

Frae that day to this we've had nocht to regret,
An' tho' gettin' auld, we're just like wooers yet ;
Oor bairns are aroun' us, baith mensefu' an' kind,
While oor happiness seems wi' the auld hoose entwined ;
An' noo, lookin' back owre the years that hae gane
Sin' the day that I spier'd her gin she'd be my ain,
I bless the auld folks wha ance lived in the glen,
An' their first welcome gi'en me to "Come awa' ben."

BE CANNY WI' THE CREAM.

It's just as muckle's I can mind,
  When but a waddlin' tot,
I've heard my worthy granny say
  Some things I've ne'er forgot :

An' thus my memory still retains
　　Her frugal, thrifty theme,
As owre oor hamely meal she'd say,
　　Be canny wi' the cream.

The mind as weel's the body aye
　　Maun hae its solid food,
An' trifles that may please awhile
　　Confer nae lastin' good :
Seek knowledge that will stan' the test,
　　An' win the warld's esteem ;
But ne'er to pleasure be enslaved ;
　　Be canny wi' the cream.

When phantom pleasures lure us on,
　　In paths where snares are rife,
Wi' promises o' joys that fade
　　An' blight the charm o' life,
See that your craft is safe an' soun'
　　Ere that ye 'tempt the stream,
Nor venture far frae shore ; but aye
　　Be canny wi' the cream.

The love-glint that lights up oor hearts,
　　When we are young an' auld,
If fanned owre free may flicker oot,
　　An' leave us in the cauld :
True love, e'en when we're up in years,
　　Should be mair than a dream :
Sae gin ye'd hae 't to last thro' life,
　　Be canny wi' the cream.

Should passion, wi' its scorpion whip
　　Hid 'neath a wreath o' flowers,
Tempt us to lea' the narrow road
　　For love's illicit bowers,
Think o' the sting that's sure to come
　　Tho' a' may pleasant seem :
An' a' thro' life tak' heed, an' aye
　　Be canny wi' the cream.

Aye try to live within your means,
    An' lay a wee aside,
Sae as to hae 't in darksome days,
    An' for auld age provide :
Gin spendthrift ways see youth's bright days
    Depart, then, puirtith grim
Your later life will joyless mak' :
    Be canny wi' the cream.

Then just tak' tent while yet there's time,
    A' ye on pleasure bent :
Seek that as weel that wisdom gies,
    An' brings ye sweet content :
I wadna frown wi' jaundiced e'e,
    An' see ye sad or prim ;
But tak' ye this advice frae me—
    Be canny wi' the cream.

HAUD THE KAIL HET.

What ploys an' pranks we used to hae
    When we were bairns at schule !
What games o' shinty, hunt the hare,
    An' peerie, ba', or bool !
Baith licht o' heart an' fleet o' fit,
    We'd loup owre ditch or yett,
While words o' cheer the laggards hear,
    To haud the kail het.

An' this was aft a motto gi'en
    For something mair than play :
To keep us at oor tasks at schule,
    Nor idle time away ;
Hoo we wad spur ilk ither on
    When irksome sums were set,
Ne'er to despair, but grind the mair,
    An' haud the kail het.

When schulin' days were owre an' gane,
    An' life's real work began,
That sayin' still wad urge us on,
    In mony a scheme an' plan :

Gin stumblin'-blocks were in oor way,
   An' difficulties met,
To clear the road we'd harder plod,
   An' haud the kail het.

Eh! weel I mind when love's first flame
   Was waukened in my breast,
An' there was ane I langed to win
   I lo'ed aboon the rest;
When ither lads were wooin' her,
   I didna sulk or fret;
But 'mang the ruck, I chanced my luck
   To haud the kail het.

Where in the race o' life we find
   That competition's keen,
We must keep movin' wi' the rest,
   Nor sit doon an' compleen;
Ne'er fear, altho' the hill be steep,
   The goal far aff as yet,
Keep up the rate, nor growl at fate,
   But haud the kail het.

I've nae use for that thowless breed
   Wha snail-like snoove alang,
An' when ill-luck owretak's them, swear
   The warl' is a' gane wrang;
Their want o' push an' energy's
   The last thing they regret;
An' fail to score, when ithers daur
   To haud the kail het.

The langer that I live, I see
   This truth stands baulder oot,
If things are worth the fash ava,
   We've got to stir aboot;
It winna dae to sit an' glunch
   When obstacles are met;
The prize is there for them wha dare
   To haud the kail het.

It's folly to rush at a thing
　　Withoot baith thocht an' tact,
But it's a greater blunder still
　　To think but never act;
Be sure before ye tak' the loup
　　There's firm grun' for your fit,
Syne dae your best an' trust the rest
　　But haud the kail het.

GRIP YOUR NETTLE TIGHT.

In a' the great concerns o' life,
　　An' e'en in sma' things tae,
There's plenty aye to tax your strength,
　　An' baulk ye on your way;
Half-hearted action winna dae
　　To haud ye in the right,
It's thoroughness an' grit yon need,
　　Sae grip your nettle tight.

Gin it is work ye hae to dae
　　To keep the hame secure,
To gain ilk day the bread ye want
　　An' keep care frae your door;
When only stern unflinching toil
　　Brings in the sup an' bite,
There's nae time then for idle play,
　　Sae grip your nettle tight.

Gin troubles come to plague ye whiles,
　　An' clouds o' care appear,
What need ye play a coward's part,
　　An' shake wi' idle fear!
Face boldly up the blast that comes;
　　Ye'll fley auld care wi' fright,
If ye'll but daur the warst he threeps,
　　An' grip your nettle tight.

The thocht o' some mishap to come
　　Will aft unnerve ye mair
Than troubles that are full in view,
　　An' hem ye front an' rear;

GRIP YOUR NETTLE TIGHT.

Imaginary troubles aft,
   An' real anes too, tak' flight,
If ye but hae the pluck in time
   To grip your nettle tight.

Worry has had mair victims yet
   Than either toil or care,
It dries the joy-springs o' the heart,
   An' leaves life bleak an' bare;
But what guid e'er did frettin' dae
   To end or mend your plight?
Keep aye a cheery heart thro' a',
   An' grip your nettle tight.

Gin scandal or ill words are aimed
   To injure your repute,
When covert hints ye aften find
   A hard thing to refute,
Face boldly up the charge, if made,
   An' gie it nae respite;
Ye'll squeeze the venom oot o't, if
   Ye grip your nettle tight.

When sair temptation eggs us on
   To dae the thing that's wrang,
Or wander in the paths of vice,
   Amid the giddy thrang,
It winna dae to toy wi't, or
   You're sure to get a bite;
But it is harmless after a',
   If ye just grip it tight.

An' when your faith in higher things
   The shafts o' doubt assail,
Wi' truth in your right hand, ye can
   'Gainst a' sic foes prevail.
Just face the error boldly up,
   An' drag it to the light,
The sting o't ne'er will harm ye, if
   Ye grip your nettle tight.

FILL AN' FETCH MAIR.

THERE surely maun be something wrang,
  An' awfu' aff the stot,
When 'mang our busy workin' hives
  Grim want is aft their lot:
While wealth is made by toil an' skill,
  An' plenty fills the land,
Starvation thins the workers' bluid,
  An' aft unnerves their hand;
    An' while they live frae hand to mouth,
      An' scanty aft their fare,
    Wi' them wha neither toil nor spin
      It's fill an' fetch mair.

While weary days an' nichts are spent
  To stem grim puirtith's tide,
Sma' chance is there for them to save,
  An' for auld age provide:
Wi' stoopin' gait an' stiffened limbs
  The aged toiler bears
The crushin' tho't that want an' wae
  Will curse his closin' years:
    Nae ease or comfort can they claim,
      Nae shield frae sordid care;
    While wi' the drones wha they've enriched
      It's fill an' fetch mair.

They've robbed us o' oor common lands,
  Where ance we wandered free,
Where coo or cuddy grazed at will,
  An' bairns could sport in glee:
Noo we can just look owre the dyke,
  An' see what we hae lost
By graspin' hands wha claimed the lot,
  An' never spiered the cost.
    They'd keep the sunshine to themsel's,
      They'd tax ye for the air;
    For to the landlord's greedy maw
      It's fill an' fetch mair.

The birds an' beasts that roam the muirs
  Are no' for you an' me;
The fish that seek the upland burns,
  An' e'en far oot at sea,
They claim them a', an' hedge them roun'
  Wi' penalties an' pains;
The earth is for the landlord's use,
  An' a' that it contains;
    But you, ye ploddin', common crew,
      They daur ye touch a hair;
    While their desires ken nae restraint,
      But fill an' fetch mair.

I wadna care for wealth mysel',
  It aft brings worryin' care,
Gin I've enough to dae my turn
  An' help the eydent puir;
For weel I ken, doon in the slums,
  By circumstances driven,
Are those wha wear the pauper's garb,
  Wi' souls as pure as Heaven.
    An' oh! it mak's me grieve to see
      That they wha weel could spare
    Aft droon the cries o' want an' wae
      Wi' fill an' fetch mair.

This curse o' greed for hoardin's sake
  Dries up the heart's best springs,
Sae that in time the joy ye had
  In life's maist simple things
Is crushed beneath the sordid weight
  O' lucre's chillin' drift,
Until there's no' a shread o' soul
  In all your being left;
    Nae generous feelin's for the weak,
      The sufferin', an' the puir;
    But self the aim an' end o' life;
      Wi' fill an' fetch mair.

An' whether it's to swell their purse,
  Or else to grease their crap,
There's aye the miser cry for mair;
  They kenna when to stap;
Self is their only aim in life,
  Self is their vulgar creed,
That may be summed up in a word
  Plain, bald, unvarnished greed.
    The warld was made for their delight,
      They claim the biggest share,
    They hae nae tho't for ought ootside,
      But fill an' fetch mair.

But there's anither class wha live
  In shiftless, spendthrift ways,
Wha never tak' a tho't hoo they
  Will spend their closin' days;
Enjoyment for the present, shuts
  The future from their view,
An' then owre late they mourn their fate
  When a' their gear's run thro';
    The present's a' they care to scan,
      The morrow brings nae care;
    As lang's their bowie hauds the meal,
      It's fill an' fetch mair.

But there will be a reckonin' day;
  Tak' heed, ye revellin' crew,
If ye hae hopes beyond this life,
  Then dae your duty noo.
"I was an hungered"—think o' that,
  An' grasp the truth in time,
For a' your specious quibbles fail
  When He unveils your crime;
    "Ye fed me not"—an' never tho't
      O' duty to the puir;
    Ye had your Dives day, wha's creed
      Was fill an' fetch mair.

Then ye wha wear the threadbare garb
  An' live frae hand to mouth,
Hae faith that right will yet prevail,
  An' error bow to truth :
But ye maun dae your part to bring
  This happy state aboot,
When they wha toil an' plant the seed
  Shall likewise eat the fruit ;
    Then there will be nae achin' hearts
      Or hopeless, starvin' puir,
    When labour stoutly daur refuse
      To fill an' fetch mair.

THE MORN'S ANITHER DAY.

It's human nature after a'
  To see life's darkest side,
Tho' there are cheery natures, wha
  Are blithe whate'er betide :
They coort the sunshine when it comes,
  An' keep cauld care at bay ;
They live in hope, for aye they ken
  The morn's anither day.

When life has donned its blackest hue
  An' a' is bleak dismay ;
While every avenue ye seek
  Shows ne'er ae cheerin' ray ;
Ne'er mind what croakers prophesy
  O' comin' dool an' wae,
Nor count your cares before they come
  The morn's anither day.

When business troubles rack the brain
  An' breakers loom aheid,
When day an' nicht nae rest you get,
  An' comin' storms ye dread ;
Keep peggin' on, an' mind that fret
  An' worry winna pay ;
There's aye some glint ayont the mirk
  The morn's anither day.

Your toil may bring but sma' reward,
   But puirtith, pinch, an' want,
The ootlook dreary, dull, an' dark,
   The stootest heart micht daunt;
To fell despair an' discontent
   It's nae use to gie way;
Brace up, a change may be at hand
   The morn's anither day.

Gin ye hae tint your lass, an' think
   That life has gane a-gee,
There's maybe yet a truer heart
   That fain wad comfort ye;
Ne'er mourn the jaud that's thrawn ye owre,
   Just let her tak' her way,
Ye'll thank her for't, an' woo again
   The morn's anither day.

The disappointments that we meet
   Are apt to mak' us fret;
But what's the guid? To pine an' sigh
   Ne'er mended matters yet.
Keep aye a stoot heart to the warst
   That ill-luck blaws your way;
The darkest hour's afore the dawn
   The morn's anither day.

Up then, an' storm the forts o' care
   That seem to block your path,
Nor heed the murky sky, or list
   The tempest's chillin' wrath;
Aye mind the calm succeeds the gale,
   An' clears the mists away;
Sae live in hope whate'er betide—
   The morn's anither day.

IT'S HARDLY WORTH YOUR WHILE.

Whate'er you dae, be sure you're richt,
   An' then gang straucht aheid,
An' dae your part, whae'er may doot
   The motive o' your deed;

But if a selfish, warldly aim
    Is a' for which ye toil,
The after-come will surely prove
    It's hardly worth your while.

Hoo true it is that gathered gear,
    When got in crooked ways,
Will sune tak' wing, or prove a curse
    An' blast your later days:
If you think happiness is bought
    By heapin' up the pile,
You'll find oot to your cost, ere lang,
    It's hardly worth your while.

If that pure love which wedlock brings
    (Or should, at least if true)
Be but a mercenary scheme
    Wi' selfish ends in view,
If you think you can reckon on
    The warld's approvin' smile,
Or ask Heaven's blessin' on your hame.
    It's hardly worth your while.

Where pious speech and conduct is
    For business ends put on,
While harmless joys ye deprecate
    Wi' sanctimonious groan;
When ready tears, aye on the tap,
    Stream *à la* crocodile,
Gin ye think that the world's deceived,
    It's hardly worth your while.

Where scenes o' sufferin' meet your gaze,
    An' puirtith's piteous cry
Rings in your ears, you shut them oot,
    An' proudly pass them by;
If pure humanity ye scorn
    As vulgar, mean, an' vile,
An' think your duty you hae dune,
    It's hardly worth your while.

The warld is fu' o' pitfa's that
  Will tax your wit to shun,
E'en when you seek to steer your course
  Wi' guidance frae aboon ;
But if in your ain strength you pride,
  An' heaven's aid revile,
Some ugly fa's will yet remind
  It's hardly worth your while.

Tak' tent then, ere it be owre late,
  An' ne'er be proud or hie,
An' gin ye fa'—as will the best—
  Let that a lesson be
For future conduct, 'mang life's ruts,
  Or help owre fortune's stile ;
But to sit doon an' mourn your fate—
  It's hardly worth your while.

LOOK WHERE YOU'RE GAUN.

See the bairnies at play as they loup an' they rin,
Or play keek-a-boo as they jouk oot an' in,
A' heedless o' dangers that lie in their way,
As careless an' thochtless their wayward feet stray
Till a stang frae the nettles, a jag frae the thorn,
Or daidlies or breeks wi' some hidden nail torn ;
Or maybe, when slap i' the glaur they hae faun,
They're aften reminded to look where they're gaun.

What are we but bairnies o' bigger degree,
An' aft as camsteerie as younkers can be ;
Aft reckless o' dangers that lie in oor road,
An' no' takin' heed e'en where ithers hae trod ?
We learn the same lesson again an' again,
Whiles aften impressed wi' some measure o' pain,
Till, brocht up fu' sudden, we sune understan'
That to steer in the right we maun look where we're gaun.

What puir feckless creatures we are at the best,
Frae the time that we first venture oot o' the nest,
To the frail totterin' step that tells nature's decay,
An' we find the road rough near the fit o' the brae !

Oor lang life's experience at maist has been lost,
For we ne'er seem to learn frae the dangers we've crossed.
An' we still fum'le on an' get upset an' thrawn,
An' we've need o' the counsel to look where we're gaun.

Hey! haud up, my man, ye look cheery an' bricht
As ye travel alang in the sun's glancin' licht:
But dinna just count on aye ha'ein' owreheid
The sun's warm glint, or bauld signposts to read;
For the mirk's sure to come, whether welcome or no'.
An' gin ye wad be safe, just gang cautious an' slow,
Or ye may get benighted an' lost, till the dawn
Ance mair gies the hint just to look where you're gaun.

If pleasure is a' that ye live for, beware!
For 'neath the blown roses lurks many a snare;
The present may be a' that ye can desire,
But think on the time when o' pleasure you'll tire,
You'll wish you could just hae the time owre again,
An' hae to confess that your chances were vain;
Sae, if ye wad be safe when life's curtain is drawn,
Let judgment hae scope, an' just look where you're gaun.

Gin the road o' ambition be that which ye seek,
Or a fame that may reach you besmirched wi' the reek:
Or love, that ye think will set life a' aglow,
An' you'd stake a' you hae for ae smile o' your jo:
Or wealth, for its ain sake, or what it can bring,
An' you think you wad just be as happy's a king:
There, stop ye an' think gin the great o' the lan'
Are as happy's ye think, an' just look where you're gaun.

There is something aboon an' ayont warldly care
That the rich canna filch frae the lives o' the puir;
There's a wealth o' contentment that springs frae the heart
That the humblest can own gin he'll act but his part:
But e'en in the struggle to reach that safe goal
There's mony a back-set the bravest maun thole:
An' if ye wi' contentment the future wad scan,
Let your life-maxim be, aye to look where you're gaun.

At e'en, when life's sunset is merged in the mist,
An' ye wait but the ca' to the lang-looked-for rest
Frae the struggles an' cares that hae marked your life thro',
An' your faith will the day-dreams o' life's spring renew,
Let doots an' perplexities crowd as they may,
Keep the soul's e'e aye fixed on a yet brichter day—
A day that will ken neither sunset nor dawn,
As the promised reward gin ye look where you're gaun.

MAIR THE MORN.

What's the use o' sittin' whinin'
  At the lot we hae to dree?
A' oor grief is mair than useless
  Gin we'll only think a wee;
We had better thole the present,
  Nourishin' a hope inborn,
That tho' present joys hae vanished,
  There will may-be mair the morn.

We hae struggled thro' the winter
  To the gladness o' the spring,
We hae banished care an' sorrow
  Till oor hearts are like to sing;
Tho' to-day there's gloom an' mirkness
  Everywhere we like to turn,
An' the sunshine's in the background;
  Weel, there may-be mair the morn.

Catch the sunbeams as they flicker,
  Nurse your joys as best you can:
Aye to seek the gloomy reaches
  Ne'er contented ony man:
Gin there be the faintest glimmer,
  Seek it oot; nor treat wi' scorn
Ony faint rays strugglin' earthward,
  For there may-be mair the morn.

Oh, hoo aften Hope eludes us,
  An' we ken-na where to steer
For a word or look o' comfort
  That will bring a glint o' cheer!

MAIR THE MORN.

Hoo we scan life's wide horizon,
  An' the sma'est glow discern,
Bringin' e'en a little promise,
  Wi' a hope o' mair the morn.

When we get at times disheartened
  That oor efforts ne'er succeed,
Tho' we dae oor best an' bravest,
  Failure seems to loom aheid ;
Dinna slacken in your purpose,
  Treat a' croakers' bodes wi' scorn :
Gin success but comes in dreepin's,
  Trust there may-be mair the morn.

Sometimes e'en the sma'est trouble
  Fairly seems to weigh us doon ;
Yet, when cares heap up the measure,
  Block oor path, an' hedge us roun',
We get roused frae oot oor dazement
  Kennin' that the tide may turn,
An' the wee-est joy's a blessin'
  That foreshadows mair the morn.

A' the frettin', a' the worry,
  Winna turn a thread that's wrang ;
It will only bring the wrinkles
  An' the stoopin' gait ere lang :
Sae, gin ye can warsle thro' it,
  Let misfortune blaw her horn,
That's the tune the Auld Coo died o' :
  Laugh, an' look for mair the morn.

Up an' at it then wi' vigour,
  "Never let the Gregor doon" ;
Face the warld's storms an' buffets,
  An' defy your cares a' roun' :
Soon you'll see them at the gallop,
  A' their jaggin' prickles shorn,
Like the mists that rise an' vanish
  When the sunshine comes at morn.

A MAN AFORE YOUR MITHER.

Langsyne, when but a bairn at schule,
   Gey dull at lesson learnin',
Aft envyin' them wi' brichter pairts
   The maister's praises earnin';
An' weel I mind my first success,
   I passed aboon anither;
He clapped my heid, an' said, "You'll be
   A man afore your mither."

I took his words as kindly gi'en,
   An' strove to win his praises;
For then I didna understan'
   The meanin' o' sic phrases;
But a' the same, it spurred me on
   Mair knowledge yet to gather,
Determined that I yet wad be
   A man afore my mither.

May-be my schulemates kenned the joke,
   An' lauched at sic a greeny,
Yet I was in real earnest then,
   Tho' but a toddlin' weanie:
Sae, let them lauch as lang's they like,
   I let them rin their tether,
An' set mysel' to strive an' be
   A man afore my mither.

Oor stern auld dominie was ane
   We seldom kenned to utter
A word o' cheer when ane did weel,
   Or urged them to do better;
An' when he did unbend a wee
   To pat you on the shouther,
His owre-come aye was this, "You'll be
   A man afore your mither."

When, aulder grown, I heard the phrase
   An' understood its meanin',
I never thocht I had been fuled,
   Nor gaed aboot compleenin';

I just turned roun' an' tell't the same
  To mony a younger brither,
"It's true eneuch, my bairn, you'll be
  A man afore your mither.

Sin' then I've aften thocht, altho'
  The words may be deceivin',
There's mony a bairn been urged to strive
  When fickle tasks were grievin';
'Twas weel they kent nae better, but
  Were helped like mony anither,
Wi' that sure prophecy, "You'll be
  A man afore your mither."

Sae lang's it helps the bairnies on,
  An' cheers their first endeavours,
I'll ne'er let on, nor mak' them think
  It's only senseless havers;
They'll soon find oot, as time rins on,
  'Mid wark an' cares together;
Sae strive, my bairnies, strive to be
  A man afore your mither.

AT THE RICH MAN'S DOOR.

We envy aft the rich an' great, an' think their life a' bliss,
That a' their lines rin smoothly, an' there's naething gangs amiss;
But yet the rosy-cheekit fruit's whiles wormy at the core,
An' there's aye a slippery stane at ilka rich man's door.

O' a' life's cares an' troubles they hae just to tak' their share,
An' puirtith's lot is aftentimes mair free frae sordid care;
For wealth brings mony worries they are fated to endure,
An' there's aye a slippery stane at ilka rich man's door.

Then there are aft temptations that the puir ken nocht aboot,
An' sinfu' pleasures toyed wi' they'd be better far without;
While simple, pure enjoyments aye mair lastin' peace secure,
For there's aye a slippery stane at ilka rich man's door.

The things that bring maist pleasure are what Heaven has
    gi'en us free,
An' nature's treasures spread aroun' are sent for you an'
    me ;
They canna shut the sunshine oot ; tho', gin they had the
    power,
Sma' glints indeed wad ever reach the puir man's door.

Gin puirtith gets a tum'le, weel, it hasna far to fa',
An' aft escapes wi' little scaith that scarcely hurts ava ;
But when the proud folk coup the creel they get an awfu'
    clour,
For there's aye a slippery stane at ilka rich man's door.

Altho' the puir aft find it hard to manage bite an' sup,
Or week to week mak' baith ends meet an' keep their
    credit up ;
Yet lang as wark is plentifu' their crowdie is secure,
While there's aye a slippery stane at ilka rich man's door.

You've heard it said that riches may tak' wings an' flee
    awa',
An' high folk when they tint their gear just founder where
    they fa' ;
No like the man wha hains his wealth, they canna tide it
    owre,
An' the slippery stane seems slipperier at the rich man's
    door.

When some by Fortune's windfa' get a heize up in the
    warl'
Aboon the heids o' neibours wha maun still drag puirtith's
    harl,
Prosperity aft proves a curse when dootfu' pleasures lure ;
An' there's aye a slippery stane at ilka rich man's door.

Then dinna covet what they hae, or their exalted place ;
For a' their great advantages aft lands them in disgrace ;
Gin principle is wantin' they are sure to bite the stour,
For there's aye a slippery stane at ilka rich man's door.

SIMMER FRIEN'S.

Life is dreich eneuch an' dreary,
    Sae the mair we prize a frien'
When the smiles o' fickle fortune
    Are baith few an' far atween ;
Kindly hearts that share your sorrows,
    Help you frae their scanty means,
Cheer you wi' their words o' comfort ;
    These are true an' trusty frien's.

There are plenty ever ready,
    When you hae a fav'rin' breeze,
To admire, an' fawn, an' flatter,
    Aye as mealy-mou'd ye please :
See them when your bark's in trouble,
    An' her timmer creaks an' streins,
They're awa' to smoother waters ;
    Vain your trust in Simmer frien's.

When your balance at the banker's
    Totals up a guidly sum,
You've nae need to whistle for them,
    Uninvited, here they come ;
While they're treated at your table
    In your heyday festive scenes,
Wha could then believe hoo hollow
    Are the vows o' Simmer frien's ?

Aye ! but should you hae a dooncome,
    An' you hae to pinch an' hain,
They're conspicuous by their absence ;
    Faith, you'll look for them in vain.
A' your kindness is forgotten ;
    You may beg for wife an' weans,
They're awa' an' owre the Borders
    Like the lave o' Simmer frien's.

You'll repent it, gin you trust them
    Ere their honest worth you prove,
An' you find their protestations
    Only spell oot cupboard love.

When you hae to plan an' reckon
  Hoo to nurse your scanty means,
Sune they'll see you've nocht to gie them,
  An' you'll lose your Simmer frien's.

You an' I, I wat, hae met them
  Thick as haws in harvest time,
Aye sae smilin', aye sae gracious,
  While your prospects loom oot prime :
Reckoned at their fullest value,
  They're no' worth a raw o' preens ;
Hearts wi' selfishness encrusted
  Turn oot ever Simmer frien's.

Ye can aye hae plenty roun' ye
  When the prospect's fair ahead,
Wha will turn tail an' desert ye
  In your anxious time o' need :
In this life's stern uphill battle,
  Daily waged for wife an' weans,
For a han' to help you onwards
  Dinna trust to Simmer frien's.

When ye find a right guid Billie,
  Stick to him, he's worth it a' :
For ye can rely wi' safety
  On his help, hoovever sma' :
Maybe he's no' much to pairt wi',
  But that little's freely gi'en,
Wi' nae thocht o' favours seekin' ;
  He's a leal an' faithfu' frien'.

An' beware o' them wha're ever
  Ready wi' their words o' praise,
Wha can see nae fau'ts, but owre your
  Sma'est virtues mak' a phraise ;
An' where'er your course may tak' you,
  In your ain han's keep the reins ;
Better far ae faithfu' neibour
  Than a host o' Simmer frien's.

IT'S A SAIR THING TROUBLE.

There are few upon this footstool
   That can claim exemption sure
Frae the ills that flesh is heir to,
   And the trials we maun endure;
For tho' ilka ane's experience
   Is as varied as can be,
It's a sair thing trouble
   When the warst ye hae to dree.

Ye may gather wealth in gowpens
   That ye kenna hoo to spend.
An' ye want for naething earthly,
   Yet it canna buy a friend;
An' should ye hae a dooncome,
   An' ye fairly lose your grup,
It's a sair thing trouble
   When there's nane to help ye up.

We seldom think o' stintin'
   Against puirtith to secure,
An' we fairly seemed to revel
   When the moothpock's rinnin' owre;
But when we've reached the bottom,
   An' oor last provision's shared,
It's a sair thing trouble
   When ye're no' owre weel prepared.

There are times in oor life's journey
   When the sky gets overcast,
When we reel an' stagger under
   Misfortune's cauldrife blast.
When we see nae glint o' sunshine
   Thro' the mists an' fogs o' care,
It's a sair thing trouble
   When alane your grief you bear.

When we look for help or succour
   To tide us owre the warst,
To friends we used to swear by
   Wha in promises were first;

They are gane like spring's first blossoms
  When the frost has settled keen ;
It 's a sair thing trouble
  When ye 're left to strive your lane.

Oh ! the hollowness an' shammin'
  That surrounds us every day ;
We never seem to gauge it
  Till misfortune blocks oor way :
An' we look in vain around us
  For a look or word o' cheer ;
It 's a sair thing trouble
  When your lanely course you steer.

E'en the rich are no exempt frae 't
  Ony mair than puirer folk ;
Trouble comes to high an' lowly,
  An' we a' maun bear the yoke :
Aye ! we a' meet on a level
  When oor hearts are stunned wi' grief ;
It 's a sair thing trouble
  E'en when wealth brings nae relief.

But gin ye hae faith to lippen
  To the word o' promise gi'en,
That your every pang is noted
  An' your every tear is seen ;
Ye can look beyond the present
  To a time when grief shall end,
While there 's Ane will share your troubles
  As a true and faithful friend.

AT THE HEEL O' THE HUNT.

It 's a maxim that 's true o' a' countries an' climes,
To succeed, ye maun try to keep pace wi' the times ;
For if ithers push past ye an' get to the front,
You 'll fin' yoursel' left at the heel o' the hunt.

We maunna look back on the past wi' its ways,
Content, like oor forebears, to tak' things wi' ease ;
We aye maun be ready to share in life's brunt,
Or languish ahint at the heel o' the hunt.

In a'thing we dae, we will fin' this is true,
Whether business or study the path we pursue ;
Gin we lag in the race, then aside we maun shunt,
An' be fated to drag at the heel o' the hunt.

In this age o' progression things move like a flash,
An' sometimes we need baith the spur an' the lash :
Nae maitter what obstacles we maun confront,
It means winnin' the race,—or the heel o' the hunt.

"A faint heart ne'er won"—weel, ye ken the auld saw,
Tho' coortin's no' tied doon to method or law ;
But the slow, cautious wooer will get leave to grunt,
An' mourn a' his lane at the heel o' the hunt.

Then be up an' daein' whate'er be your lot ;
Be eydent, an' mak' for your mark like a shot ;
Keep the goal in your e'e as ye push to the front,
Or mak' up your min' for the heel o' the hunt.

NEVER GO BACK ON A FRIEND.

As you journey through life, though the road may be rough,
   And with trouble you have to contend,
True friendship will smooth all the crosses you meet,
   So never go back on a friend.

Let brotherly love be your motto where'er
   A kind-hearted neighbour you find ;
For firm true affection is rare in this world,
   So never go back on a friend.

If once he was wealthy, but now broken down,
   And his riches all gone like the wind ;
Though poor, if his heart be as true as of yore,
   Then never go back on a friend.

When calumny raises a cry 'gainst his name,
   To scandal an ear never lend ;
Always speak a good word, or say nothing at all,
   And never go back on a friend.

Always stretch out a hand to those in distress,
    But an empty hand never extend ;
Advice may be good, but the hungry 'twont fill,
    So never go back on a friend.

So remember wherever your lot may be cast,
    Let your motto be, "leal to the end,"
And you'll never have cause to mourn the loss
    Of a good, honest, true-hearted friend.

IT'S A' THE SAME TO ME.

Let fortune smile or fortune froon,
    It's a' the same to me ;
I never let my spirits doon,
    But lauch wi' hearty glee :
Auld care gangs doiterin' by my door,
He daurna show his nose oot owre :
Nae matter though he glunch an' glower,
    It's a' the same to me.

Tho' I hae neither lands nor gear,
    It's a' the same to me :
I've something that I haud mair dear
    Than a' that wealth can gie :
I toil alang for what I hae,
Tho' that but serves frae day to day ;
An' while grim puirtith keeps away,
    It's a' the same to me.

The rich ride past in gilded state,
    It's a' the same to me ;
I jog alang my humble gate,
    Tho' rough the road may be :
I note the charm that nature flings
Owre vale an' hill, the bird that sings ;
While free to share sic pleasin' things,
    It's a' the same to me.

I hae nae hankerin' after fame,
    It's a' the same to me ;
Let ithers rise an' mak' a name,
    I'll cast nae envious e'e :

But in my place I'll be content,
An' count my days an' years weel spent:
If free frae woe, an' safe frae want,
   It's a' the same to me.

I never heed what neibours say,
   It's a' the same to me;
I never care what ithers dae,
   I let the boddies be:
Gin they'll but keep their ain gate en',
An' lea' me to jog on my lane,
O' them an' theirs I'll ne'er complain,
   It's a' the same to me.

Gin Maggie gies me the go-bye,
   It's a' the same to me;
I'll treat her just as saucily,
   An' let the lassies be:
Gin she can fin' anither jo
To lo'e her better, what for no';
She's free to choose her laddie O,
   It's a' the same to me.

Tho' frien'ship flit like morning dew,
   It's a' the same to me;
I'll sune fin' ithers, leal an' true,
   To share life's joys wi' me:
If them that I hae trusted lang
Get cauld as ice, there's something wrang:
I'll ne'er tak' tent the road they gang,
   It's a' the same to me.

THE MORN WE NEVER SAW.

That thief, Procrastination,
   Maun hae mony a hearty laugh
When he sees us unco ready
   Ony duty to put aff.
What does't matter—thus we reason—
   If we lose an hour or twa?
We can mak' it up the morn;
   But the morn we never saw.

Hoo we waste the precious minutes
　Till they stretch oot into hoors,
An' forget the weel-thumbed maxim
　That the present time is oors:
We are lavish o' a treasure
　That we never can reca',
Tho' we aft re-hear the adage,
　That the morn we never saw.

Weel! there's maybe some excuse for 't,
　When the task we hae to dae
Isna just sae awfu' pleasant,
　An' we shun 't as lang 's we may;
But gin we are bound to face it,
　Tak' the job on richt awa',
Wait na that convenient season
　On the morn ye never saw.

Is it business care that worries,
　An' ye hope 'gainst hope that sune
That everlastin' burden
　O' hard times will change its tune?
It will only come by effort;
　Put your back against the wa',
An' tak' time by the forelock,
　For the morn ye never saw.

Altho' time heals mony troubles
　That are aften hard to bear,
Dinna count on help frae ithers,
　For ye hae to dae your share:
Tho' the tide may turn withoot ye
　That is ruled by Nature's law,
Tak' it at the flood, an' trust na
　To the morn ye never saw.

In oor youth what thochtless wastrie,
　Aye! an' even in oor prime;
Ane wad think there was nae end o't,
　We're sae prodigal o' time:

But when up in years, my callants,
    Ye wad fain the past reca',
Then nae mair are moments squandered,
    For the morn we never saw.

Just a word in application—
    As the parsons say—to teach
Hoo we prize the years that's slipt us,
    An' are far ayont oor reach :
But 'twill dae nae guid to grumble
    That oor chances noo are sma' ;
Set to wark to mak' the best o't,
    For the morn ye never saw.

KISS THE SAIR PLACE.

SEE the wee bit toddlin' bairnie
    Staggerin' owre the cottage floor,
Quits its grip an' tines its balance,
    Gies its wee bit head a clure ;
See the mither rin to raise it,
    Croodles owre 't, an' strokes its broo,
"Let your mammy kiss the sair place ;
    There, my bairn is better noo."

When, as laddies, we were promised
    Whiles a treat in schulin' days,
An' admonished to be eydent
    Owre oor "Lennie's" an' oor "Gray's" ;[1]
Gin we risked to play the truant,
    We for this were richtly ser'ed,
For the Maister left a sair place,
    An' oor faither did na spared.

When in calf-love days you're jilted
    By some lassie you admire,
An' you think the warld's grown dreary,
    An' you'd fain frae it retire ;

---

[1] Lennie's Grammar and Gray's Arithmetic ; two classics in school fifty years ago. I remember them well ; bound in full leather. Books were books then.—J. P.

Foolish laddie, you're but learnin'
  What your elders ken owre weel:
Women's wiles leave mony a sair place
  Time alone can kiss an' heal.

When misfortune's blast has found us
  Cowerin' neath some scanty beild,
When oor erst-while frien's desert us,
  An' to dark despair we yield;
Gin some kindly, generous nature
  Gies us e'en a word o' cheer,
'Tis a balm that soothes the sair place
  Better far than gifts o' gear.

When the heart is bowed wi' sorrow
  Aftentime owre deep for words,
An' the warld, that ance could cheer ye,
  Noo nae solid peace affords,
Then some neibour's kindly action
  Seems to lift a load o' pain,
Brings ance mair the smiles an' sunshine,
  As the mither soothes the wean.

Let us, then, where puirtith pinches,
  Gie what little help we can,
An' tho' clad in tattered garments,
  Dinna let's despise the man;
For beneath these rags there may be
  Truer heart as e'er was born,
Which will feel its sairs mair keenly
  When the world has nought but scorn.

COME IN AHINT.

You've nae doot seen a flock o' sheep
  In canny shepherd's care,
Whiles nibblin' in the grassy ditch
  As 'yont the road they steer;
The watchfu' collie rins an' youffs
  When some wee lammie strays,
Till ordered to "come in ahint,"
  When promptly he obeys.

E'en like the shepherd wi' the doug
　　That minds its maister's words,
We hae to watch oor life's desires
　　Just like sae mony herds ;
An' should we ance owrestep the mark,
　　Before we gang owre far,
A timely stern "come in ahint"
　　May save frae something waur.

If we could aye oor passions guide,
　　That aft wad lead us wrang
In ways o' sinfu' pleasures, bought
　　Wi' mony an after-stang ;
When slee temptation whispers saft,
　　"The warl' will never ken,"
Then conscience cries, "Come in ahint,"
　　An' saves us muckle pain.

Oor bairns wad sune be maisters gin
　　They gat their wilfu' way :
Sae we can ne'er begin owre sune
　　To teach them to obey :
An' when rebellious, as at times
　　The maist o' them will be,
The faither's stern "come in ahint"
　　Will curb their wills a-wee.

Sometimes when lovers quarrel, an'
　　The breach no' like to heal,
Tho' pairted, as if ne'er to meet,
　　They like ilk ither weel ;
Throw pride aside gin you're to blame,
　　An' own your faut richt oot ;
A whispered saft "come in ahint"
　　Will bring them back nae doot.

If we hae wandered frae the faith
　　Oor faithers held sae firm,
An' speculative themes hae lured
　　Wi' their seductive charm ;

There comes a time when we are fain
　　To hae the auld faith back,
An' reason cries "come in ahint,"
　　In humbler ways to walk.

Gin there's a deil to tempt puir folk
　　To whiles gang off the straucht,
Just keep a sharp lookoot, an' set
　　Your conduct as you ought ;
Ne'er be beguiled by honeyed words
　　To dae what brings disgrace,
Just mind him to "come in ahint,"
　　An' keep his proper place.

HUNT THE GOWK!

The fules are no' a' deid yet, as
　　Frae day to day appears—
Young fules, for whom there's some excuse,
　　An' waur anes up in years ;
They 're a' on bubble schemes engaged,
　　Or fulish errands bent,
Whilk turn oot but a hunt the gowk,
　　When time an' siller's spent.

The phantom pleasures that we seek,
　　An' strive for late an' ear',
Aft turn oot like the Deid Sea fruit,
　　Or bring us nocht but care ;
The prospects aye seem bright eneuch,
　　Until we reach the goal,
An' then it's but a hunt the gowk
　　To gull some silly fule.

See yonder youth wi' anxious e'e
　　The sportin' paper scan,
To find the stakes he risked are gane,
　　An' he's a puirer man ;
Could he but see ahint the scenes,
　　Hoo wires are deftly pulled,
He'd find himsel' a hunt the gowk—
　　Anither greeny fuled.

The love ye lavished nicht an' morn
   On yon fair blushing queen
Gied promise o' a sweet return,
   An' a'thing looked serene;
But when she left ye in the cauld,
   An' chose anither mate,
Ye fand 'twas but a hunt the gowk,
   But fand it oot owre late.

We sometimes dream o' climbin' up
   To heights o' wealth an' fame,
An' naething will content us but
   A much belauded name;
Mair like we'll flounder in the bogs
   Where social wrecks are rife,
To find it's but a hunt the gowk
   That's blighted mony a life.

Gin we wad be content to plod
   An' tak' oor pleasures slow,
An' seek the simple joys that leave
   Nae aftermath o' woe,
We'd hae nae cause to grumble then
   An' rail at Fortune's froon;
We wadna play the hunt the gowk,
   An' aye be hauden doon.

What tho' we toil baith nicht an' morn
   To hoard a pickle gear,
An' lea' oor minds to rin to weeds
   For want o' healthy lear;
When youth's bricht days are past an' gane,
   We'll at the last repent;
For siller's but a hunt the gowk
   That brings nae pure content.

It's no' alane on April first
   They fulish errands gang,
For there are some sae warped an' thrawn
   They're sure to choose the wrang;

Some see their error, an' reform
    Gin they've been fuled but ance ;
But there are life-lang hunt the gowks
    That never can learn sense.

WAIT AND HOPE.

CEASE repining, troubled heart,
Time will soothe the bitter smart ;
Now, though dark the clouds may lower,
Summer comes with sun and shower ;
    Wait and hope.

Though thou may'st have loved and yearned
For a love yet unreturned ;
Though thy wealth of love were wasted
For a mutual love untasted,
    Wait and hope.

Kindness wins a kindred feeling,
And the heart, yet unrevealing,
Love's mute mysteries may yet
True felicity beget ;
    Wait and hope.

May-be thou hast loved and lost,
Shadows o'er thy pathway crossed ;
Though forlorn thy life may be,
There are brighter days for thee ;
    Wait and hope.

Come, no longer sadly shun
Summer breezes, summer sun ;
Let not winter's storm-clouds roll
O'er thy dark, despairing soul ;
    Wait and hope.

And as sure as summer brings
Flowers and fruits and pleasant things,
So thy path will bloom anew
With a mutual love and true ;
    Wait and hope.

HEAVEN IS NO' SAE FAR AWA.'

This world has mony beauteous spots,
　And wonders rare that reach the heart:
We cannot gaze on God's great work
　An' think o' Him as far apart;
We see His footsteps 'mang the flowers,
　An' hear His voice when breezes blaw,
While nature everywhere affirms
　That Heaven is no' sae far awa'.

An' there are mony worthy souls
　Amang the puir aye dacin' guid,
To cheer the widow 'mid her tears,
　An' children in their orphanhood;
On Christ's example they rely,
　To teach the world that after a'
Kind words an' deeds are valid proofs
　That Heaven is no' sae far awa'.

Amid the darkest city slums,
　Where vice an' greed together herd,
Where foul debauchery shuns the licht
　An' human lives are warped an' blurred,
There still are hearts like jewels bricht,
　Forced low by puirtith's iron law,
Wha's lives nae foulness can besmirch,
　For Heaven is no' sae far awa'.

I put nae trust in them wha preach
　That power for guid is gi'en to few,
Yet hug some dim uncertain dream,
　'Twill a' be richt ayont the blue:
Noo is the sure accepted time
　To labour at the Maister's ca',
An' show, amid life's darklin' scenes,
　That Heaven is no' sae far awa'.

'Tis no' the creeds which men profess,
　Nor yet the shibboleths they preach,
But heart-communin's true an' guid
　The Faither's listenin' ear will reach;

For human hearts are grander far
    Than mightiest creeds the world ere saw:
While humble upright lives proclaim
    That Heaven is no' sae far awa'.

While listenin' to the prattlin' words
    That give a charm to babyhood,
You tell me that their nature 's vile,
    That there is no' a trait o' guid ;
I care not what your creeds assert,
    Christ's words I deem a higher law.
An' childhood's innocence to me
    Proves Heaven is no' sae far awa'.

Let men hae but some end in view,
    To raise the fallen, aid the puir,
Sae then, when they are ca'd awa',
    They 'll lea' the world mair bricht an' fair :
To-day 's the time for labour's task,
    An' tho' your efforts be but sma',
E'en here you 'll reap a rich reward,
    For Heaven is no' sae far awa'.

WHEN THE DAYS ARE CREEPIN' IN.

The simmer flowers are withered,
    The simmer winds are gane,
An' yellow leaves lie scattered
    On upland an' in glen ;
The burnie lilts sae dolefu'
    As its drumlie waters rin,
An' the sun curtails his glances
    When the days are creepin' in.

The stacks hae a' been thackit,
    We 've laid aside the plough,
The tatties a' are howkit,
    An' the simmer dargs are thro' ;
An' noo beside the ingle,
    In the neuk sae snug an' clean,
Sae canty we foregather
    When the days are creepin' in.

Noo winter's comin' surely,
    Wi' cauldrife win's an' snaw,
We're thankfu' for oor biggin',
    Altho' oor cot's but sma';
We envy nae the riches
    Sae mony try to win:
We hae oor simple pleasures
    When the days are creepin' in.

An' for the helpless ootcasts
    We never grudge a bite:
We're fain to gie them shelter
    Frae the nippin' winter's night:
For we think o' oor ain laddie
    Far frae a' his kith an' kin,
Amang strangers may be fendin'
    When the days are creepin' in.

Auld age comes on us creepin',
    For oor simmer days are past,
An' sune we maun be sleepin'
    Amang the mools at last:
But yonder, where oor hope is,
    Free frae a' stains o' sin,
There will be nae cheerless winters
    When the days are creepin' in.

I'LL FECHT TILL I DEE.

I'm a peaceable chap when I'm tethered at hame,
Wi' the ties o' my bairns, an' my couthie guid-dame:
I quarrel wi' nae ane, nor yet interfere
Wi' the neibours at han', act they ever sae queer;
But should they misca' me, or wreck my guid name,
Or seek to bring discord among us at hame,
I'm ready to gie them as guid as they gie,
An' for hame, wife, and weans, faith, I'll fecht till I dee.

If ye're coortin' a lass that ye think muckle o',
An' she in return thinks the warl' o' her jo,
Ye surely wad shield her frae a' kinds o' scaith,
An' listen to naething to weaken your faith;

But should some mean suitor, wi' underhan' airts,
Endeavour to sinder your twa trustin' hearts,
Ye're nae man ava, gin ye no say wi' me,
For the lassie I lo'e I will fecht till I dee.

Ye're puir shauchlin' creatures that ken na their mind,
But are just like the leaves blawn a' airts wi' the wind,
Wha hae nae richt principle guidin' their acts,
An' retail idle gossip as gin it were facts.
Awa' oot my gate, I've nae use for sic crew :
Gie me the upricht man that's faithfu' an' true,
Wha'll stick to the straucht road tho' a' gang agee,
An' for honour's sake's ready to fecht till he dee.

There's nae word I ken that's sae muckle abused,
Or oftener by the base-spirited used,
Than Loyalty oh! but it covers a lot
O' ill-deeds that leave on oor standard a blot :
Sic wrang daein', tho' dune in the name o' oor Queen,
Is a thing I'm ashamed o'—despicable, mean ;
They may prate o' sic loyalty wha like for me,
But for honour and justice I'll fecht till I dee.

There are folks wha can talk o' their friendships fu' gleg,
Wha to help ye in trouble will no lift a leg,
Their offers o' help come when a' thing is fair,
When your purse is weel lined an' you haena a care :
But the first cloud o' sorrow sends them a' adrift,
An' ye're left to yoursel' 'mid misfortune to shift ;
But for frien's wha wad share their last shillin' wi' me,
Should I need it, for them I wad fecht till I dee.

I winna boo doon to the greatest on earth,
If a' he can boast o's his fortunes an' birth,
Nor yet to a party that bolster up wrang,
An' ignore puirtith's cry in the grip o' the strang ;
But where they bring fairly their deeds to the licht,
Redress grievous ills, and conserve what is richt,
They'll get my support, tho' it's a' I can gie :
But 'gainst legal oppression I'll fecht till I dee.

V.

Miscellaneous Poems.

"Accept my best thanks for your book, into which I have looked with great pleasure. Your songs are full of nature, and love, and truth, and pious wisdom, and genuine Scottish feeling. 'The Thistle' is an excellent glorification of our kingly weed; and the 'Royal Mouse' is a poem that would have done credit to Burns."—*Letter from Professor Blackie*.

V.

MISCELLANEOUS POEMS.

THE ROYAL MARRIAGE.

While fevered nations cease their burning strife,
And war-worn veterans seek their homes again :
While mourning widows 'mid their blighted life,
    And orphans in their prayers,
Think of the loved who fell on battle plain,
    Unmoved by sighs and tears :
And patriot hearts with holy feelings swell
For the brave ones in duty's cause who fell ;

Within our peaceful kingdom, far and near,
'Mid city life, in rural cot and hall,
A nation's voice is raised in loyal cheer
    On the bright bridal morn :
God bless the fair Louise resounds from all—
    God bless the Lord of Lorne ;
And Scotland sees with patriotic pride
Her son united to a peerless bride.

On mountain tops the lurid bonfires blaze,
As when of old to herald war's alarms,
But now the thoughts of peace and joy they raise,
    And call the happy free
Not to repel a proud invader's arms—
    'Tis England's jubilee ;
And peer and peasant join with one accord
To hail the maiden and her happy lord.

Our fair dominion, loyal to the core,
Vies with our mother-land to wish them joy ;
And Scottish hearts, where'er the wide world o'er,
    One sentiment express,
That heaven will watch them with a loving eye,
    And guard, protect, and bless
With love felicitous that will abide ;
Not the cold form which mocks a purchased bride.

If such were needed, 'twill our hearts unite
In closer bond to our beloved Queen,
Whose virtues shine with a refulgence bright,
    Though sorrow clouds her heart ;
A mother to her people she hath been,
    And we must act our part,
Like loving children ready to obey,
When called to peaceful scene or battle fray.

Campbell, the scion of a noble race,
Whose deeds of valour shine on history's page,
May'st thou through life their worthy footsteps trace .
    Though now in battle-field
No longer clansmen glorious warfare wage
    Or deadly claymore wield :
Thine be the path which art and science claim :
Here add new lustre to thy honoured name.

For thee, fair daughter of a noble Queen,
We wish thy life as happy, pure, and good :
Thine be the Christian's better part to win,
    And shine in all thy deeds ;
May never grief within thy heart intrude,
    As 'neath thy mother's weeds :
Thine be the queenly virtues we admire :
Thine be the genius of thy noble Sire.

So when thou hear'st our acclamations peal ;
So when thou see'st torch and taper gleam,
Know that our hearts are ever staunch and leal,
    And true to all that's free :

Deem not our vows an empty worthless dream ;
      We will be true to thee,
Long as thou keep'st thy wifely honour bright,
And hold'st thy lord's heart as thy love's true right.

And we, though parted from our fatherland—
The land thy mother loves with many ties—
With willing hands and willing hearts will stand
      To guard thy happy home :
Our country's stainless memories we prize
      Wherever we may roam,
And dearer for all time because of thee
Will be to us that land across the sea.

ROBERT BURNS.

(WRITTEN FOR A CALEDONIAN SOCIETY GATHERING.)

While gathered here frae a' the airts,
Wi' mirth an' sang to cheer oor hearts,
Ae name, 'boon a', a lowe impairts
      To Scottish veins ;
He wha auld Scotia's fame asserts
      In Doric strains.

Dear Ploughman Bard, wha's meteor flicht
Gleamed but a span, then sank in nicht,
Yet left ahint a glamour bricht
      O' sang sublime,
An' gilded wi' poetic licht
      The stream o' time ;

Thy name an' fame become mair dear
As time rows roun' the circling year ;
An' Scotia's sonsy bairns, where'er
      They may foregather,
Delichted, list thy lilts to hear
      Frae ane anither.

In youthfu' hearts thy love-strain sweet
Gars the warm bluid aye faster beat
At gloamin' hour, when lovers meet
    O' simmer days,
An' "sighs an' vows" again repeat,
    By "banks an' braes."

Still, patriot hearts are nerved for war,
When lowers the thunder-cloud afar,
An' Scottish heroes dae an' daur
    As in the past;
Nae coward hearts thy fame shall mar
    In "war's rude blast."

Thy thunder-blasts, langsyne sent forth
Against the pride o' rank or birth,
Still find an echo o'er the earth,
    In ilka lan',
An' prove, wi' honest, sterling worth,
    "A man's a man."

Where crawling hypocrites are rife,
Smooth o' the tongue, yet vile o' life,
Thy satire pierces like a knife
    In flesh an' bluid,
An' bares the root o' cantin' strife
    I' "the unco guid."

But piety, wherever pure,
Ye noted 'mang the simple puir,
An' pictured i' the reading hour,
    In cottar's hame,
Warm love for Him wha did endure
    The cross an' shame.

An' sympathy thou didna lack
Where stern oppression bowed the back;
For serf or slave, or white or black,
    Thy heart did yearn,
An' curst the tyrant wha could mak'
    "A brither mourn."

Aye, e'en thy sympathy went oot
To puir dumb creatures—bird an' brute,
Nor heard their suffering cry withoot
  A pang o' grief;
An', ever watchfu', kindly tho't
  To gie relief.

Thou hadst thy fau'ts; an' wha is there
Wad hae his inmost thochts laid bare,
Or show his words an' actions square?
  Sic saint, alane,
Daur ought against thy fame declare,
  Or cast a stane.

Na, Robbie, had ye been a saint
Withoot a flaw or sin's mirk taint,
I fear me, we'd hae looked asklent
  To hear ye rave;
Your words an' guidin', baith ill-spent,
  "Amang the lave."

Thy very fau'ts are beacons bricht
To help us forward to the licht,
When thrawart hearts wad frae the richt
  On ill-rades gang,
Yet scorn to hide if e'er sae slicht
  "A kennin' wrang."

Still a' thy glowin' words endure,
Bricht glints o' rare poetic power,
To lichten mony a weary hour
  O' puirtith sair,
Till stern oppression, fell an' dour,
  Can harm nae mair.

Noo, far frae a' our praise or blame,
We guard wi' jealous e'e thy fame,
While fancy haunts oor far-off hame,
  An' Ayr-ward turns;
In gentle tones we speak the name
  O' Robbie Burns.

A ROYAL MOUSE.

On the publication of this poem in *The Chatham Banner* (Ontario), the following note was printed by way of introduction:

A fellow-boarder, who belongs to the Grenadiers' Band, was stationed at Windsor Castle for a time, going and returning every day. On his arrival one evening, he entered our room for a chat, when, in taking off his overcoat, a mouse jumped out from his shoulder and disappeared. He said he had felt a strange feeling about him all the way from Windsor, and then recollected that in one of the rooms of the Castle he had been fondling a cat, which had caught a mouse and was playing with it. Pussy having dropped the mouse for a moment, it disappeared, and its escape could not be accounted for until our friend's arrival home. Some weeks after, in overhauling the room, the poor mouse was found dead. The lines are founded on this incident.

    Wee beastie, wham our Scottish bard
    Look'd on' wi' tenderest regard,
    Tho' nobly born, an' gently rear'd,
        Let nocht alarm ye;
    There's nae occasion to be fear'd,
        I wadna harm ye.

    Whatever made the sodger loon
    Entrap ye frae the royal toun,
    Frae 'neath the shadow o' the croon
        An' castle ha',
    To live ilk day the same dull roun'
        O' here awa'?

    I fear 'twill be an unco change,
    Tho' here, you're free to romp an' range.
    Yet a'thing will be dull an' strange
        For some wee while;
    Tho' here ye need na boo nor cringe
        To lordly style.

    But warst o' a', you'll miss your meat,
    The little tit-bits choice an' sweet
    At royal feasts— some extra treat
        Frae maid or lackey:
    While here, there's little ye can eat
        But books or baccy.

But still there's comfort even here,
Altho' the larder's scant o' cheer :
Nae cakes, nor kebbuck, meal nor bear
   To fill your maw ;
Yet murderin' cats ye need na fear
   In Bachelor's Ha'.

If ye can find a corner snug,
Safe frae the fear o' cat or dug,
In drawers or cupboard, chair or rug,
   In plaid or quilt,
Then tak' your ease, nor fash your lug :
   You 're welcome til't.

But mind ye, here you'll find nae state,
Nae booin' to the rich an' great ;
Nae fetes nor feastin', pride nor plate,
   An' grand display,
Wi' sodgers guardin' ilka gate
   Baith nicht an' day.

Ye maun just tak' things as they are,
Nor grumble at your scanty fare,
An' tho' I haena much to spare,
   You're welcome to't ;
My crust or crowdie you can share,
   Or gang withoot.

An' may-be when we're mair acquent,
Oor mutual feelin's better ken't,
Just gambol to your heart's content,
   Withoot a swither ;
Sae lang as I can pay the rent
   We'll fend thegither.

Try to forget what ye hae been,
The pomp you've shared, the wealth you've seen.
An' at your dooncome ne'er compleen,
   Nor care a whistle ;
You're safer here than wi' the Queen
   In Windsor Castle.

EPITAPH.

Here lies a puir unfortunate beast,
Wham royal cats ance deem'd a feast,
Wha cuddled in the sodger's breast
   Frae pussy's fangs,
To find as cruel a fate at last
   Frae hunger's pangs.

An' may-be, too, it felt the blow,
The fa' frae high estate to low ;
An' wi' this ranklin' sense o' woe,
   An' cruel smart,
It pined for bygane pomp an' show,
   An' broke its heart.

Sae like the feck o' mortals here,
Aye pinin' for some grander sphere,
Forgettin' a' the joys sae near
   On every side :
Or mournin' owre a past career
   O' cursed pride.

Heaven save me aye frae sic a fate :
I want na, crave na wealth nor state,
Nor for the favour o' the great ;
   An' should I do it,
Then may misfortune warm my seat
   Until I rue it.

― ― ―

WELLAND STREAM.

On Welland banks I loved to stray,
When closed the summer's sultry day,
When twilight over vale and plain
Her sombre curtain drew again ;
When by the grove, the glade and hill,
The warbler's song was hushed and still :
Where bending flow'rets kissed thy wave,
I loved to list thy limpid lave,
   Sweet Welland Stream.

There, many hours of sweet delight
I've passed, when first the shades of night
Came spreading o'er the verdant vale,
When balmy winds waft on thy tale:
There, 'neath an ancient elm, I'd lie,
And list thy murmurings bubbling by,
Or slowly wending by thy side,
Where, o'er the vale, thou flowest wide,
   Sweet Welland Stream.

But sweeter far the hours I strayed
With Mary, lovely, peerless maid;
I thought not then of streams and tides,
Nor culled the flow'rets by thy sides:
By mossy bank, where oft we'd rest,
My Mary to my heart I pressed,
While all her charms I praised in song,
Sweet echo sighed thy groves among,
   Sweet Welland Stream.

Glide on, sweet stream, glide on, and tell
Where Mary sleeps in yonder dell;
Tell how she faded in her bloom,
Like flower to spring-tide's early tomb:
Tell how I wandered lonely here,
My clouded heart and spirits drear:
Tell how my sigh and grieving wail
Thou wafted on thy twilight gale,
   Sweet Welland Stream.

Where willows to the night-winds wave,
I often muse by Mary's grave,
And often, as the tell-tale breeze
Whispers amid the clustering trees,
It bears my joyful message on;
When with this path of tears I'm done,
Beside thee laid, I'll peaceful dream,
While thou shalt sing my requiem,
   Sweet Welland Stream.

THE SUNSET HOUR.

When the village bells are chiming
    The approach of twilight's gloom,
And the labourer is returning
    To the comforts of his home,
Then, alone, I love to wander,
    Or recline beneath the bower,
Pondering on the scenes around me
    At the balmy sunset hour.

I have wandered at the day-dawn,
    When Aurora's golden beams,
Glowing o'er the eastern hilltops,
    Pierced the mist in fitful gleams:
But I feel a happier pleasure,
    Yea! I love that soothing power
Breathed o'er Nature's scenes, enchanting,
    At the balmy sunset hour.

I have wandered at the noontide,
    When the sun, in all his might,
Lighted up, with fairy grandeur,
    Scenes of ever-dear delight:
But yet fairer were the valleys,
    Sweeter fragrance filled the bower,
Gentler blew the genial zephyrs
    At the balmy sunset hour.

At that hour how clear the dewdrops
    Sparkle o'er the forest glade!
Sweetly sings the mellow blackbird,
    Welcoming the twilight's shade;
Merry laugh the village children
    As they cull the wildwood flower,
Sweetest even is echo's answer
    At the balmy sunset hour.

'Tis the hour when faithful lovers
    Seek the fairy-haunted dell;
There, where all is calm and silent,
    Each their joys and sorrows tell;

But no care can there disturb them,
  Grief or sorrow's withering power;
All is happiness and pleasure
  At the balmy sunset hour.

Thus I love alone, at even,
  O'er these woodland scenes to rove,
When my heart is sad and downcast,
  Far away from her I love.
O'er my grief my spirit rises,
  And tho' sorrow's clouds may lower,
They like morning vapours vanish
  At the balmy sunset hour.

DREAMING OF MOTHER.

On a pallet, weak and dying,
  A little orphan lay,
While through the open window
  He watched the fading day;
Till, weary with his vigil,
  His head to rest he laid,
And lost in airy fancies,
  In murmurs soft he said:
    "I love to dream of mother,
      To feel her loving hand
    Stretched out to smooth my pillow
      From that happy spirit land.

He closed his eyes in slumber,
  And rested calm and still,
Just as the sun had vanished
  Behind the purpled hill;
A smile played o'er his features
  Like sunshine's wintry beam,
While scarce above his breathing,
  He murmured in his dream:
    "I'm coming, dearest mother
      I see thy beck'ning hand
    Stretched out to give me welcome
      To that happy spirit land."

DRAW IN YOUR STOOL AN' SIT DOON.

When young widow Glen lived awa' up the cleuch,
I thocht an' I dreamed o' her aften eneuch;
If I met her by chance, I looked sheepish an' shy,
She wad nod, say guid-mornin', an' aff she gaed by.
But at last I plucked courage to gie her a ca',
Sae dressed in my Sunday claes, breeks, hose, an' a':
Oh! my heart it felt queer when I gat to the toun,
An' she said to me, "Draw in your stool an' sit doon."

I drew in my stool an' sat doon by the fire,
An' naething could I dae but look on an' admire:
My tongue wadna wag, sae a word I ne'er spak',
Till the widow sat doon, an' the silence she brak'
By spierin' for mither an' faither at hame,
An' hoo the auld crummie got on that was lame,
O' the sheep in the fauld, an' the hens on the bank;
While "aye, no, an' imphm," was a' that I spak'.

She brocht oot the bottle, an' gied me a dram
Whilk opened my mou' like an' oyster or clam:
I praised her white han', an' her een o' deep blue,
Then crap closer till her an' pree'd her sweet mou'.
She never resisted, but gied me her han',
An' said that her riches, her houses, an' lan'
I should share, gin I'd leave the auld folks in oor toun,
An' cannily draw in my stool an' sit doon.

I tell't her hoo lang an' hoo fondly I'd lo'ed her,
Hoo fu' was my joy noo I'd sought an' had woo'd her:
A lang fond embrace an' a kiss sealed oor vow,
Sae my heid has been lichtsome frae that time till now.
Neist week I've appointed to mak' her my ain,
For I canna thole langer her living her lane;
Sae I'll dae as she tauld me when first I ca'd roun',
I'll cosily draw in my stool an' sit doon.

INDIAN SUMMER.

The glorious days of summer
    Are numbered with the past,
And the giants of the forest
    Their withered leaves have cast;
In garden and in wildwood
    The flowers their bloom have shed,
And the maple tree is blushing
    And hanging down its head.

The parching summer sunshine
    No longer lights the scene,
The summer dews no longer
    Refresh the meadows green.
At morning and at evening
    The hoar-frost decks the spray,
Like the signs of old age coming
    When the locks are turning gray.

The bees have ceased their humming
    The meadow flowers among,
And hushed in grove and greenwood
    The feathered warblers' song.
Though blue the sky above us,
    And mild the midday sun,
'Tis the summer's lengthening shadow
    And the twilight coming on.

As the candle in the socket
    Gives its last expiring glare,
As hope beams out the brightest
    Near the clouds of dark despair,
As the soul's ecstatic visions
    When the snows of age appear,
So the glorious Indian Summer
    Proclaims the waning year.

HOW SHALL WE HONOUR HIM?

How shall we honour him now he is gone?
　How shall we show that we cherish his name?
Shall it be cut in memorial stone
　　The tribute we pay to his fealty and fame?
Shall it be blazoned on pillar or scroll?
　Shall it be sounded in speech or in song?
Nay, let his deeds be the theme of our soul,
　Like him, loving right and despising the wrong.
　　Bow down the head, reverently tread,
　　　Garfield has gone to his last silent rest;
　　Here let us plight our souls to the right,
　　　Thus shall we honour him, bravest and best.

Mourn we not, then, as do those hope-bereft,
　Learn we the lesson his pure life has taught:
High let us prize the example he left,
　Thus shall his memory ne'er be forgot.
Thus shall his fame and unsullied name
　Still in our memories ever be green;
Be our life's aim free from censure and blame,
　And may our record be stainless and clean.
　　Bow down the head, etc.

High was the standard he sought to attain,
　High was the trust that the nation bestowed;
And though cut off in the dawn of his reign,
　Mighty the power that he wielded for good.
Then let the nation, the rich and the poor,
　Follow his steps on the pathway he trod;
Thus shall we honour him, noble and pure,
　And live for our country, our people, and God.
　　Bow down the head, etc.

ON THE DEATH OF DAVID KENNEDY, THE SCOTTISH VOCALIST.

FAREWELL, sweet singer of our Scottish songs,
　No more thy lilting shall our spirits cheer,
Nor tell of Scotia's triumphs and her wrongs,
　　To wake the smile or tear.

To those in exile, far in other lands,
    In cold or sunny climes, thy tender lay
Felt like the clasp of warm embracing hands,
        Of loved ones far away.

How oft in listening to some matchless strain
    Has fancy round us wove her magic spells,
And wafted us to childhood's scenes again,
        'Mid cowslips and bluebells!

Thy martial lays have nerved us for the fight,
    And made the Scotch blood leap in every vein,
Inspiring in the cause of freedom's right,
        Our birthright to maintain.

And then thy melting strains, so soft and sweet,
    That told of love in many a humble cot,
Of trysting hours when faithful lovers meet,
        Or vows too soon forgot.

Again, with laughter have our hearts been stirred,
    And slumbering echoes of the past awoke,
As mimicked action, or some quaint old word,
        Pointed the quip or joke.

How have we hung upon thy varying tones,
    And seen new beauties in the poet's song,
Which told the doughty deeds of Scotia's sons,
        Their struggles against wrong!

Here, where we met and clasped thy kindly hand,
    We gave thee hearty welcome as a friend,—
A messenger from that dear distant land
        Which we have left behind.

Now still, the manly heart, and cold the hand,
    Hushed is the voice of sweet melodious tone;
And Scotia's sons afar in many a land
        Will mourn a brother gone.

Fitting the end,—when death had dealt the wound,
    Not darkling through the valley didst thou grope;
Thy weary spirit passed away, attuned
        To songs of faith and hope.

WHERE SHALL OUR LOVED ONES REST?

(SUGGESTED BY THE CHOICE OF A CEMETERY GROUND.)

Where shall our loved ones rest
   In their last unbroken sleep?
Shall it be by the river's brink,
   Where it is still and deep;
Where its murmurs waft along
   'Mid the zephyr's gentle sigh,
Where the night-bird's scream is heard,
   And the echoes make reply?

Where shall our loved ones rest?
   Shall it be in the fragrant shade,
In the leafy waving dome,
   By the spreading maple made;
Where the grass grows fresh and green,
   And the cricket's chirp is heard,
Where the leaves are trembling low,
   Like a lover's whispered word?

Where shall our loved ones rest?
   Shall it be where the night-dews weep,
And the twinkling stars above
   Their silent vigils keep:
Where the winding stream below,
   And the waving pines o'erhead,
Join in a mournful strain,
   A requiem for the dead?

Where shall our loved ones rest?
   Shall it be by the wintry wold,
Where the driving clouds are dark,
   And the storms blow bleak and cold;
Where the sere and yellow leaves
   At the north wind's breath shall fall,
And a spotless shroud descends
   So gently over all?

Where shall our loved ones rest?
   Shall it be where the summer flowers
And the merry songs of birds
   Are first in the sylvan bowers?

Ah! yes, let us lay them there,
    Where flowers shall each grave adorn,
And tell of the life renew'd
    On the resurrection morn.

MITHER'S BONNIE LASS.

We hae a fair-haired lauchin' wean,
    As fu' o' mirth and glee
As ony friskin' lamb that sports
    Upon the gowany lea ;
An' should ye spier her name, she 'll look
    Wi' roguish, lauchin' face,
And say, "I 'se dot no usser name—
    I 'se mither's bonnie lass."

Ay, 'deed, she 's mither's lassie noo,
    The younglin' o' the fauld,
An' oor hearts cling closer till her,
    As we feel we 're growin' auld ;
We watch an' guard wi' ceaseless care
    Frae a' the storms that pass,
That no' a bitin' blast can harm
    Oor mither's bonnie lass.

An' when she says her prayers at nicht,
    An' cuddles 'mang the claes,
We ask kind Heaven to be her guide
    In a' her comin' days ;
We nichtly plead that she may hae
    The Spirit's savin' grace,
To keep her pure as she is noo,
    Her mither's bonnie lass.

Her mither's heart aft pleads wi' Him
    Wha blessed the bairns langsyne,
To hae a watchfu' e'e upon
    This wee, wee tot o' mine ;
To shield her in His lovin' airms
    Frae a' sin's foul disgrace,
An' be thro' life a Guide an' Frien'
    To mither's bonnie lass.

NAE MAIR.

Slowly and sadly the muffled bell
Rings oot a solemn funeral knell
    On the bitin' winter air,
A mournfu' dirge for the loved and gane,
While the funeral march, wi' its sad refrain,
Tells o' ane wha will march again
    Nae mair.

Slowly the crowd o' mourners go
Thro' the eager air an' the drivin' snow
    To the kirkyaird, bleak an' bare,
Where the elm tree points, wi' bony arms,
To the joyless river an' dreary farms,
Owre ane wha'll hail spring's buddin' charms
    Nae mair.

He is laid to rest, the salute is fired,
The train o' mourners hae a' retired;
    While the band, wi' lively air,
Wakens the echoes frae grove an' plain,
Whilk silently listened the funeral strain ;
But, gay or sad, *he* will listen again
    Nae mair.

Cauld in death is his kindly heart,
Silent his tongue ; frae street an' mart
    His frien's will miss him sair.
But as the years roll swiftly by,
We'll lo'e the spot where his ashes lie,
While his name shall fade frae oor memory
    Nae mair.

The nicht is sad wi' the widow's wail,
An' infant fears are soothed wi' the tale
    (A light 'mid the dark despair),
If faither comes not, they'll go to him,
Where their cup o' joy will be fu' to the brim,
Where hearts are sad, and eyes grow dim
    Nae mair.

FAITHER'S AIN BAIRN.

Faither's ain bairn is a blue-e'ed lassie,
    Wi' lint-white locks hingin' doon owre her broo,
An' the blush on her cheeks like the roseate dawnin',
    Or the crimson flowers wat wi' the simmer dew.
Her step is as licht as the breath o' the zephyr
    That scarce stirs the grass by the brae-side or cairn;
As she rins thro' the meadow, the gowans she tramps on
    Spring up frae the tread o' faither's ain bairn.

Her voice is as sweet as the sang o' the mavis
    Whilk sings aye sae saft at the close o' the day,
An' she'll lilt an' she'll sing the hale day thegither,
    As she gathers flower-wreaths by burnie or brae.
The ither wee lassies will toddle thegither,
    Awa' thro' the woods amang heather or fern,
To meet my wee lassie; for nocht they lo'e better
    Than the sangs an' the stories o' faither's ain bairn.

In the lang winter nichts she'll sit by the ingle
    Watchin' the flare o' the dancin' lowe,
Or wi' saft dimple fingers she smooths oot the wrinkles
    That she wunners to see in her faither's brow.
It cheers me to list to her innocent prattle;
    An' her sweet winnin' ways, to a' sae endearin',
Sune mak' me forget the cares o' life's battle,
    As I kiss the fair cheek o' faither's ain bairn.

Ilk mornin' an' nicht, when the knee we are bendin'
    To Him that's the Giver o' a' that we hae,
Wi' deep, fervent zeal I press the petition,
    That oor lassie may never be taken away:
That she may be kept frae a' trial an' temptation,
    As pure as she's noo, is my deepest concern,
Till some likely laddie may woo her an' win her;
    Tho' she'll aye be to me her faither's ain bairn.

WHEN DADDY COMES HAME.

I ken a camsteerie wee laddie, wha keeps
    Baith auld folks an' young folks at hame on the gang;
Frae the time that he waukens, straucht on till he sleeps,
    There's nae rest where he is the weary day lang.
His playthings are constantly shifted aboot,
    An' tho' the cart's broken, the cuddie is lame,
He's as happy's a king either indoors or oot ;
    But his greatest delight is when daddy comes hame.

Sae cheery's the rogue, tho' on mischief aye bent,
    He's a general favourite wi' strangers that ca';
Gin new toys are gi'en him, he's never content
    Till he sees the inside, be 't engine or ba'.
An' tho' the last present be never sae braw,
    Before the day's owre wi't the novelty's tame,
Then the cat gets a thro'-gaun that ends in a claw :
    But a'thing is changed when his daddy comes hame.

When he gangs for a walk wi' his auntie or me,
    His cat, like a collie, comes trottin' alang,
Then hear hoo he'll lauch when it rins up a tree,
    An' jumps like a squirrel the branches amang ;
But listen the yells when he sees a stray doug,
    An' no' for himsel' is he feared for the same,
But Girsie, wee Girsie, he shields wi' a hug,
    An' he'll watch it an' guard it till daddy comes hame.

The laddies, wha pass as they gang to the schule,
    Will sometimes look in just to play for a wee,
An' he'll lend them his toys—bat, barrow or bool,
    An' the way they enjoy't is a pleasure to see ;
For hours after schule-time the fun's at its height,
    Their lessons forgotten when thrang wi' their game ;
It ne'er troubles them hoo the time tak's its flight,
    An' their ploys dinna cease until daddy comes hame.

But see him at e'en on dad's knee in the neuk,
    A smile on his face an' his een open wide,
He listens to stories ne'er learned frae a buik,
    O' giants an' fairies—an's ne'er satisfied ;

He'll try to keep wauken when Nature says na!
　Whiles noddin' an' winkin', ilk nicht it's the same,
Till at last, to the fair land o' Nod he's awa',
　In the arms he lo'es dearest, when daddy's at hame.

Aye! aften I whisper a prayer by mysel',
　That Heaven may protect him where'er he may gang;
When—his laddie days owre—he maun fend for himsel',
　An' oot in the warl' he maun mix wi' the thrang:
May the vices an' sins that are ilka where rife
　Ne'er lure him aside to the byways o' shame:
But, pure as his bairnhood, ilk day o' his life
　Be as happy as noo wi' his daddy at hame.

THE BAIRNIE TAK'S AFTER HIS FAITHER.

We hae a bit laddie doon bye at the hoose,
An' the mither aboot him is cantie and crouse:
As for me, wha am generally sober an' douce,
　They say I am prood o' him raither:
Wi' his carroty pow he is unco like me;
He's a kip to his nose, an' a cast i' his e'e,
An' a' the auld wives in the clachan agree
　That the bairnie tak's after his faither.

O' the wee ane's complaints he has had his full share,
The kink-host an' measles,—an' twenty things mair;
Yet he's stoot an' weel-faured a' the howdies declare,
　Whilk comforts the heart o' his mither:
Yet 'mang a' the troubles, an' drawbacks sae rife,
He tak's to the bottle as nat'ral as life,
An' aften I smile as I tell the guidwife
　That the bairnie tak's after his faither.

When the lassies drap in hoo he coo's an' he craws,
An' glams at their ribbons, their gum-flowers an' braws,
Or expresses his joy wi' goo-goos and da-das,
　While the lassies guffaw to ilk ither:
As for me, when I see a' the cuddlin' gaun on,
I think o' the days afore Kirsty was won;
For in a' this curdooin' sae early begun,
　The bairnie tak's after his faither.

Your rattles an' toys he no cares for a preen,
Nor dolls whilk the lassocks are fond o', I ween:
But see hoo he'll warstle an' cock up his een
    When I jingle the siller thegither:
An' should I a bawbee an' saxpence haud oot,
He'll grab at the wee ane withoot ony doot:
This auld-farrant weanie ken's what he's aboot,
    For the bairnie tak's after his faither.

There's ae thing peculiar to Scotchmen a' owre,
They're unco strong-wulled an' inclined to be dour:
They winna be driven, dae a' i' your pooer,
    Tho' they'll follow withouten a swither:
An' young as he is, I can see i' the wean
He'll stan' to his point just as steeve as a stane,
An' he'll try a' he can to toddle his lane;
    For the bairnie tak's after his faither.

Let us hope, as the years come an' gang, he will be
Aye lovin' and kind to his mother an' me;
Nor frae the straucht road gangin' meikle aglee.
    Nor wi' dootfu' companions foregather:
Aye firmly the wiles o' the warl' to withstand,
As saft as the doon, yet as gritty as sand,
An' haud up his head wi' the best i' the land,
    For the bairnie tak's after his faither.

TO PLEASE THE BAIRNS.

My bonnie wife an' sonsie weans
    Are a' the warl' to me;
I canna boast o' muckle gear,
    Yet blither could na be;
The lowe o' love lichts up my hame,
    An' seek thro' a' the Mearns,
Ye winna fin' a happier pair,
    Or bonnier toddlin' bairns.

Just see me when I'm hame at e'en
    A-spranchlin' on the floor,
An' playin' bools wi' a' my micht
    Wi' lauchin' younkers four;

An' then I'll mak' them paper kites,
   Or totums oot o' pirns;
I'm just a bairn again mysel',
   An' a' to please the bairns.

To music I mak' nae pretence,
   I dinna ken a note,
But when I try to lilt a song
   It seems to come by rote;
The tune may no' be classical,
   An' hae some queerish turns,
But what does't maitter after a'—
   It serves to please the bairns?

An' when I take my keelievine,
   An' on the jam-stane draw
A horse or hoose, or something else,
   Just hear the younkers craw;
Nae artist yet wham fame has reached,
   An' gowden honours earns,
Could frae his patrons win mair praise,
   Or better please the bairns.

Then never let the bairnies think
   Ye dinna share their joys,
An' dinna think yoursel' demeaned
   To join their childish ploys;
Far better to unbend awee,
   Forget life's dull concerns:
'Twill tak' the kink oot mony a care
   To try an' please the bairns.

The time will come, fu' soon atweel,
   When we maun lea' them a'
To bear alane the warl's cares,
   As fortune kicks the ba';
An' maybe, when we're auld an' frail,
   Oor love will bring returns,
In helpfu' care for totterin' age
   Frae kind an' lovin' bairns.

THE WANING YEAR.

SWIFTLY to its close
The old year goes,
And nought that we can do its step retard :
Still it, with many a groan,
With struggle, sigh and moan,
'Mid life's last ebbing throes,
Dies hard.

Oh ! it hath seen sad sights,
This fading year,
Brought many woful plights
To nations and to men :
Bloodshed and war to some,
And blackest gloom :
To others woe and fear,
A prospect drear
Of want and misery,
Sad heart and tearful eye,
That we
Hope ne'er to see
Again.

And it hath had bright days,
And sunny skies o'erhead.
Full many a mother gave to heaven
Her heartfelt praise :
While on her lowly bed,
When, pain and travail past,
She gazed with joy at last
Upon the lovely child kind Providence had given.

And marriage bells have pealed
A merry peal,
As in the solemn church
The holy man of God
Spoke of the pledges sealed
In Heaven—exhorts them to fulfil
Each unto each the vows they take ;
Then to their new abode

The prancing steeds soon whirl them away ;
 And anxious crowds, around the porch,
Wish life an' love for the young couple's sake,
And all seems glad and gay.

But let the curtain fall
 Upon the woes of war,
And awful waste of life that did appal
 The world both near and far,
And let us pray that, in the coming year,
 No tear
May fall upon a murdered victim's bier ;
 But over all the earth
Peace and good-will to man will reign ;
 As from out the ark of hope goes forth.
With olive branch, the peaceful dove,
Proclaiming heaven's love
 To fallen man ;
Pointing to gloomy wrecks of days gone by,
Warning of guilt's undying misery,
And leading to the cross of Calvary
All nations, slave and free,
A Saviour's all-atoning death to see.

Thus would the coming year
Witness, alone, contrition's hopeful tear,
 And the "good time" by sages often sung
 With poesy's sweet tongue,
Come with the infant year's bright smile,
 When all our flickering hopes and fears,
 And anxious toil,
Would dissipate before the genial ray
 Of a millennial day.

 Alone I sit and dream
 Upon this solemn theme :
The passing moments, with a sigh,
 Rush swiftly by ;
Around me all is darkness and repose,
As to the year's sad close
The clock with warning finger points,
 And wisely hints

Of that time when my little year shall cease,
Exhorting me to make with heaven my peace,
    That so,
When parting from this weary world below,
    Hope's bright illumined star
May lead my thoughts from Time's sad scenes of woe,
And through the valley's gathering gloom
Guide on and up afar to an unfading home.

BIRTHDAY MUSINGS.

This day have twenty years flown by
Since first I ope'd an infant eye
  On this sad vale of tears;
And, ah! what changes have been wrought
Since first a loving mother sought
  To guide my tender years!

I cannot help the rising sigh
While back I cast a wistful eye,
As fain some token to descry
  Of youth's unclouded joys;
And I can see a summer sky,
O'er which no threatening storm-clouds fly,
And watch that time pass swiftly by—
  The time when we were boys.

And fain I'd be a boy again
  Amid those scenes of yore,
To roam by heathy moor and glen,
By wildwood, mead, and stream,
And from the cloudlet's summer beam,
The morning breeze, the warbler's song,
The opening flower with dewdrops hung,
The fairy nook, the hillock green,
And every loved and cherish'd scene,
  To learn poetic lore.

But no; alas! it cannot be
That e'er this heart shall be as free
  From worldly grief and care;

For fancy's fairest pictures fail
   To paint the world as fair
As when, by streamlet, hill, and dale,
With hearts as free as summer gale,
Sweet nature's charms cheer'd heart and eye,
Imparting hope, and peace, and joy,
Yea, happiness without alloy
   Or sin's delusive glare.

And where are those who with me play'd
   Upon the village green,
And oft together careless stray'd
   The still, sequester'd scene,
Where 'mong the springing flowers we lay,
By meadow green, or mossy brae,
And told our tale, or sung our song,
   Or cull'd the fragrant flowers,
While, happy as the day was long,
   We pass'd the fleeting hours?

They, too, are scatter'd far and wide;
   In many lands they roam;
In backwoods wild, or torrid clime,
   Or on the foaming tide;
   Far from their native home
They pass their manhood's prime.

But 'tis in vain to sigh
For those bright hours, now fled,
   To come again;
The future path doth lie
Before me, where I can descry
   Shadows dark and dread;
But then the battle **must** be fought,
   And it is all in vain
To live in dreams, and labour not.
Then "up and doing" be the cry,
Clouds and darkness to defy,
And soon the shadows dark shall fly,
And bring a clear and sunny sky,
   As sunshine follows rain.

Now I shall hope and pray
  That, come what may,
    The coming day
Shall open calm and fair,
And find me ready for the fight,
To do and battle for the right,
  Nor nurse desponding care,
But, journeying along life's way,
  Tho' dark the clouds above,
Some hopeful ever-cheering ray
  Shall guide me where I rove:
  And may the future prove
That, though 'gainst sin and pride
  But feebly yet I've striven,
Each coming dawn shall beam more clear,
Shall chase away the gathering gloom,
    And in its room
    Bring light and life
To nerve me for the world's strife,
  And bring me nearer heaven!

THE WAY GAUN O' THE YEAR.

I'm anchored in my arm-chair beside a bleezin' fire,
  An' a' the sports o' Mayfair wadna lure me frae the spot,
For I'm buildin' airy castles o' the days that are to come,
  Or travellin' backward o'er the time that marked a chequered lot:
I've had the swing an' whirl o' my boyhood's happy time,
  I've had my joys an' sorrows—the pleasure an' the tear,
An' tasted "love's young dream" that flickered oot ere manhood's prime,
  An' it a' comes back sae vivid at the way-gaun o' the year.

Oh! the cherished schemes o' boyhood that we tho't wad yet come true,
  The harder cares o' manhood that obscured the simmer sky,
The loves an' disappointments that brought wrinkles to the broo,
  The failures an' successes o' the past are flittin' bye:

An' yet a thread o' glamour rins through the tangled skein,
  For things might hae been darker, tho' guid kens they're unco drear;
But the hope that looks for blossoms when the weary winter's past,
  Still cheers me as I ponder on the way-gaun o' the year.

What need to seek the darker side? The mirk will surely come,
  An' sma' may be the glints o' light that beam across oor path;
But it's satisfaction surely just to nurse the joys we hae,
  An' mak' the maist o' simmer that succeeds the winter's wrath.
What need to magnify oor cares till they loom mountains high,
  An' steep oor souls in gloomy tho'ts when there's sae much to cheer?
Far better wad it be to tak' a rosier survey,
  An' reckon up oor pleasures at the way-gaun o' the year.

The circle o' oor frien'ship shows mony a mournfu' gap,
  For some hae slipt their anchors, and hae drifted on the rocks;
An' some, noo in a foreign land, hae sought a fairer hame,
  An' settled doon contented amang hamely couthie folks;
An' Death has snapped the thread o' some ere they had passed their prime,
  O' them wha humbly plodded, or attained a grand career;
An' the tears will come unbidden as we count the grassy mounds,
  An' oorsel's yet spared to miss them at the way-gaun o' the year.

Still, there are left staunch frien'ships that grow stronger year by year;
  The farther we get on in life the closer are we knit;
We share ilk ither's confidence as in oor boyhood days,
  Or help by word or action where misfortune's dart has hit.

Ah! this is what mak's life sae sweet, e'en when oor cares
    are rife,
  When times are hard, an' puirtith's pinch is grievous
    hard to bear,
To find we're no' deserted when their kindly help we need,
  An' oor hopes hae almost perished wi' the way-gaun o'
    the year.

The young may pass it lightly, this time o' tho'tfu' change,
  An' only see the jollity it brings to cot or ha';
Their hearts are yet unseared by cares that pass them
    lightly by,
  Nor wad I hae it itherwise, sae joy I wish them a';
But we wha've passed life's keystane canna help a back-
    ward glance,
  For we live on memories o' joys that come nae mair to
    cheer,
An' altho' we hae nae forecast o' comin' weal or wae,
  Oor thankfulness is deepened at the way-gaun o' the year.

Then let us raise a fervent prayer, that what life has in store
  May be nae waur than what has gane wi' a' its ups an'
    doons,
An' a hope it may be brighter than we ever dared to dream,
  An' that we may be shielded frae misfortune's wintry
    frowns;
Let's help ilk ither onward where the road is kind o' steep,
  An' raise some fallen brither wi' a welcome word o' cheer;
For the burdens we can lighten will a blessin' bring us back
  Ere circlin' time has brought again the way-gaun o' the
    year.

Memorial Stone in Polwarth Church.

Publications of J. & R. Parlane, Paisley.

**JOHN MENZIES & Co., Edinburgh and Glasgow.
HOULSTON & SONS, London.**

1 Vol., Crown 8vo., 360 pp. Price 3/6.

MINSTRELSY OF THE MERSE
By W. S. CROCKETT, F.S.A.Scot.

SOME OPINIONS OF THE PRESS.

"It is a work of which the natives of the Border county ought to be proud."—*Glasgow Evening Times.*

"The work is one of the most charming and interesting which we have perused for many a day, the sketches of the principal persons mentioned in it being written with great beauty, a just discrimination of their distinctive merits, and with true poetic taste."—*Ayr Observer.*

"The work is a valuable addition to current literature."—*Scottish Border Record.*

"There was ample room for such an anthology as the Rev. W. S. Crockett has so successfully brought together."—*Scotsman.*

"The whole work has been in the hands of one who has evidently dipped deeply into history, and whose research of the beaten paths of literature is abundantly manifest."—*Dumbarton Herald.*

"The sketches of the poets are written in excellent style, and the various illustrative poems given show good selection, discretion, and taste."—*People's Friend.*

"The whole book is agreeable reading."—*Glasgow Weekly Citizen.*

"This book deserves to find a favoured place in every house in Berwickshire; and for school prizes it is worth dozens of those commonly used for that purpose. It is of perennial interest."—*Kelso Chronicle.*

"This is a book to buy. It is so cheap as to be within the reach of all. No Merse home, with any pretension to love of its native hills and vales, can possibly be without one."—*Berwickshire News.*

"Mr Crockett has earned the gratitude not only of the Merse, but of Scotsmen everywhere, by his admirable collection. He has spared no pains, grudged no labour in research. He has his reward."—*Perthshire Advertiser.*

"Such a volume cannot fail in winning general and hearty appreciation."—*Perthshire Courier.*

"It is a volume that is bound to take very high rank in works of this class." *Berwickshire Advertiser.*

"Mr Crockett has laid all who love Scottish song and ballad under a debt of gratitude." *Oban Times.*

"The author does his work well, writing with enthusiasm, yet without too effusive exuberance." *Literary World.*

"It is a book to read for its first-rate biographical notices, and the many excellent verses scattered throughout its pages."—*The Scottish Weekly.*

"A book to give genuine pleasure, and that deserves the heartiest thanks." *Edinburgh Evening Dispatch.*

"The editor has been singularly successful in treating his subject, and the reading public generally will feel that a worthy theme has been handled here in a manner to inspire the fullest confidence and admiration." *Forfar Herald.*

"We confidently commend the collection." *Kelso Mail.*

"Mr Crockett is to be commended for the quality of his biographical notices; and it may be added that his volume is a credit to his judgment and editorial industry." *Glasgow Herald.*

"It should be found both as a souvenir and as an educator in every home in the Merse." *Border Advertiser.*

"It will serve to show that this Borderland can boast as well of its songsters as it could, in days of yore, of its warriors." *Daily Mail.*

"That this anthology of the Merse will be received with much acceptance, we have not the slightest doubt."—*The Scottish Leader.*

"This book gives information concerning the poets of this Borderland, which is not to be found in any other single work. We congratulate Mr Crockett on the successful completion of his task." *The Scottish American.*

"The book is altogether admirably got up, reflecting great credit on editor and publishers." *Kilmarnock Standard.*

"An admirable volume." *North British Advertiser.*

Homely Rhymes, &c., from the Banks of the Jed. By AGNES STRAIRT MABON. Preface by Rev. JAMES KING, M.A. Crown 8vo. Price 3/6.

"A genuine poetic spirit breathes through all the poems, and that the author has a heart alive to the sympathies and affection of friendship is to be seen in very many of her productions." *Hawick Advertiser.*

The Bards of Angus and the Mearns. An Anthology of the Counties. By ALAN REID, F.E.I.S. With Numerous Illustrations. Cap. 4to., 660 pp. Price 10/6.

The Harp of Stirlingshire. By WILLIAM HARVEY, Author of "Kennetherook: Some Sketches of Village Life," "Scotch Thistles," &c. Crown 8vo., 530 pp., Price 7/6.

The Poets and Poetry of Linlithgowshire. An Anthology of the County By ALEX. M. BISSET. Crown 8vo., 352 pp., with Illustrations. Price 4/6.

Songs and Poems. By AGNES CHRISTALL DEY. With Introduction by Rev. J. H. WILSON, D.D. Crown 8vo., Price 2/.

History of the Life of Fénelon (Archbishop of Cambray). By ANDREW MICHAEL RAMSAY, D.C.L. F.R.S., Author of "The Travels of Cyrus," &c. Translated from the French Edition of 1723, with a Biographical Memoir of the Author, Bibliography, and Notes, by DAVID CUTHBERTSON. Fcap. 8vo., with Portrait. Price 7/6.

Agnes C. P. Watt: Twenty-five Years' Mission Life on TANNA, NEW HEBRIDES. Biographical Sketch and Introduction by Rev. T. WATT LEGGATT, New Hebrides. 385 pp. 8vo., Cloth boards. Numerous Illustrations. Price 6/

"A notable volume in many respects, and worthy to be placed alongside of those written on Tanna."

Holiday Fortnights at Home and Abroad. By G. E. PHILIP, Glasgow. Numerous Photo Illustrations. Crown 8vo. Price 2/6.

The Poetical Works of MICHAEL BRUCE, with Life and Writings (including Discussion of the Bruce-Logan Controversy). By Rev. WILLIAM STEPHEN, Kelty, Blair Adam. With Illustrations. Price 2/6.

In PENNY NUMBERS—Staff or Sol-fa.

THE NATIONAL CHOIR:

Standard Songs for Part-Singing, Original and Arranged, adapted for Choirs and Secondary Evening Classes. Specimen post free.

YEARLY PARTS, with Notes to the Songs—Historical, Personal, and Critical. Price 1 each.

Volumes I. & II., each containing **Four Yearly Parts,** with Notes to the Songs, interesting Prefaces, and upwards of 600 Musical Gems, harmonised for Part-Singing. Price 5 each.

Nothing better could be selected as gift books for friends at home or over the sea than this large and varied collection of our finest National Songs.

"A monument of National song."
"The arrangements are ably written."
"Really a National Handbook of Part Music."—*Press Notices.*

The National Choir contains more of BURNS'S SONGS arranged for Part-Singing than any other book published.

Specimen No. sent post free to any address.

BOOKS BY REV. R. LAWSON,
MAYBOLE.

The Capital of Carrick and the District about it. Numerous Illustrations. Price 1/.

A Minister's Life. Crown 8vo. With numerous Illustrations. Price 2.

Glimpses of Norway: Being Notes of a Trip in the S.S. St. Sunniva, July, 1894, with Fifteen Photographic Reproductions and Four Norse Songs with Music. Cloth, 1/.

Ailsa Craig: Its History and Natural History. *New Edition—Enlarged.* Map and Illustrations. Crown 8vo. Cloth, 1/.

Places of Interest about Girvan, with some Glimpses of Carrick History. Illustrated. Price 1/.

Places of Interest about Maybole, with Sketches of Persons of Interest. With Illustrations. Cloth, 1/.

Crossraguel Abbey: A History and a Description. With Illustrations. Cloth, 1/.

The Sacred Places of Scotland: Being an Account of a Personal Visit to Them. With Illustrations. Cloth, 1/.

The Famous Places of Scotland (including the Shetland Islands). From a Personal Visit to Them. With Illustrations. Cloth, 1/.

The Covenanters of Ayrshire: Historical and Biographical. With Illustrations. Cloth, 1/.

What I Saw of India and its People. Being Notes of a Tour in 1888-89. Map and Illustrations. Cloth, 1/.

Fifty-four Views of Carrick, with Description. Price 6d.

The Romance of Missions. A Popular Reading, containing a short Biographical history of Christian Missions from the first century to the present. With 18 Musical Illustrations Arranged for Part-Singing. Staff or Sol-fa, 3d.

Homes and Haunts of Robert Burns. A Popular Reading, with 19 Musical Illustrations from Burns's Songs, specially arranged for Part-Singing. Staff or Sol-fa, 3d.

"It may be doubted if the Story of Burns's Homes and Haunts has ever been better told." *Scotsman.*

The Ballads and Songs of Carrick, with Nineteen Musical Illustrations arranged for Part-Singing; and Introductory Notes. Staff or Sol-fa, 3d.

The National Anthems of the World. A Popular Reading. With Eighteen Musical Illustrations Arranged for Part-Singing. Staff or Sol-fa, 3d.

www.ingramcontent.com/pod-product-compliance
Lightning Source LLC
Chambersburg PA
CBHW022027240426
43667CB00042B/1211